A PASSION FOR DEMOCRACY

OTHER BOOKS BY BENJAMIN R. BARBER

Jihad versus McWorld (1995)

An Aristocracy of Everyone (1992)

The Conquest of Politics (1988)

Strong Democracy (1984)

Marriage Voices (A Novel) (1981)

Liberating Feminism (1975)

The Death of Communal Liberty (1974)

Superman and Common Men (1971)

COLLABORATIONS

The Struggle for Democracy
with Patrick Watson (1989)

The Artist and Political Vision
edited with M. McGrath (1982)

Totalitarianism in Perspective
with C. J. Friedrich and M. Curtis (1969)

A PASSION FOR DEMOCRACY

AMERICAN ESSAYS

Benjamin R. Barber

PRINCETON UNIVERSITY PRESS   PRINCETON, NEW JERSEY

Third printing, and first paperback printing, 2000
Paperback ISBN 0-691-05024-4

The Library of Congress has cataloged the cloth edition of this book as follows

Barber, Benjamin R., 1939–
A passion for democracy : American essays / Benjamin R. Barber.
p. cm.
Includes bibliographical references (p.   ) and index.
ISBN 0-691-05766-4 (CL : acid-free paper)
1. Democracy—United States.   2. Democracy.   I. Title.
JK1726.B27   1998
320.473—dc21   97-52582

This book has been composed in Galliard
by Wilsted & Taylor Publishing Services

The paper used in this publication meets the minimum requirements of
ANSI/NISO Z39.48-1992 (R1997) (*Permanence of Paper*)

http://pup.princeton.edu

Printed in the United States of America

3   5   7   9   10   8   6   4

Contents

Preface

AMERICA has been working at democracy, if a little unevenly, for over two hundred years. I have been working at thinking about American democracy, also a little unevenly, for fewer than thirty years. Fortunately, thinking about it, although tough, is still a good deal simpler than practicing it.

In these American essays written over several decades, I have been hard on my country. Like most ardent democrats, I want more for it than it has achieved, despite the fact that it has achieved more than most peoples have dared to want. I can plead for a more participatory democracy because we are blessed with a strong, liberal constitution that protects us from too much government and from democratic enthusiasts like me. I can preach the new gospel of citizenship because we are already a nation of ancient, practiced laws in which citizens cannot appeal to what they think is their virtue to defeat justice or order. I can reach out for equality and community because our individualism is deeply enough entrenched to withstand a far stronger dose of the commonweal than we have offered it. As my teacher Louis Hartz liked to say, the American majority has forever been a puppy dog tethered to a lion's leash. As we struggle to stretch the confining tethers, we may still appreciate their sturdy resilience.

In this collection, I am often impatient with those who distrust government as well as with those who insist on securing foundations for democracy that legitimate popular sovereignty only by disempowering people from governing themselves. My impatience is tolerable, however, only because we enjoy the fruits of liberalism—a regard for the freedom of the individual that trumps every common cause. In the eternal struggle to balance liberty and equality, we Americans have done enough for freedom to be able to strive incautiously for greater equality.

More than most nations, America can afford self-criticism, even—from time to time—outright rebellion, because it is strong. It is confident in its uncertainty, principled in its pragmatism, united in its diversity. The true mark of democracy is its capacity to withstand and benefit from a noisy and fractious citizenry; the true test of democracy is whether it can educate a citizenry with enough competence and judgment to understand that it bears the ultimate responsibility for the success of its representative institutions.

Because of the nature of my subject, I owe a special debt to my critics and adversaries. Our spirited disagreements, confined always to those modest arbitrators of all we say and do in a democracy—words and words alone—

pay tribute to the reality of liberty and the necessity of civility, even as they reveal again the elusiveness of justice.

I cannot claim that the essays collected here all hold up equally well over the years, but they do hint at the underlying continuity of concern that has propelled me from an early obsession with democratic Switzerland (in *The Death of Communal Liberty*) to an attempt at a definitive confrontation with democracy here in America in both its thin and its strong versions (in *Strong Democracy*), and more recently to a contemplation of the perils presented to democracy worldwide by the twin totalisms of market materialism and dogmatic communitarianism: McWorld and its fratricidal mirror-opposite twin, Jihad (in *Jihad versus McWorld*).

On this journey without a destination, I have felt comforted by the hovering spirits of earlier democrats Jean-Jacques Rousseau, Mary Wollstonecraft, Thomas Jefferson, Frederick Douglass, Walt Whitman, and John Dewey; and of recent democratic liberals (now gone) I have been fortunate enough to know: Hannah Arendt, Louis Hartz, Michael Oakeshott, Ghita Ionescu, and Judith Shklar. What they share is that they have all written about democracy without pretending they can escape contradiction and have practiced it without pretending they can avoid the hypocrisy endemic to our human inadequacy. I would like to think that in their hearts what they shared with other democrats was the conviction that every human being possesses both a right to and, when properly educated, a capacity for self-governance. And that no mere mortal may take from any other mortal this precious gift of liberty.

Acknowledgments

An earlier version of "Liberal Democracy and the Costs of Consent" appeared in *Liberalism and the Moral Life,* edited by Nancy L. Rosenblum, copyright © 1989 by the President and Fellows of Harvard College; reprinted by permission of Harvard University Press, Cambridge, Mass.

An earlier version of "Foundationalism and Democracy" appeared in *Democracy and Difference: Contesting the Boundaries of the Political,* copyright © 1996 by Princeton University Press; reprinted by permission of Princeton University Press, Princeton, N.J.

An earlier version of "Why Democracy Must Be Liberal: An Epitaph of Marxism" appeared in *Society* 33, no. 1 (November–December 1995); reprinted by permission of Transaction Publishers, New Brunswick, N.J.

An earlier version of "The Compromised Republic: Public Purposelessness in America" appeared in the *Moral Foundations of the American Republic* (1986); reprinted with permission of the University Press of Virginia.

An earlier version of "The Rights of We the People Are All the Rights There Are" appeared in *To Secure the Blessings of Liberty* (Boston: University Press of America, 1988).

An earlier version of "Have Rights Gone Wrong? The Reconstruction of Rights" appeared in the *American Prospect* (spring 1991).

An earlier version of "Neither Leaders nor Followers: Citizenship under Strong Democracy" appeared in *Essays in Honor of James MacGregor Burns* (Englewood Cliffs, N.J.; Prentice-Hall, 1989).

An earlier version of "Command Performance: Where Have All the Leaders Gone?" appeared in *Harper's* (1975).

"The Undemocratic Party System: Citizenship in an Elite/Mass Society" appeared in *Political Parties in the Eighties;* reprinted with the permission of the American Enterprise Institute for Public Policy Research, Washington, D.C. (1980).

An earlier version of "One Nation Indivisible or a Compact of Sovereign States? The Two Faces of Federalism" appeared in *New Federalism and Long Term Health Care of the Elderly* (Center for Health Affairs, Project Hope, 1984).

An earlier version of "The Civic Mission of the University" appeared in the *Kettering Review* (1989).

"Service, Citizenship and Democracy: Civic Duty as an Entailment of Civic Right" is reprinted from *National Service: Pro and Con,* ed. Williamson M. Evers with the permission of the publisher, Hoover Institution Press, Stanford, Calif. Copyright © 1990 by the Board of Trustees of the Leland Stanford Junior University.

An earlier version of "Cultural Conservatism and Democratic Education: Lessons from the Sixties" appeared in *Salmagundi* (winter 1989).

An earlier version of "America Skips School: Why We Talk So Much about Education and Do So Little" appeared in *Harper's* (November 1993).

An earlier version of "Education for Democracy" appeared in *The Public Purpose of Education and Schooling* (Jossey-Bass, 1997).

An earlier version of "The Second American Revolution" appeared in *Channels* (February–March 1982).

An earlier version of "Pangloss, Pandora, or Jefferson? Three Technology Scenarios" appeared in *Information Technology: The Public Issues* (Manchester University Press, 1991).

Part I

AMERICAN THEORY:
DEMOCRACY, LIBERALISM,
AND RIGHTS

CHAPTER 1

Liberal Democracy and the
Costs of Consent

IN ITS ERRATIC, often glorious, political history since 1688, liberalism has forged many alliances: with rationalism and with empiricism, with revolution and with bureaucracy, with enlightenment and with romanticism, and with laissez-faire economics and with nationalism. But no alliance has served it better than the one it established with democracy. For, by itself, liberalism was a struggle for emancipation from religious and political absolutism that exacted costs liberal principles could not contend with. In establishing the solitary individual as the model citizen, liberalism shortchanged ideas of citizenship and community, and contrived a fictional self so unencumbered by situation and context as to be useful only in challenging the very idea of the political.[1] In emphasizing freedom as the absence of all governmental restraints, it impeded the march of popular sovereignty. In combating higher ecclesiastic and secular authority, it attenuated the capacity of religion and tradition to sustain and integrate.

As Tocqueville noticed, societies organized around the anarchic blessings of freedom are more rather than less in need of the unifying blessings of religion.[2] Yet liberalism's virtues—the wall between church and state, the toleration of conflicting confessions, the acknowledgment of uncertainty, even skepticism, in public thinking—could only further undermine the religious principles whose consolation it needed. Liberalism created a safe haven for individuals and their property, but a poor environment for collective self-government. As liberals were quick to remonstrate, if traditional authoritarian governments endangered the rights and freedoms of individuals, the tyranny of "legitimate" majorities founded on popular sovereignty could be still more onerous. Equality obviously might be an entailment of the idea of the common liberty of individuals, but in its political form (rectification, redistribution, government intervention, social justice) it endangered liberty understood as being left alone. Even friends of democracy such as William Connolly worry that democracy "contains danger" and that it is a danger that "resides within the ideal itself."[3]

The pure liberal state was in fact an oxymoronic conundrum. Anarchy—the absence of all government—was liberalism's purest expression, to be found in principles like the ones inhering in Robert Nozick's minimalist Protective Association, or in the Watchdog State (the state as arbitrator, umpire, regulator or free market rule-keeper).[4] In this pure sense, Hobbes—who is sometimes construed as a liberal by virtue of the instrumentalism with which he makes absolute authority prudentially serve absolute liberty—is no liberal at all.[5]

Of course there has never been an actual state constituted by pure liberal principles. From the start, liberalism forged (at times, was thrown into) a working relationship with democracy, which seemed to share so many of its goals (the welfare and freedom, differently understood, of the individual), even as it created problems for their realization.

Western liberal states are in fact all liberal democracies, combining principles of individual liberty with principles of collective self-government and egalitarianism. And, as a matter of practice, such states have done comparatively well, both by liberty, property, and individualism, on the one hand, and by equality, justice, and self-government, on the other. Many observers would attribute their success precisely to their hybrid form.

Yet in England and North America, the mix has been less than judicious, the balance less then dialectical. Although liberalism has benefited from democracy, it has rarely acknowledged the benefits and has generally treated democratic practices (if not also democratic ideas) as perilous. Rather then permitting democracy to complement liberty, liberty has been given lexical priority over all other principles. Even the manner in which the central problem of politics in the West is formulated is liberal (this is Rousseau's version of that formulation): how to find a form of association that defends and protects the person and goods of each individual, by means of which each one, uniting with all, nonetheless obeys himself alone and remains as free as before.[6] This assumes the priority of the individual and his freedom over the community and its rights, and makes the accommodation of the individual, regarded as an a priori, the task of the community, regarded as an artificial contrivance.[7]

The priority of the "liberal" in liberal democracy has rendered democracy vulnerable to modernity's most devastating political pathology: deracination. The impact of the Enlightenment on religion and the impact of epistemological skepticism and post-Enlightenment science on nature and natural law have left modern women and men to live in an era after virture, after God, after nature, an era offering neither comfort nor certainty. Freedom has been won by a ruthless severing of ties ("all that is solid melts into air," wrote Marx) and an uprooting of human nature from its foundations in the natural, the historical, and the divine.[8]

The specific pathologies that have been occasioned by deracination need little comment, for they are by now a very old story. Yet they still are frequently overlooked by those who champion liberalism's defensive properties as a protector of individuals against communities gone awry and states run amok.[9] Indeed, it is arguable that the forces that created the greatest pressures on the liberty of individuals in the twentieth century are, at least in part, the consequences of deracination, social anarchy, and rampant individualism—the consequence not of too much democracy and too little liberalism but of too little democracy and too much liberalism. Fascism in Germany was preceded by the Weimar Republic's wan liberalism; and the authoritarian personality would seem to be at least in part the product of deracination.[10]

I believe that liberal democracy has been given an insufficiently dialectical reading in modern political theory, as a result in large part of the theorists' reliance on the notion of consent as the crucial bridge between the individual and the community (between liberty and justice and between right and utility). The doctrine of consent was originally intended to give obedience a justification rooted in the interests of individuals rather than in the authority of states (in the rights of the ruled rather than the rights of rulers) and did not necessarily entail democratic arrangements. But it also created principled grounds for democracy by making all political legitimacy a function of popular will. The consent device skewed the relationship toward liberal individualism from the outset, however. It deprived liberals of the comforts of democracy as they tried to accommodate the communities produced by individuals (whom they recognized as such) with the individuals produced by communities (which they refused to recognize).

Unlike pure liberalism of the Nozickean variety, in which the individual stands as the sole measure of right, liberal democracy claims both to unite individuals with the community and to preserve individual liberty in the face of community—leaving men "as free as they were before" (Rousseau's formulation). In Michael Sandel's language, it aspires to mediate the extremes of the "radically situated self" (presumably the collectivist conception) and the "radically disembodied subject" (the libertarian conception).[11] Moreover, it seeks a bridge that does not depend on some foundationalist conception either of right or good. Liberal democrats are not unmitigated voluntarists, but per force they eschew traditional foundationalism of the kind that makes politics depend entirely upon ideas derived from grounds independent of and anterior to the political. The liberal democrat prizes justice but believes justice without consent is a form of heteronomy incompatible with the moral responsibility of the individual. Consent becomes the crucial link: for Locke, for example, what men will consent to in the state of nature binds them henceforward; for Rawls, what men will consent to in a hypothetical original position, before they know the actual identities they will assume in society, binds them to the rules they will live by in society.[12]

By consenting to the substantive rules to which he will subordinate his will, the liberal individual obeys without compromising his freedom. The conception of democracy that emerges from contract—that is to say, from consent theory—does provide some security for liberty and rights, by rooting them in a voluntarism that is immune from the immediacy of popular will. The arbitrary whimsy (the subjectivism) of pure voluntarism is avoided without embracing discredited forms of metaphysical foundationalism.

Consent plays a central role in all liberal theory, but it is differently construed in Hobbes, in Locke, in Nozick, and in Rawls. As consent changes the forms it takes, liberal democracy changes its colors. Yet in every form it permits liberal ideas to take precedence over democratic ideas. Moving from the weakest to the strongest, three primary forms of consent can be discerned: we may understand them as original consent, periodic consent, and perpetual consent. The first, in which individuals offer consent once in the form of a covenant that obliges them henceforward to obey whatever rules the civil society they have thus created may promulgate, is original consent, or the doctrine of the social contract. Original consent embraces both the form where individuals agree to procedures by which rules are made (social contract constitutionalism), without consenting to the actual rules, as well as the form where individuals agree in advance to the actual rules, as with Rawls. The second major form taken by consent theory, calling for a kind of ongoing commitment to the contract, engages individuals in periodic rehearsals of consent, most often through the election of representatives. This form is periodic consent, or the doctrine of representative government. It employs elections not merely to assure the accountability of representative governors but also to elicit periodic fidelity from citizens whose commitments might otherwise weaken. The third, and strongest, form requires consent to each and every collective act (each law, contract, bargain, encroachment, and so on). It approaches the spirit of pure liberalism, where government exists and acts exclusively at the pleasure of each individual with whom it interacts. This is perpetual consent, or the market doctrine of libertarianism (a stone's throw from what I earlier called "pure liberalism").[13]

In terms of the hypothetical politics they produce, the three regimes that emerge from these three forms of consent look very different. Social-contract theorists may be satisfied with highly authoritarian and illiberal regimes that are still legitimate by liberal standards because they are authorized by an original contract to which all subjects initially give their consent (if only tacitly). One thinks of Hobbes or Hamilton. Advocates of representative government, such as Locke, require that citizens reaffirm their government and thus their civic commitment from time to time by periodically reauthorizing the governors (who are only trustees of their electors). Libertarians are fierce and constant consenters who demand perpetual vigilance by individuals for whom every new social act is a potential encroachment.

Social-contract theorists take a tacit and relatively passive view of the role of consent—once suffices for all time—which raises issues of compliance (covenants without the sword, free riders, and so on); advocates of representation take the middle ground, enhancing the autonomous activity of citizens as individuals while limiting their common power to the act of selecting rulers, but otherwise discouraging ongoing self-rule; and libertarians make consent a cudgel with which they beat the very idea of collective governmental activity into senselessness.

However different they are in theory, all three versions of consent theory merge in the practice of Western governments, almost all of which are "mixed" regimes with respect to original, periodic, and perpetual consent. Indeed the pluralism of such governments arises in part out of jurisdictional quarrels between these conflicting forms of consent—as when the Supreme Court intervenes in the name of original consent (the integrity of the Constitution, representing the original voice of the people) to overrule elected officials operating in the name of periodic consent (they represent the citizens who have elected them to office) in order to uphold the complaint of a private citizen who has challenged the government in the name of his own liberty (embodying the principle of perpetual consent). These mixed liberal democratic regimes share certain fundamental weaknesses that take us to the heart of the problem with consent as the liberal linchpin.

Perhaps most disconcerting among the defects of liberalism that arise out of its dependence on consent is the reactivity—and thus the negativity—consent imparts to liberal politics. Politics becomes purely defensive; the model political act is resistance to encroachment on a private sphere defined by the autonomous and solitary person. And while the radically isolated individual may originate a purely logical priority, the ideal individual's sphere of activity in the real world seems always to be expanding, as the domain of the person is enlarged by outward pushing liberties and rights, and then enlarged still more by that extension of the person and its liberties liberals call property—ownership of things as an entailment of self-ownership.[14] The ultimate battle cry of the liberal is "Don't cross this line!" The political slogan always reads "Don't walk on my turf!" Liberalism is a politics of negativity, which enthrones not simply the individual but the individual defined by his perimeters, his parapets, and his entrenched solitude. Politics is at best a matter of "Let's make a deal," where the stakes are exclusively private ("What will it take to get you to honor my liberty?").

Politics understood as reactive negativity and the denial of every commonality other than that of aggregated individuality reduces the role of will to one of obstinate resistance. Hence it obstructs common willing—what Rousseau called general willing—where communities essay to disclose common purposes or discover common ground through the political interaction of active wills. The very idea of sovereignty, construed as the paramountcy of a common will, cannot exist in a setting defined by the primacy of the right of the individual to unlimited resistance (that resistance being seen as a property of essential—and hence rightful—human nature). Politics becomes a matter of "not doing" rather than of "doing," and the individual becomes sovereign, always trumping the community.

Historically, the focus on resistance had powerful political uses in emancipating individuals from feudal authority. The priority of the individual was an artificial device, which (although everywhere contradicted by the real life dependency of individuals on hierarchical social structures) helped to free men from bondage. The fiction preceded the reality: in fact, the fiction created the reality, for it was meant not as a defense of preexisting individuals against encroaching authority, but as a justification for the forging of individuals from socially constructed subjects. The point was not to legitimize natural individuals, but to legitimize individuation in the face of "natural" (historical and traditional) collectivism. The "natural" man was merely a hypothetical contrivance whose wholly rhetorical significance was not to be mistaken for the kind of anthropological conjectures that would in time be favored by the romantics (noble savages and all that).[15]

The useful fiction of the independent person soon hardened into a supposed reality of naturally autonomous men, and this new and contrived "reality" became the basis for denying both the historical legitimacy of unfree commonality (feudalism, ancient slavery, traditional tyranny) and thus the future possibility of a free commonality. Abstract personhood, so fruitful as an emancipatory hypothesis, subverted ideas of democratic community and democratic cooperation in its inevitable reification. We have traditionally worried about the consequences of the reification of the collectivity or the state. I am suggesting that we might also have some reason to worry about the political consequences of the reification of the individual—an idealized abstraction given a concrete incarnation if ever there was one. Individuals, merely separate in the hypothesis, became competitive and adversarial in the anthropologized version, where they were confounded with bargainers in the new capitalist economy and predators in the dawning age of imperialism. And where every individual faces every other individual not merely as distinct but as an adversary, where possessiveness and aggressiveness are primary and highly prized social traits, where the Other is seen first as an antagonist and last (if at all) as a neighbor, where suspicion of encroachment is the chief political motive, there can be no politics of cooperation. Nor is a viable conception of a public sector or a common good likely to emerge. Crippled from the outset by the very framework that made it liberating, liberalism needed democracy. It had to have a politics to complement its antipolitics. Yet it was averse to the democratic ideas that provided it with that politics.

The tensions have persisted. Anxious witnesses to our century's statist and collectivist depredations may understandably perceive in the resisting negativity of pure liberalism our best defense against every form of unfreedom. Judith Shklar reminds us how often some noble common purpose has been employed to hurt vulnerable bodies, as if their animal fragility made them ignoble.[16] But it is also true that twentieth-century collectivism is in part a consequence of the failure of liberalism to offer a healthy politics of community. There is a deep yearning, well known to liberals, for a more supple and intersubjective identity than that offered by the hollow shell of legal presonhood; when it is not satisfied by some safe, democratic form of mutualism, the door is wide open to unsafe, totalitarian forms of mutualism. By construing politics exclusively in terms of reaction, liberals limit it to resisting Others (or the political incarnation of Others, the state)—an antipolitical act at best—or to acquiescing to them—politics understood as compliance, agreeing to but not doing. Even Robert Nozick's self-interested anarchist busybodies, perpetually examining potential bilateral exchanges with others for signs of encroachment, are limited to a political vocabulary of "OK, I'll buy it" or "No deal!" In these one-shot yea/nay situations, the role of common deliberation, general willing, and public judgment is negligible. There is little room for anything resembling public space—except for those who seize it for their own private purposes.

Indeed, for liberals, public space has an exclusively prudential feel (that space ceded to government which permits government to enforce the integrity of private boundaries) and is not intended to convey a rich sense of publicness or commonwealth or res publica. Contrary to historical reality, where public space was the condition of the emergence of individuals, it exists in liberal theory only as a concession reluctantly proffered by individuals pursuing self-preservation or self-aggrandizement. It is at best the domain of prudence where individuals strike public bargains (like the Social Contract) in the pursuit of private interests. Even in Hobbes's authoritarian version, every act of the omnipotent, irresistible sovereign finds its ultimate justification in the original authority of those self-interested authors of the contract who are struggling to avoid lives which, in the state of nature where liberty is theoretically uncompromised, are solitary, poor, nasty, brutish, and short.[17] American pluralist theory does not advance much beyond Hobbes in this regard, since the Madisonian formula is distrustful of democracy and places its faith in dividing power (and interest) against itself so as to safeguard liberty from its putative governmental protectors. Madison emulates Locke in worrying more about the peril to liberty presented by the sovereign Lion than about the small mischiefs polecats and foxes might do to their common liberties. In general, liberals deploy a political language drawn from the menagerie, reenforcing with metaphor their essentially adversarial (what could later be called Darwinian) conception of the social relations of their fictive "persons."

To be sure, the language of consent is in principle an attempt at bridging the liberty of liberalism and the demos of democracy, but the foregoing survey of what consent actually entails suggests that it does little to bring individual and commons into equilibrium. Its final result is the dogmatic justification of the priority of liberty (liberty understood as the absence of all external—read public—constraint),[18] and thus the priority—even in Rawls—of right over utility, of the liberty of the abstract individual over the needs of community-created citizens.[19]

For some time, critics of the skewed liberal version of liberal democracy have been urging an alternative formulation, one centering on participation rather than consent. My own elaboration of the theory and practice of "strong democracy" is intended to help conceptualize this alternative view.[20] Participation turns out to provide a much more dialectical account of the relation between individuals and the community than consent can possibly hope to. It offers a framework for institutions that safeguards the liberty of individuals without alienating them from public space—since their liberty is constructed in and with respect to that public space.

Taking participation seriously does not reverse the priority of individual and community (which would produce some form of totalist collectivism) but strikes a genuine balance between the two.[21] To do so acknowledges the interdependence of individuals on one another and on the communities from which they derive sustenance of their identities and their (socially constructed) rights, and thus makes of morally autonomous citizens the aim rather than the premise of liberal democratic politics.

Participation is less a way of linking previously or "naturally" autonomous persons to an artificial and sovereign collectivity than it is of characterizing and legitimizing the provisional autonomy that real men and women living under conditions of actual dependency can elicit from the social milieus in which they are embedded. Participation is a form of belonging in which active agency is transferred from the whole to the parts, which, however, possess a capacity for effective action by virtue of their membership in the whole.

The hypothetical act by which the community based on the consent of "naturally free" individuals is formed must be: "Let's make a state we all obey, in return for which it will protect us from each other [Hobbes] and from itself [the prudent Locke]." The hypothetical act by which the community based on participation is formed is "Let's take this collectivity into which we were all born and to which, willy-nilly, we all are bound and legitimize it by subjecting it to our common will." Where with consent, the archetypical political act is *resistance against or acquiescence to encroachment,* with participation, the archetypical political act is *disclosing and legitimizing common ground,* or *willing common action in the absence of common ground.* In a word, it is collaboration rather than antagonism, learning to live with conflict rather than constructing a geometry and vector physics of conflict.[22]

Underlying the model of participation is a conception of the person radically distinctive from the one underlying the model of consent.[23] The liberal person is a fixed being with an identity arising out of theoretically constructed interests made legitimate by the heightened language of rights. Liberal rights are in fact individual interests posturing as moral claims. (This is an oddity, in that moral claims presuppose a moral-social environment in which claims have meaning—the point T. H. Green makes in his work.)[24] The force of this conception lies precisely in the fixity and immutability of interests, which define the natural and unchanging social monads who constitute liberal persons.

The participating citizen, however, is a being with a mutable nature, whose evolution is in part a function of its social habitat. It is this very talent for self-transformation that enables the citizen thus conceived to engage in the process of individuation: not merely to engage in bargaining and exchange over fixed and permanent interests but to modify the notion of what those interests actually are. Participation entails change—a faculty for self-transformation—for the community as well as for the participating member. The bachelor who becomes a spouse is not a bachelor who has made a bargain, but someone who has given up the identity and interests appropriate to bachelorhood and assumed the identity and interests of someone participating in a life partnership. Spousehood supplants bachelorhood as a point of view, so that the spouse ceases to think or act like a bachelor. A spouse who in turn becomes a parent is not a spouse who has cut a deal with pushy and self-preoccupied (that is, infantile!) newcomers who were not parties to the original marital contract. He is someone who has given up the identity of spouse in favor of an identity that includes the interests and concerns of children. In moving from bachelor to parent, the man and the woman are transformed by the relations they enter into, even as, by virtue of their participation, they transform the character of the community they belong to. The compass of their sympathies enlarges; their capacity to identify the concerns of a growing "neighborhood" as *their* concerns alters their own sense of identity.

Participatory citizenship is an extension of the same principles to strangers. The moves from parent to neighbor, from neighbor to townsperson, from townsperson to citizen of the United States, all have the same potential of self-transformation, when the link to the community is participatory and not merely consensual. As the sphere of identification grows, identity undergoes a change. The office of citizen is not just a role assumed momentarily by the individual; it is a mantle that settles over the shoulders and in time becomes an organic epidermis of the skin on which it rests. The state is a neighborhood of strangers. It cannot deal with its constituents through the intimate roles of friendship or kinship because they are strangers; yet it need not treat them as adversaries, one to the other, because they are also neighbors.

If the individuals who participate are changelings whose consciousness grows (or can potentially grow) as the sphere of their activity enlarges, then their activity when they participate is far more demanding—more engaging, more enthralling, more disquieting—than their activity when they merely consent, when they act exclusively to resist or to acquiesce. Participation entails constant activity, ceaseless willing, and endless interaction with other participants in quest of common grounds for common living. The one-time contract offends the idea of participation, which demands with Jefferson that principles be constantly remembered, deliberated, reembraced, even reinvented, if they are to earn their legitimacy among the living.[25] Nor is the sometime contract called representation an adequate surrogate for civic participation. For while the election of representatives requires some periodic activity from citizens, it is a political act whose purpose is to terminate political action for all but the elected delegates. It achieves accountability by alienating responsibility, and leaves elected politicians as the only real citizens of the state.[26]

The perpetual consent demanded by libertarians would on first inspection seem better to approximate the vigorous civic activity associated with participation, and the libertarian is certainly a busy fellow as he rushes to and fro, defending his perimeters against the endless encroachments of his hungry neighbors. But not only is his activity limited to fight/flight reactions (yea/nay judgments on potential encroachments), whatever he does lacks public import of any kind. Public relations become private relations, and commonality is reduced to a series of trustless bilateral exchanges.

This liberal vision calls to mind a kind of Brownian motion by agitated human molecules that results in random movement with no consistent or patterned (that is, public) character. On the other hand, participation is by its very nature public activity whose aim is to produce publicity or public-mindedness. Participation is participating in public discourse (finding discourse that is public) and participating in public action (action possible only when actors act together) in the name of creating public things res publica. The language of consent is *me* language: "*I agree*" or "*I disagree*." The language of participation is *we* language: "Can we?" or "Is that good for us?"

The libertarian damns the contractarian for being satisfied with a single act of willed compliance and then sitting in torpor for eternity. How can a man speak but once and then remain forever mute? The libertarian knows he must sing on, and so, on and on he sings (on and on and on and on). But chirping away from his solitary branch against the din of rival birds he produces only cacophony.

Noise is of course a concomitant of democratic politics, and the citizen has nothing to fear from a little high decibel cacophony. But the aim is harmony: the discovery of a common voice. Not unity, not voices disciplined into unison, but musical harmony in its technical meaning. Liberals grow particularly anxious at what they believe is a democratic penchant for consensus and unity. William Connolly, for example, insists that democracy must be limited by ambiguity and open to discord.[27] He might recall, however, that in music, harmony is not a matter of a single voice but of several voices, of distinct notes, which complement and support one another, creating not the ennui of unison but a pleasing plurality. Harmony is not monism, and the consensus reached by democratic deliberation and action has nothing in common with the unity imposed by the collectivist demagogue armed with a plebiscite.

Democratic politics need not be limited by ambiguity because it embraces and teaches us how to live with ambiguity. It is precisely about common decision making in the face of ambiguity and uncertainty. (Certain knowledge would transform politics into an exercise in expertise and promote a Platonic government of the most knowledgeable.) It is precisely where we cannot know for sure that we must act democratically. In the best of circumstances we may achieve a harmony within our civic communities that preserves our hard-won individuality but permits us to support and complement the individuality of other participants. In those rare moments where inevitable cacophony is transformed briefly into harmony (but not totalitarian unity), participation achieves its greatest civic victory, realizing an egalitarian community that accommodates individuals without destroying their individuality—an achievement which, though perhaps beyond the liberal imagination, is deeply satisfying to the liberal spirit.

These images, I know, are redolent of a kind of democratic idealism that is worrisome to liberals, whose chief political concern remains the abuse of individual bodies (and spirits, but bodies first of all) by illegitimate power. But the possibility of harmony is a by-product of participatory politics: a remarkable achievement when accomplished, but not essential to the argument on behalf of participation. For, as I have suggested, participatory politics is in the first instance simply a more realistic way of understanding the actual relationship that obtains between individual and community, as well as a more dialectical way of envisioning how that relationship (which by nature is one of dependency) can be made legitimate (just). In fact, it is the most prudent defense liberty can deploy in an era uprooted from foundations in religion, history, or tradition.

In a world after virtue, where the foundational certainties of God and Nature have gone the way of metaphysics, and where men and women are compelled to live together and find both mediators for their conflicts and a forge for their commonality, liberal democracy in the participatory mode may be humankind's safest form of politics. The individual is a paltry vessel when torn apart from within by doubt and vacillation. Liberty rings hollow to women and men whose lives lack purpose and meaning: it is then only the right to do everything in a world where one has no idea of what to do. In emancipating us from authority, liberalism separated us from one another. Resistance was a powerful instrument in taking on popes and kings and their ex cathedra arguments, but when the very idea of God withers and when, freed from arbitrary authority, women and men grow desperate for almost any authority at all, resistance ceases to be a useful political tool. To the creature trapped within the fortress, the impregnable redoubt may come to feel like a prison. Liberals, ever wary, still preach "Defend yourselves! The enemy is everywhere!" And, to be sure, wherever there are policies, policemen, and power, there lurk potential enemies of liberty. Yet the price we pay for this vigilance is also to see enemies where there are only neighbors, antagonism where there may be cooperation. In safeguarding our separate bodies, we neglect the body politic; in expressing our dignity as individuals, we fail to dignify our sociability and give it a safe form of expression. The alternative to legitimate community is not natural liberty but illegitimate community. The alternative to democratic politics is not the absence of all politics but undemocratic politics. An unhealthy polity is not an occasion for a righteous return to prepolitical individuality: it is the occasion for the destruction of individuality tout court.

Our human strength lies in our capacity for community. Abandoned by God and nature, we must depend on each other; yet we are saddled with a residual politics of emancipation that forbids us mutual consolation or cooperation. In the long freedom wars, liberalism won a thousand important battles, securing first the individual and his rights, and then the rights of others long excluded from liberty's fruits. But the costs of victory are now being paid: the price of liberal reliance on contract and consent has been the impoverishment of its politics. The argument for participation is thus not idealistic but brutally realistic. It is how liberals can safely pay the piper—who, one way or the other, *will* be paid.

A more dialectically balanced liberal democracy employing the language and institutions of participation can respond to modernity's losses by reenforcing the individual from within and by offering artificial membership in new contrived communities of common will from without. Participation subjects standards, whose roots in natural or metaphysical foundations have withered, to the voluntary and common conventions of a democratic polity, permitting artifice to achieve what nature no longer can. And if artifice is to be safe, it is clear, it must be democratic: the subject of common deliberation and decision. Participation greets the loss of certainty with neither cynicism nor despair but with a novel epistemology of political judgment: concrete processes by which our convictions can be measured by something firmer than private prejudice in a world where cognitive certainty is no longer vouchsafed us.[28]

If we are to learn to live with what Clifford Geertz has called the vertigo of relativism, participatory democracy can be an instructive teacher. It offers hope without making foolish promises. It proffers not a civic religion but a civic life that binds without enslaving, that ties together the frayed pieces left behind by the unraveling of religion. It instructs us to look to common invention for the social sustenance we once derived from tradition.

Strong democracy cannot replace the loss of foundations that is modernity's legacy, but it promises a certain prudence in place of mores, tradition, and history. It is a politics of modest hope in a world of despair. And, liberal skepticism notwithstanding, liberty remains today what it has always been: the hope we fling into the teeth of sovereign necessity to make a small space for human will and for the virtue will enjoins.

NOTES

1. This is a now familiar criticism put forward in its classical form by Comte, Marx, and the nineteenth-century sociological tradition, and given modern philosophical expression by Charles Taylor, Michael Walzer, William Sullivan, Alasdair MacIntyre, and many others—for example, Michael Sandel, who in his critique of Rawls's liberal conception of the self writes: "But a self so thoroughly independent as [Rawls's] rules out any conception of the good (or the bad). . . . It rules out the possibility of any attachment (or obsession) able to reach beyond our values and sentiments to engage our identity itself. It rules out the possibility of a public life. . . . And it rules out the possibility that common purposes and ends could inspire more or less expansive self-understandings and so define a community."

Michael J. Sandel, *Liberalism and the Limits of Justice* (Cambridge: Cambridge University Press, 1982), p. 62.

2. "Despotism may govern without faith, but liberty cannot. Religion is much more necessary in the republic . . . than in the monarchy. . . . [I]t is more needed in democratic republics than in any others. How is it possible that society should escape destruction if the moral tie is relaxed?" Alexis de Tocqueville, *Democracy in America,* ed. Phillips Bradley, 2 vols. (New York: Vintage, 1960), II, 318.

3. William E. Connolly, *Politics and Ambiguity* (Madison: University of Wisconsin Press, 1987), p. 3.

4. Thus, when in *State and Revolution,* Lenin (what irony!) writes that "while the state exists there is no freedom. When there is freedom there will be no state," he is speaking quintessentially liberal language.

5. Liberals rightly pall at the idea of Hobbes as a liberal predecessor because his fear of anarchy leads him to embrace an authoritarian conception of the state incompatible with limited government. Yet inasmuch as the state serves a liberty the natural condition imperils, Hobbes does share a crucial liberal premise: that the legitimating political principle is in the service of individual self-preservation, which is the sine qua non of liberty. For a recent, subtly argued construction of Hobbes as a defender of the individual and his fragile body, see George Kateb, "Hobbes and the Irrationality of Politics," *Political Theory* 17, no. 3 (August 1989): 355–91.

6. Jean-Jacques Rousseau, *The Social Contract,* bk. I, chap. 6.

7. Will Kymlicka defends liberals against communitarian charges that their conception of the individual is abstract and atomistic. But, in addition to turning every liberal from Rawls to Dworkin and Nozick into John Stuart Mill, he misses the essence of the criticism, which is not simply that liberals neglect community or the constraints of encumbered selves, but that they consistently treat both as secondary to and logically and morally dependent on prior conceptions of unencumbered individuals. See Will Kymlicka, "Liberalism and Comunitarianism," *Canadian Journal of Philosophy* 18 (June 1988): 181–204.

8. See Marshall Berman's splendid essay on modernity and disorder, which uses Marx's phrase in its title: *All That Is Solid Melts Into Air* (New York: Simon and Schuster, 1982).

9. Judith Shklar's essay "The Politics of Fear," in *Liberalism and the Moral Life,* ed. Nancy L. Rosenblum (Cambridge: Harvard University Press, 1989) is representative. Both Richard Flathman and, from a very different point of view, George Kateb champion freedom without entering into a full discussion of its costs to community and identity, although Kateb acknowledges the debt liberty owes to citizenship in "The Moral Distinctiveness of Representative Democracy," *Ethics* 91 (April 1981): 357–74.

10. This argument was first advanced after World War II by Theodor Adorno and his colleagues in *The Authoritarian Personality* (New York: Harper, 1950), and by psychologists such as Erich Fromm, Robert Jay Lifton, and Viktor Frankl.

11. Sandel, *Liberalism and the Limits of Justice,* p. 54.

12. John Rawls, *A Theory of Justice* (Cambridge, Mass.: Harvard University Press, 1971). As I have argued elsewhere (*The Conquest of Politics* [Princeton:

Princeton University Press, 1988], pp. 54–55)—Kymlicka, "Liberalism and Communitarianism" notwithstanding—Rawls's logical prioritization of liberty entails a psychological and political prioritization that defeats the attempt at mediation.

13. Robert Nozick is the most vociferous recent advocate of this brand of strong liberalism. See his *Anarchy, the State and Utopia* (New York: Basic Books, 1974).

14. C. B. Macpherson's account of possessive individualism (in *The Political Theory of Possessive Individualism* [Oxford: Oxford University Press, 1961]) may not always be creditable as intellectual history, but it remains a persuasive vision of the liberal democratic conception of the self, and how the self-possessing individual becomes the acquisitive (property-owning) individual.

15. The social contract theorists tried to have it both ways, surrounding their ruminations about the possible historicity of the social contract with caveats about the hypothetical character of the state of nature. Rousseau is typical here, offering an anthropology of natural man in the *Second Discourse* that he studiously avoids in *The Social Contract,* where he makes it clear not only that the state of nature is hypothetical, but that man's actual condition is one of dependency (man is "everywhere in chains").

16. See Shklar's powerful defense of the liberalism of fear, n. 9 above.

17. The familiar portrait of man's life in the state of nature in *Leviathan,* chap. 13.

18. "Liberty, or freedom, signifieth, properly, the absence of opposition; by opposition, I mean external impediments of motion. . . . [A] freeman, is he, that in those things, which by his strength and wit he is able to do, is not hindered to do what he has a will to." *Leviathan,* chap. 21.

19. The lexical ordering of the principles of justice "means that a departure from the institutions of equal liberty required by the first principle cannot be justified by, or compensated for, by greater social and economic advantages" (Rawls, *Theory of Justice,* p. 61).

20. Benjamin R. Barber, *Strong Democracy: Participatory Politics for a New Age* (Berkeley: University of California Press, 1984).

21. Reversing the polarity and giving community the priority that, for liberal individualists, the individual enjoys, only reverses the imbalance and creates a different set of problems well known to critics of communitarian (totalitarian) collectivism. Most recent communitarians respect the dialectical interplay of individual and community, however, and do not dispute the ultimate concern for individuals. The question is not the normative priority of the individual, but how the individual is morally and politically constituted. This is the essence of Michael Sandel's critique in *Liberalism and the Limits of Justice,* and is a position that Rawls himself moves toward in his recent work (see note 23).

22. The collaborative character of participatory politics does not, as liberal critics sometimes seem to suppose, require that conflict be wished away or denied. On the contrary, as Rousseau observed, without conflict there would be no politics and thus no need for government at all (the anarchist premise, which is closer to libertarian liberalism than democratic communitarianism). Connolly typically exaggerates the democratic penchant for conflict-free harmony; see also note 27.

23. Philosophers have come to appreciate that the rigid conception of the person

demanded by the fiction of the legal person or the free agent needs to be supplemented by a richer conception of the moral and social person. This is particularly apparent in John Rawls's recent work, which, as it pushes a morally constructed person toward its center, distances itself from hypothetical persons bent into abstract Archimedean positions. See, for example, "Kantian Constructivism in Moral Theory" (The Dewey Lectures), *Journal of Philosophy* 77 (September 1980): 515–73; and "Justice as Fairness: Political, Not Metaphysical," *Philosophy and Public Affairs* 14 (Summer 1985): 223–51, as well as *Political Liberalism*.

24. "There can be no right without a consciousness of common interest on the part of members of a society. . . . Without this recognition or claim to recognition there can be no right" (T. H. Green, *Lectures on the Principles of Political Obligation* [London: Longmans, 1941], p. 48).

25. "No society can make a perpetual constitution, or even a perpetual law. The earth belongs always to the living generation. . . . [E]very constitution then, and every law, naturally expires at the end of 19 years," Thomas Jefferson to Madison, 1789. Jefferson and John Stuart Mill share with libertarians like Nozick an affection for perpetual consent, but whereas for the libertarians this suggests private consent to public acts, to Jefferson and Mill it suggests the importance of active citizenship and ongoing participation.

26. This line of criticism has an impressive pedigree. In *Political Parties* (Glencoe: University of Illinois Press, 1915), Robert Michels turns Rousseau's disdain for representation into a profound critique of the party system.

27. "We need a theory and practice of democracy," writes Connolly, "that appreciates [the] element of disharmony. One that understands harmonization to be normalization." *Politics and Ambiguity*, p. 8, "Normalization" as used here is highly pejorative, suggesting the kinds of leveling, routinization, and noncoercive repression (*gleichschaltung*) long associated with both democratic conformism (in Tocqueville's critique) and bourgeois liberalism (in Foucault's critique). But the harmony that issues from the interplay of democratic wills has the richness of a seven-tone chord and is neither unitary nor repressive.

28. See Benjamin R. Barber, "Political Judgment: Philosophy as Practice," in *The Conquest of Politics* (Princeton: Princeton University Press, 1988), where I have tried to spell out a political theory of judgment in greater detail.

CHAPTER 2

Foundationalism and Democracy

THE LEADING political philosophical question of the eighties—Does democracy have foundations?—may not be the leading political philosophical question of the nineties. But it remains critical in that it compels an ongoing debate about the meaning of democracy itself. Whatever the merit of foundationalist approaches, they tend to mandate a construction of democracy that favors natural liberty and absolute rights. I wish here to ask not only whether democracy has foundations but what sort of democracy it is that can do without foundations or, indeed, repudiates foundations precisely because of what it requires politically.

The very question, "Does democracy have foundations?" is dangerous for democrats of my tendencies, because it mandates a discussion on the turf of epistemology that leans toward an answer in the affirmative, and yields an understanding of democracy hostile to what I believe are its necessary participatory attributes. But if democracy is concerned with a form of knowledge (say, knowledge of political things such as power, or political values such as rights, or political ends such as justice) or constituted by institutions and procedures that rest on knowledge (say, constitutions or the principle of majoritarianism), then unless we wish to invite an abject politics of relativism or arbitrariness, to the question of whether democracy has foundations we are perforce obliged to reply, "Well, yes, democracy must have foundations in truths antecedent to and not dependent upon it." How, after all, can any cognitive moral or political system function without roots in a prior understanding of what constitutes true knowledge?

By my lights, however, it is the character of politics in general, and of democratic politics in particular, that it is precisely *not* a cognitive system concerned with what we know and how we know it but a system of conduct concerned with what we *will* together and *do* together and how we agree on what we will to do. It is practical not speculative, about action rather than about truth. It yields but is not premised on an epistemology and in this sense is necessarily pragmatic. Where there is truth or certain knowledge there need be no politics, even though (as Plato warns) politicians and citizens may wantonly ignore truth and certain knowledge in pursuit of base interests or raw power. But democratic politics begins where certainty ends. As I suggested in *Strong Democracy,* the political question always takes a form something like: "What shall we do when something has to be done that affects us all, we wish to be reasonable, yet we disagree on means and ends and are without independent grounds for making the choice."[1]

This, then, is the sense in which politics is ineluctably pragmatic and so, as William James says of pragmatism, turns its back resolutely and once and for all "upon a lot of inveterate habits dear to professional philosophers . . . away from abstraction and insufficiency, from verbal solutions, from bad a priori reasons, from fixed principles, closed systems, and pretended absolutes and origins."[2] As democratic politics are pragmatic, so pragmatism is democratic: "See already how democratic [pragmatism] is," James rhapsodized; "Her manners are as various and flexible, her resources as rich and endless."[3]

Politics occupies the domain of practical action. As Dewey suggests, "the distinctive characteristic of practical activity . . . is the uncertainty that attends it."[4] The philosophical quest for certainty inspires a longing "to find a realm in which there is an activity which is not overt and which has no external consequences. 'Safety first' has played a large role in effecting preference for knowing over doing and making." Like the Greeks, our foundationalists continue to believe that the "office of knowledge is to uncover the antecedently real, rather than, as is the case with our practical judgment, to gain the kind of understanding which is necessary to deal with problems as they arise."[5]

What Bertrand Russell said ruefully about the quest for mathematical truth seems to me to fit perfectly the quest for political truth in the form of foundations antecedent to democratic politics:

> Real life is, to most men, a long second-best, a perpetual compromise between the ideal and the possible; but the world of pure reason knows no compromise, no practical limitations, no barrier to the creative embodying in splendid edifices of the passionate aspiration after the perfect from which all great work springs. Remote from human passions, remote even from the pitiful facts of nature, the generations have gradually created an ordered cosmos, where pure thought can dwell as in its natural home, and where one, at least, of our nobler impulses can escape from the dreary exile of the actual world.[6]

Politics is not an ordered cosmos in which our nobler impulses can be given expression; it is how we try to govern ourselves in "the dreary exile of the actual world." Here we are, to use a metaphor favored both by Charles Sanders Peirce and Michael Oakeshott, afloat on an open and endless sea where, in Peirce's words, we must rebuild our ship "on the open sea, never able to dismantle it in dry dock and to reconstruct it out of the best materials."[7]

Notice already how, despite my intentions, in replying pragmatically to the imperatives of epistemology I am entrapped by its language. Because philosophy always seeks to "create the world in its own image" (Nietzsche), its tyranny is to transform the discussion of politics into a discussion of knowledge, even among those wishing to defend the autonomy and sovereignty of politics. In order to make my case for democracy as a foundationless commitment to a certain form of politics, then, I will shift the argument from the pragmatic/philosophical critique of philosophy, which can only remind us of the power of philosophy, to a political discussion in which the sovereign force of politics becomes evident. Since (Daniel Webster reminds us) governments are instituted for practical benefit and not for subjects of speculative reasoning, let us turn away from the epistemology and toward the politics of democracy. The question is not which politics is legitimated by a certain epistemology, but which epistemology is legitimated by a certain democratic politics.

If epistemological concerns enjoin a definition of democracy in terms of its root values and antecedent normative foundations, democratic politics defined by active citizenship and ongoing deliberation moves in a different direction. Politically, we may define democracy as a regime/culture/civil society/government in which we make (will) common decisions, choose common conduct, and create or express common values in the practical domain of our lives in an ever-changing context of conflict of interests and competition for power—a setting, moreover, where there is no agreement on prior goods or certain knowledge about justice or right and where we must proceed on the premise of the base equality both of interests and of the interested. Voting involves not a discretionary decision about what is true but a necessary decision about what to do. This political definition suggests certain attributes of democratic politics that help explain why democracy cannot and does not rest on "foundations" in the way that (say) natural law or Platonic justice do. These attributes include:

> **1.** the revolutionary spirit of democracy, which is tied to its spontaneity, its creativity, and its responsiveness to change;
> **2.** the autonomy of democracy, which entails a commitment to engagement, participation, and empowerment; and
> **3.** the commonality or publicness of democratic judgment (decision-making with respect to common action) in a democracy, which mandates some form of democratic communitarianism and common willing.

Revolutionary spirit. We need to distinguish several aspects of "revolution" in assessing the role of a zealous revolutionary spirit in democracy. Revolutionary resistance, for example, often is rooted in foundationalist claims that are used to assail an illegitimate or arbitrary politics. Thus resistance to seventeenth-century British absolutism was couched in natural rights rhetoric with a strong foundationalist flavor—the absolute monarch understood as a transgressor of inviolable rights antecedent to all political convention. Here revolution is quite literally—in consonance with the astronomical use of the term—a return to an original starting point: the recovery of a foundational prepolitical moment to challenge an illegitimate present politics. Tom Paine thus argued that the American Revolution was actually a "counter-revolution" aimed at recovering ancient British rights violated by a tyrannical monarch.

While this captures an important moment in revolution, I am concerned here rather with the revolutionary spirit associated with political spontaneity—that sense of fresh ownership that each generation brings to a constitution or political order by reembracing its principles.[8] The object here is to make revolution a *permanent* feature of the political landscape rather than just a founding mechanism for a new, more legitimate politics of stasis (the locus classicus of law and order!).

Benjamin Rush reminded would-be democrats that though in the American system "all power is derived from the people, they possess it only on the days of their elections."[9] Thomas Jefferson, who always loved "dreams of the future more than the history of the past,"[10] had a special sensitivity to the centrality (and fragility) of this dimension of revolutionary ardor. He warned against looking "at constitutions with sanctimonious reverence, and deem[ing] them like the ark of the covenant, too sacred to be touched,"[11] and he is known famously for his insistence that "the tree of liberty must be refreshed from time to time with the blood of patriots and tyrants. It is its natural manure."[12] These sentiments were linked both to his conviction that constitutions must change with the times[13] and to his belief that "the earth belongs in usufruct to the living" and "that the dead have neither powers nor rights over it."[14] But it was finally the preservation of the revolutionary spirit itself that was at issue: a "little rebellion now and then," he had argued, was a "good thing" in and of itself.[15]

There is of course a paradox here, since a revolution is always a founding (and thus a foundation) as well as the kindling of a certain spirit of spontaneity hostile to foundationalism. As Hannah Arendt has observed, in America the revolutionary spirit founded a constitution that in time came to be at odds with that spirit—as social contracts and fixed laws are always likely to grow at odds with the spirit of innovation that creates them.[16] Jefferson saw democracy itself, more particularly ward government and active participation by citizens in self-governance, as the remedy to the ossification of the democratic constitution. Like Rousseau before and Robert Michels after him, Jefferson worried that representative government could swallow up a people's liberties and lead to an elective despotism, the worse for being legitimized by a social contract rooted in the very notion of consent being violated by representation. The call for ward government and full participation by citizens "not merely at an election one day in the year, but every day" was to Jefferson the key to the preservation of revolutionary ardor.[17]

The lesson taught by Jefferson is that original consent, derived from the foundational principles of natural right (the essence of social contract reasoning), is inadequate to the democratic mandate—which is why I have spent so much of my career trumpeting the benefits of strong, participatory democracy. By this logic, it is not just foundationalism but foundings themselves that imperil the democratic orders they establish. The tension between constitutional order and the revolutionary spirit has been the subject of two recent books that pointedly capture the contradictions between founding and democracy: Gordon Wood's *The Radicalism of the American Revolution* (winner of the 1993 Pulitzer in history) and, even more suggestively, Bruce Ackerman's *We the People: Foundations.*[18] In the latter book, Ackerman offers a provocative version of "dualist democracy" in which "Rights Foundationalists" face advocates of the actual exercise of popular sovereignty in a contest over the meaning of democracy and of the revolution that made it. Ackerman sees in historical moments like the Founders' rejection of the Articles (and the procedural principles the Articles mandated), or Roosevelt's New Deal, revolutionary emblems of the nation's true democratic spirit. Foundationalism, even where it represents an authoritative establishing of the credentials of democracy, tends then to undermine democracy, and democracy both requires and entails an immunity to its own foundations if it is to flourish.

Michael Oakeshott once said rationalists are "essentially ineducable," by which he meant that, wedded to formal models of truth and cognition, they were closed to the evidence of their senses about the here and now, and the commonsense conversation of those around them.[19] In a similar way, foundationalists may be said to be ineducable and thus immune to democracy for they know their truths up front and have nothing to learn from the democratic process. Foundations immobilize whatever rests on them: that is their purpose. Democracy enjoins constant, permanent motion—a gentle kind of permanent revolution, a movable feast that affords each generation room for new appetites and new tastes, and thus allows political and spiritual migration to new territory.

Autonomy. The autonomy necessary to democracy reinforces the sense of foundationalism's incompatibility with democracy. There is always something heteronomous about roots, antecedents, and a prioris even when they belong to democracy's genealogy. They tell us what is what and order us what to do ("Make no laws abridging speech! Respect private property!") rather than permit us to choose or create by willing into existence (Kant's realm of ends) our values and common objectives, or, minimally, to test fixed rules against changing reality ("Is advertising to count as speech? How about child pornography? Are slaves property?") It is in the name not just of revolution but of autonomy that Jefferson insists that the earth belongs always and first of all to the living.

The principle of liberty, often grounded in foundational reason, none-theless demands liberty from its foundations. Minimally, the free must freely choose (rechoose) their principles to make them their own. Founda-tions dug up, reconsidered (perhaps redesigned), and regrounded (perhaps in new or different soil) are not exactly what foundationalists mean when they speak of foundations. And while in seeking common ends, democracy processes prospective norms, values, and rationales that may be rooted in metaphysics, religion, or foundational ethics, their *legitimacy* is a function not of their genealogy but of their status as products of democratic choice. In this sense, their origins are neither arbitrary nor relativistic, just irrele-vant to their democratic legitimacy.

This is an important point: John Rawls validates principles of justice through the contractualist (consensualist) logic of the original position, which, nevertheless, have independent intuitive and historical status in conceptions of the person. Equal liberty and the difference principle can be argued from a number of persuasive perspectives: but their political validity for Rawls derives from their capacity to survive the consensualist test of reasoning in the veil of ignorance. Likewise, democratic principles originate in historically important, psychologically pertinent, and morally admirable ways: but their legitimacy—how we *know* them politically—depends on the democratic process. Political knowing here meets Dewey's standard: "Knowing," he writes, "is not the act of an outside spectator but of a participator inside the natural and social scene [so that] the true object of knowledge resides in the consequences of directed action."[20] The crite-rion by which this form of knowledge is judged "lies in the method used to secure consequences and not in metaphysical conceptions of the nature of the real."[21] The method turns out to be democracy itself. Dewey thus concludes that "the method of democracy . . . is to bring . . . conflicts out into the open where their special claims can be seen and appraised, where they can be discussed and judged in the light of the more inclusive interests than are represented by either of them separately."[22]

Dewey is portraying something like a general will, where the coinci-dence of particular wills describes a common good that can be willed on behalf of the community. The process modifies and legitimates as "public" not only the interests and principles that adjudicate them but the process itself. Hence Article V of the American Constitution renders the Constitu-tion itself subject to revision via a difficult but specified democratic proce-dure. The operating principle of democracy produced by the imperatives of autonomy is then *reflexivity*: democratic rules, the definition of citizen-ship, the character of rights—however they originate—become legitimate only when subjected to reflexive scrutiny—democratic deliberation and decision.

This means that democracy is self-correcting: its insufficiencies are corrected democratically rather than by the imposition of externalities on the democratic process. The process is dynamic because it is self-transforming; educative. Dewey not only links democracy and education but suggests that "popular government is educative as other modes of political regulation are not. It forces a recognition that there are common interests, even though the recognition of *what* they are is still confused; and the need it enforces of discussion and publicity brings about some clarification of what they are."[23] Clarification can take a long time, but democracy holds out to those with the patience to struggle through rather than against it the promise of reform from within. It took nearly 150 years for American citizenship to be extended from propertied white males to all adult Americans. But the struggle that led to the gradual expansion of the civic ambit was a democratic struggle in which the rules of democracy were used to modify the rules of democracy. A benevolent king or a Platonic Guardian seeking to secure greater equality would have acted far more quickly and decisively, but at the expense of the liberty of those in whose name democracy was evolving. Jefferson's notion that the remedy for the ills of democracy is more democracy speaks to its self-correcting character.

Commonality of political judgment. Perhaps the clearest way to differentiate democratic from foundationalist reasoning is to contrast cognitive judgment and political judgment; the former reverts to epistemological modes of understanding while the latter is firmly rooted in politics and publicity. I will not rehearse the arguments I have offered in defense of political judgment as an enterprise distinct from other forms of judgment elsewhere,[24] but there is much to be said for the view that political judgment is defined by activity in common rather than thinking alone and is hence what democratic politics produces rather than (as with foundations) what produces democratic politics. Democratic political judgment can be exercised only by citizens interacting with one another in the context of mutual deliberation and decision-making on the way to willing common actions. What is required is not foundational mandates or individual mental acumen in rigidly applying fixed standards to a changing world, but such political skills as are necessary to discovering or forging common ground. What is right, or even what a right is, cannot in itself determine political judgment. Rights themselves are constantly being redefined and reinterpreted, dependent for their normative force on the engagement and commitment of an active citizen body.

Bills of Rights, Madison warned, are parchment parapets from which real liberty cannot be defended—more covenants without the sword! In any case, the citizen wishes only to act in common in the face of conflict, not to know with certainty or to uphold ancient norms that claim to be foundational. The object is to resolve or find ways to live with conflict, not to discover the grounds of bliss or a path to eternity. Civic judgment is thus always provisional, constrained by a sense of uncertainty. It is a form of judgment made uneasy by every form of absolutism, including foundational rights absolutism. Democratic politics is what men do when metaphysical foundations fail rather than metaphysical foundations reified as a constitution.

My earlier argument is apposite here: "If political judgment is understood as artful political practice conducted by adept citizens, then to improve our judgment we must strengthen our democratic practices. To think aright about politics, we must act aright, and to act aright calls for better citizens rather than better philosophers. If we find our political judgment defective, it may be the fault of too little rather than too much democracy."[25] Democracy may be established by a foundational logic but it is sustained only by a logic of citizenship. It is made in Athens but enacted and practiced in Sparta (the Athenians, said Rousseau, knew how to think aright; the Spartans how to act aright). Citizens are men and women who have learned to live freely and in common under rules they make for themselves, and who are thus capable not just of survival but of flourishing both in spite of the foundations that have supported their birth and in the absence of all foundations. Like every political system, democracy too has a birth mother, and thus rests on foundations. Unlike every other political system, however, democracy is necessarily self-orphaned, the child who slays its parents so that it may grow and flourish autonomously. This may dismay those like Burke who believe that in hacking up its aged parents democracy destroys its soul; but it will be seen by all those who wish to assure the sovereignty of the political in a setting of equality and liberty as a melancholy necessity. Reflexivity once again turns out to be democracy's great virtue. Democracy is the debate about what democracy is; democratic citizenship entails an argument about whom democratic citizenship includes; democratic politics debates and ultimately defines the limits of the democratic polity, thus adjudicating issues of private and public, society and state, individual and community. Courts may enforce "natural" or "higher" rights but do so finally at the pleasure of the democratic sovereign. If that sovereign believes the judiciary has become overzealous in its exercise of independent judgment, it can amend the judiciary's constitutional position (as Roosevelt threatened to do in his first term).

Persuasive as these three elucidations of nonfoundational democracy may be, to critics in the liberal tradition of natural rights hegemony they may nonetheless seem something of an evasion. To be sure, spontaneity, flexibility, autonomy, and commonality are features of democracy that seek to elude foundations; yet surely, it will be argued, they describe a set of democratic values that condition and so cannot originate in the democratic process. This puzzle, which threatens to return us to the turf of epistemology, needs addressing. Is it not obvious, goes the objection, that democracy's procedures and institutions, which constitute and guarantee the creativity, autonomy, and commonality of democracy and manifest themselves as the principles of equality, right, and liberty, require a grounding in something antecedent to democracy? If democracy is not to become an arbitrary choice in a relativized political cosmos, must it not be anchored in something other than its own procedures? After all, even William James acknowledged that pragmatism has "no dogmas, no doctrines, *save its method*."[26] And even Jefferson, for all his devotion to changeability and popular will, wrote that "nothing is unchangeable . . . except the inherent and unalienable rights of man."[27] Might we not say that democracy, while foundationless with respect to public judgment and political outcomes, rests on procedures whose legitimacy is a function of prior arguments and agreements? And that those procedures, resting firmly on the idea of equality as an expression of the equal worth of individuals and their interests, are justified by recourse to principles antecedent to the democratic politics they engender, principles that are hence foundationalist? Is not equality, as democracy's guiding value, best thought of as the application to debate about public action of the foundational premise that all human beings, born free, are equal and have a right to equal opportunity and treatment? Finally, is this not simply another way of formulating what philosophers call the lexical priority of liberty?

No, it is not. In a democracy, living popular will is always trump. It operates under constraints, to be sure, but these constraints are themselves conditional: the product of a will to self-regulation by a prudent popular sovereign. Engines can be prevented from turning at too high a speed (rpm) through the installation of a governor, to be sure, but the governor can be removed by those who installed it. Democracy's most sacred values surely do have status and being prior to politics. However, in Dewey's formulation, "we come back to the fact that the genuine issue is not whether certain values . . . have being already . . . but what concrete judgments we are to form about ends and means in the regulation of practical behavior."[28] In pursuing concrete judgments and regulating practical behavior, values are themselves subject to democratic validation and revision. Democracy *is* for the living, and the living are always democratically empowered to change their founding democratic constitution. Democracy's decisions are validated post hoc.

Russian President Yeltsin's refusal to acknowledge the constraints of the 1977 Russian (ex-Soviet) constitution, and his insistence on turning to a popular referendum (in April 1993) to validate his "illegality" is a potent instance of how democracy justifies itself (although his use of force in October 1993 or his subsequent cancelation of presidential elections is another matter: when democracy is the topic and a people unschooled in citizenship is the pupil, tanks make poor tutors). Yeltsin's earlier action, however, is redolent of the 1787 Philadelphia Convention's illegal decision to revise fundamentally the Articles of Confederation that it was supposed only to modify and amend and then, against instructions, to permit ratification by the vote of only nine of the thirteen states. These are instances of democracy's post hoc legitimacy, aptly described in Gordon Wood's *The Radicalism of the American Revolution*.

Thomas Jefferson, we noted earlier, thought constitutions should not be objects of reverence, and in practice they rarely have been. Even noble democratic principles like the priority of liberty and equal rights are constantly subject to political debate and adjustment. Whose liberty? Which equality? Current debates about abortion, AIDS, the death penalty, and even NAFTA are at least in part debates about these questions. That the Declaration of Independence declared, "All men are created equal" did not preclude a bloody history of struggle for enfranchisement first by white non-property holders, then by blacks and finally by women. The "equality" Americans actually established was a product not just of a presumptive logic of natural rights but of political (and military) struggle in the name of rights not just recognized by but brought into being by that struggle, which in time led to a gradual redefinition of the inclusiveness of the democratic body politic. Exactly who the "men" were who were created equal had to be determined by democratic struggle. Justice Taney saw no incongruence between natural rights and Negro slavery because the *political* issue was not whether humankind had natural rights but who was included in humankind (African-Americans were not). The question of inclusion remains democracy's most controversial question today.

Democracy both does and must define its categories (including the category of democracy itself) through democratic struggle. There is a sense in pragmatism in which all knowledge—all reality— "depends on the ultimate decision of the community."[29] We need not necessarily accept Peirce's more radical intersubjectivity, to recognize that *political* or *public* reality has this character, *by definition*. Rights arise out of a politics of liberty, and liberty itself is a product of social struggle. That we are "born free" is a useful fiction in opposing the empirical realities of natural (physical, genetic) inequality and was a crucial weapon in the war against absolute authority. That was its great power as a premise of dissent ideology in the seventeenth century, when it first manifested its modern revolutionary potential. But in fact rights gain substance and credibility only as they are clothed in civic garments. Ironically, the rights by which we claim access to citizenship are themselves given force only by citizenship. Natural rights *are* paper parapets, and are defensible only when manned by citizens willing to pay for them with their civic engagement, their social responsibilities, and often their lives. This was once a familiar argument in the defense of positive liberty by writers like T. H. Green. The recent penchant for rights absolutism has led many to neglect or forget such arguments.[30] The simple fact is, whatever its historical genealogy and intellectual heritage, as a system of legitimacy, democracy produces itself. Democracy is the regime within which the struggle for democracy finds legitimacy—legitimates itself, that is to say, without the help of foundations, whose purposes can only be to explain but never to justify a democratic polity.

NOTES

1. Benjamin R. Barber, *Strong Democracy* (Princeton: Princeton University Press, 1984), 120–21.

2. William James, *Pragmatism and the Meaning of Truth* (Cambridge: Harvard University Press, 1978), 31.

3. Ibid., 44.

4. John Dewey, *The Quest for Certainty* (New York: Capricorn Books, n.d.), 6.

5. Ibid., 19.

6. Bertrand Russell, "The Study of Mathematics," in *Mysticism and Logic* (New York: Doubleday Anchor, 1957), 57–58.

7. Peirce cited in Israel Scheffler, *Four Pragmatists* (New York: Humanities Press, 1974), 57. Michael Oakeshott's imagery is equally captivating: for him too, we are sailors "on a boundless and bottomless sea; there is neither harbour nor shelter nor floor for anchorage, neither starting-place nor appointed destination. The enterprise is to keep afloat on an even keel." *Rationalism in Politics* (New York: Basic Books, 1962), 133.

8. I am working on a project on the revolutionary origins of democracy that discriminates between at least four distinctive moments in revolution, of which only one is highlighted here. I call it the moment of "release."

9. Cited by Hannah Arendt, *On Revolution* (New York: Viking, 1965), 239. Also see Robert Michels, *Political Parties* (London, 1915).

10. Letter to John Adams, August 1, 1816; note that this was later in his life, when some claim his revolutionary ardor had cooled off.

11. Letter to Samuel Kercheval, July 12, 1816.

12. Letter to Colonel William Stephens Smith, November 13, 1787.

13. "I know also that laws and institutions must go hand in hand with the progress of the human mind. . . . We might as well require a man to wear still the coat which fitted him when a boy, as civilized society to remain ever under the regimen of their barbarous ancestors." Letter to Kercheval.

14. Letter to James Madison, 1789.

15. As Jefferson suggested in his letter to James Madison of January 30, 1787.

16. "Paradoxical as it may sound," wrote Arendt, "it was in fact under the impact

of the Revolution that the Revolutionary spirit in this country began to wither away, and it was the Constitution itself, this greatest achievement of the American people, which eventually cheated them of their proudest possession." Arendt, *On Revolution,* 242.

17. Letter to Joseph Cabell, February 12, 1815.

18. Gordon Wood, *The Radicalism of the American Revolution* (New York: Knopf, 1992); Bruce Ackerman, *We the People,* vol. 1; *Foundations* (Cambridge: Harvard University Press, 1990).

19. Oakeshott, *Rationalism in Politics,* 32.

20. Dewey, *The Quest for Certainty,* 196.

21. Ibid., 220.

22. Dewey, *Liberalism and Social Action* (1935; reprint, New York: Capricorn Books, 1963), 79.

23. Dewey, *The Public and Its Problems* (New York: Holt, 1927), 201–2ff.

24. In *The Conquest of Politics* (Princeton: Princeton University Press, 1988).

25. Ibid., 211.

26. James, *Pragmatism and the Meaning of Truth,* 31–32. Emphasis added.

27. Letter to Major John Cartwright, June 25, 1824.

28. Dewey, *The Quest for Certainty,* 46.

29. *Philosophical Writings of Peirce,* ed. Justus Buchler (New York: Dover Books, 1955), 249.

30. The political dimensions of this argument about rights in their relationship to democracy are argued in my "The Reconstruction of Rights," *American Prospect* (Spring 1991): 36–46, reprinted as chapter 6 below.

CHAPTER 3

Why Democracy Must Be Liberal:
An Epitaph for Marxism

LIBERALISM, with its focus on the hypothetical rights-bearing individual, is far more suited to founding than to sustaining democracy. But its great virtue is its durability as a ground for resistance and rebellion. It is too negative, too skepticist, too hypothetical to nurture community institutions and the kinds of robust citizenship needed to give democracy staying power. Yet those very qualities make it a formidable philosophical adversary of dogmatic political regimes; the same qualities mark democratic foundings with an immunity to orthodoxy and certainty that helps protect democracy against its tendencies to imperious majoritorianism and utopianism.

I have often celebrated (and celebrate in many of the essays in this volume) the affirming communitarian elements of the democratic way of life, but it is precisely this slightly utopian quality of democratic thinking against which democrats most need to guard. Liberalism in its Burkean and Madisonian variations, where it is suspicious of all power, above all popular power, offers the needed safeguards. Social democracy and Marxism (not the same thing, to be sure) have not been similarly protected, and that has turned out to be their single most troubling feature.

If then we ask whether, in the wake of communism's inglorious historical collapse, social democracy has a democratic future, the answer would seem to be: Only if it can disentangle itself from communism and its ideological affiliation with Marxism; only if it can forge stronger links to the philosophical liberalism it has often despised. The proponents of social democracy have of course often eschewed the linkage to communism, insisting that communist regimes have nothing to do with philosophical Marxism or that Marxist historicism has nothing to do with social democracy. "Social democracy? Never really been tried!" say the embarrassed refugees from the living history of Marxism.

Yet that is to claim a historical exemption from culpability that is itself a part of social democracy's problem. Political systems, unlike philosophical systems, must be measured by their political success or failure. When ideas fail in practice, it is not enough to mutter "all the worse for practice!" The "political" in "political theory" means that the failure of the practice *is* to some degree the failure of the theory. To the extent that theology is social theory, the death of God as theory followed upon the decay of the worldly church as practice; it did not occasion that decay.

With a little help from Friedrich Nietzsche, God began to die in the years after 1848 when the First International tried to realize Karl Marx's diagnostic principles as positive political philosophy. With a great deal of help from a series of corrupt regimes established in his name, Marx's positive philosophy died about a century and a half later, when the high ideals of social democracy in its statist version were revealed as rickety ghosts of the glory that once was supposed to have been communism's worldly empire.

There was nothing wrong, and much that was right, with communism as an idea. The idea embodied a magnificent and beneficent principle that has appeared and reappeared throughout history as the brotherhood of man, the natural equality of all humans, the common right of individuals to an autonomous life, or the quest for fair distribution and social justice through political command structures. Philosophical Marxism took these ideals and embedded them in a theory of history that made politics subordinate to economics. Communism failed not because it represented less than just principles but because it represented unrealizably just principles wedded to an all too realizable set of historical practices that eschewed democracy in the name of class. The ends its power coveted were beyond the capacity of power to achieve, but power as an end in itself turned out to be easy enough to secure.

Communism as a practice was social democracy's most extensive, most vivid, most telling political experiment: It was social democracy taken from the pages of books and put into political practice, egalitarian ideals embodied in historical inevitability and institutionalized as worldly power. Communist social democracy shares with Marxism the doctrine that democracy must first be social and economic if it is ever to be meaningfully political. It talks "democracy" but practices class war and state ownership. Its priorities allow equality to trump liberty. Marxist communism, too, rationalizes an undemocratic politics aimed at a just society that might one day in turn generate a genuinely democratic politics. It is certain that equality must precede freedom and that only class power can forge equality.

SOURCES OF COMMUNIST FAILURE

It was not evil or malevolence that undid communism as a political philosophy. Communism failed not because it denied but precisely because it rested squarely on high but unachievable principles—principles that in turn permitted and in fact required an end run around democracy. Bertolt Brecht worried that "man is not bad enough for this world." By the same logic, Brecht's own Marxism was too good for this world. The lesson of Brecht, ignored in his own politics, is simple enough: Our ideals and aspirations must be cut close enough to the pattern of the actual to give hope to the aspect of the possible. Without noble ambitions, we are yoked to the present as bequeathed to us by a burdensome and deterministic past; yet with a too exalted ambition, we are bound to be disappointed, and, what is worse, in political terms, we are likely to transform our impatience and frustration into a dictatorship in the name of the good—that gentle tyranny of reason that transformed one utopian moment of the Enlightenment into the Jacobin Terror. Bad as we are, we cannot afford aims too very much better than we are.

The tyranny of the ideal is both less noxious and more sinister than simple tyranny. A great deal of confusion has arisen out of our tendency to confound the two, to consider the dictatorship of the good as just another hypocritical version of tyranny *tout court*. This has been the essence of the totalitarian critique of idealism at least since Karl Popper took on Plato, G. W. F. Hegel, and Marx as enemies of the open society. What Popper failed to see in indicting Marx as a Platonist was that the lust for power is far more corrosive to the soul than is the lust for truth and goodness, for, rather than ennobling, it debases us; there is nothing redemptive or admirable about it. On the other hand, the tyranny of reason is not merely coercive, it is seductive. Pursuing hegemony, even at its most malevolent, is transparently exactly what it is, nothing more and nothing less: an easily recognized feature of the human heart, what Thomas Hobbes named the "quest for power after power that ceaseth only in death."

Zeal for goodness is another passion altogether, the more dangerous exactly because it is enshrouded in benevolence and driven by good will. Not all tyrannies are alike, and the seductions of idealism should elicit both greater admiration and greater caution than power-mongering for its own sake. Historically, there has been a tendency among critics of fascism and communism to equate the two. "Totalitarianism" is the common name that writers from Popper to Hannah Arendt have given what they took to be the common hegemonies and overlapping brutalities of the two systems. Twenty-five years ago (in my contribution to *Totalitarianism in Perspective*), I argued that the very term "totalitarianism," used to associate communism and fascism, was invalid because it confounded communism's libertarian ideals with its liberty-destroying practices, which seemed indistinguishable on their face from fascism's liberty-destroying practices. I would still insist on the difference. For although the urge to rationalize force that is used to subordinate individuals to collectivist and corporatist identities and the need to rationalize force that is used in the name of liberating individuals from collectivism and collectivist history may entail equal amounts of repression, they entail two very different kinds of politics.

This is not to exculpate the leftist legacy, however, but rather to indict it on quite different grounds. Fascism and other forms of radical collectivism are dangerous because they urge our complicity in what Erich Fromm called our predilection to "escape from freedom," luring us down a path that is all too easy for us to follow. Radical communist idealism of the kind represented by Marx is dangerous because it calls us to a standard of liberty—one rooted in perfect equality—that we cannot meet. In its clarion call, it opens up an abyss between our actual natures and its high-minded goals. Marx's utopianism, no more "scientific" than that of the German rivals he demolished in *The Poverty of Philosophy,* presented men and women who lived in a real political world with ideals utterly unsuited to that world. It is not, as some critics have tried to say, that a political philosophy that ordains the transformation of humanity as a premise for a benevolent state cannot work. All political philosophy, John Stuart Mill's as well as Thomas Jefferson's, understands that political men and women— call them "citizens"—are in some sense beings who have undergone or must undergo a transformation. All education entails growth and change, and citizenship is simply an intense and particular form of education predicated on a certain mutability in human nature. We are not exactly born free, but we become so only over time as a consequence of what Alexis de Tocqueville called that most arduous of all apprenticeships, the apprenticeship of liberty.

THE MELIORATIVE NATURE OF POLITICS

The issue is not whether human beings are seen as changeable or not; rather it is whether the changes proposed in a political theory correspond with or overreach the human capacity for growth and the cumbersome, slow-moving faculty of self-improvement; whether those changes acknowledge the parameters within which education and growth actually occur; and whether they conform to the pace of change dictated by how we live our actual lives.

When they are not simply conservative, politics are meliorative. But to be successfully meliorative, they must rest on the possible. We can be better but not best; we can be good but will always fall short of being angels; we can reach, sometimes even a little beyond our grasp, but we cannot reach the stars. To ask too much of men and women is to risk not just failure but the resentments and fears that are failure's poisonous cousins. In politics, the best is not just enemy to the good. It is its true nemesis. To push beyond the limits of the better in pursuit of the best may invite a politics of the worst.

Take Brand, Henrik Ibsen's remarkable and fanatic pastor in the play of the same name: When Ibsen's preacher asks his congregation to help him build a new church, he brings them with him. And when he abandons that project, too material, too callow, not worthy of God, in favor of a far more challenging physical and spiritual journey into the mountains, his parishioners make the sacrifice and accompany him up the glacial cliffs. But when he asks them to "give all"—not just to surrender comfort and material well-being but to sacrifice their families and climb to the highest reaches of the ice-cave, where they will risk death and transfiguration not for God but for Brand's version of God—he drags them a step too far. When they resist, he judges and condemns them as too small for his great deeds, and they in turn abandon him in disgust and return to the valley, to their ordinary lives, where they revert to diurnal and material concerns. Only then, as he confronts death in solitude on the mountaintop, does a voice remind him that the harsh God in whose name he demands impossible sacrifices from his followers is no friend of stern martyrdom. Humbled, dying, Brand learns that the God he seeks is "the God of love."

Ibsen's parable in Brand recalls the need to frame our aspirations with an eye to our frailties, asking enough of ourselves that we become stronger but not so much that we stumble and fall. Love is a call for tolerance, an acknowledgment of the weakness that troubles us even in our greatest moments of strength. The same lessons apply with a vengeance to the organization of our worldly civil society around high political ideals. Democracy begins not with the certainty that we are right but with the acknowledgment that we may be wrong; it demands not perfect justice but less injustice. Fallibilism rather than certitude is its modus operandi. Whig skeptics and their American imitators like James Madison asked too little of humanity's better side and surrendered too much to its worse side. But they erred on the side of prudence. Communist strategies in the nineteenth century asked too much of humanity. Social democracy today must ponder exactly how much it dares require of men and women. It needs to turn them into citizens, into practitioners of democracy, before it can expect them to rise to the demands of justice. Humility, regret, and a recognition of the possibility of error are high political virtues, above all in a politics of ambition such as the politics of social democracy. To demand that liberty precede equality (the essential tenet of liberalism) may mean that only a few will be equal (liberalism's great defect). But to demand that equality precede liberty may mean that none will be free. Liberty and equality are entangled and can be secured only through a dialectical democratic politics that favors liberty when equality seems triumphant (John Stuart Mill and Alexis de Tocqueville) and privileges equality when liberty is secure (Jean-Jacques Rousseau and Thomas Jefferson).

THE LAW OF INCOMPLETE REALIZATION

To organize civil society around aspirations that are too one-sided, too noble, too removed from the possibilities of dialectical balance is to doom the politics of good intentions to disastrous outcomes and to guarantee its replacement by the gentle terror of reason and certitude. "If you cannot become as good as we know you are," proclaim the revolutionaries of self-transfiguration, "we will MAKE you that good, even if it kills us; even if it kills you." And usually it does. Too often, philosophers of social democracy have driven us to denigrate the men and women we would have follow us on the path of justice and righteousness when they turn out to be too weak and paltry to live the righteous ideals mandated by reason. Greed is an enemy of equality, but we must take care in making greed our political enemy that along with their avarice we do not dismiss human beings. Self-interest can be extended by political imagination to encompass the shared interests of others and can thereby be transformed. But it can be erased only at the risk of pretending that people are angels and that citizens are altruists. They are not and cannot be. Nor does a democratic politics re-quire them to be. Indeed, when we try to force them to rise to a higher plane—often by a form of coercion that, because it is psychological as well as physical, structural as well as substantive, is far worse than the coercion of merely malevolent, power-lusting dictators—we risk losing them alto-gether. There are two routes to hell: There is the direct path taken by sinners, but there is also the indirect path described by the fall of failed angels who have overreached their capacity for goodness.

The Soviet Union existed for seventy-five years, caught between awe-some ideals and the most awful realities, unwilling to contemplate that there might be a connection—more than just etymological—between the awesome and the awful. The post-historical world of pure freedom on which the historical struggle against capitalism was waged failed to arrive. That failure meant that, in time, the dictatorship of the proletariat would fossilize into the dictatorship of the Party, and that the long-awaited dis-placement of the government of man by the administration of things that the new age was supposed to bring would, in reality, turn into the adminis-tration of humans *as* things—another way to say the tyranny of man over man. What is ironic in the story of communism is that, though commu-nists were unequal to the challenge of their high ideals, they were much better than the assumptions of communism's actual practice. They could not live up to the aspirations, but they also refused in the long term to live down to the political failure of its aspirations. This gives to communism's historical failure an aspect of tragedy, of Icarus flying too near the sun, of our hubristic quest for the best annihilating our realizable taste for the common good.

Communism's failure is exemplary of what I would call "The Law of Incomplete Realization." This law states simply that political principles are to be tested against their capacity to operate when they are incompletely realized. States, like automobiles, need safety features that assume there will be accidents, that anticipate failures of engineering or inept drivers or untoward circumstances. Given the imperfection of human nature, all political ideals are likely to be imperfectly realized and therefore must be tested by their capacity to function in a state of incompletion or under circumstances that misrepresent or distort original intentions.

American democracy, as I have been imprudent enough to argue, is a thin and incomplete version of what any good democratic theorist will mean by democracy. But in the present context, I must confess that in its incomplete and thin form it meets the test of incomplete realization. Compared to the alternatives, under conditions of uncertainty, it works, if not terribly well. That presumably is what Winston Churchill meant when he said that democracy as he knew it was the worst form of government in the world except for all the other forms. If social democracy is to rival thin, liberal democracy, it must show itself capable of working even when its users fail to follow directions properly. It is not enough to say, "the premise of class conflict is not meant to entail the brutalization of the dictatorship of the proletariat," or to insist that "social equality need not require state ownership of property," if theories embodying the initial propositions are somehow forever deflected historically into these very "unintended" consequences.

Since they cannot be foolproof, our social theories must be inoculated against foolishness. The price, for progressives, is high: Prudent principles inured to abuse tend to be conservative, taking the form "Don't monkey around with the status quo; you're only going to make things worse." Edmund Burke's quip that those who destroy everything are sure to remedy some grievance can easily become "the best way to preserve the good we possess is to preserve *everything* we possess: to remedy no grievance whatsoever." To refuse to take chances with history because radicals and revolutionaries have so often made things worse is to permit history (that is to say, the hegemonies that makes our history) to govern unopposed and to guarantee that things will never get better. Those with nothing to lose in the first place may be understandably impatient with such a strategy.

TASKS OF SOCIAL DEMOCRACY

The task of social democrats is to challenge the status quo without inviting imprudence—to attach to their engines of change a governor weighted with humility and regret, to call for reforms knowing that their call is likely to be heard only by people in a hurry who will misunderstand half of what is being said and understand their own deafness as a tribute to their incorruptibility. Maximilien Robespierre was known as "the Incorruptible," which meant he listened to nobody. To be sure, to indict progressives for their nobility is to take the glamour and the glory from their calling, and it may even rob them of the spirited zeal that they need to challenge deeply embedded injustice. Moreover, it is to expose them to the danger of being outflanked by zealots, as cautious reformers have so often been in the great historical epochs of revolution. How many Girondists and Mensheviks and social democrats have tried to act with prudence, only to be overtaken and run down by imprudent fanatics rationalizing their immoderation by appealing to their idealism? Moderation is no easy road: Conservatives serve prudence better and radicals curry the favor of destiny, succeeding in the short run where the moderates fail.

What does it mean, then, for social democrats to avoid zealotry without succumbing to stasis? Above all, it means that they must act as democrats first and as social egalitarians second. It is to insist that without the safeguards of liberalism, no struggle for inclusion will be worth winning. It is to require that they take upon themselves the burdens of injustice by being patient in their work, by recognizing that politics, however incomplete and unfair, is a domain of potential autonomy in which every citizen can exert pressure on behalf of social justice. To say "slow down" to men and women without liberty outrages morals, but as politics it is nonetheless obligatory. When Niccolò Machiavelli first insisted that politics and morals answered to different standards (Montesquieu, Rousseau, and many others agreed), this is what he meant. For politics to have outcomes that conform to morals in the long term, it must sever itself from purely moral standards in the short term. As Rousseau wrote long ago, liberty is a food easy to eat but hard to digest. Those who are too hungry may wolf it down, only to vomit it up again, while those who gorge themselves on it may have perpetual indigestion.

DEMOCRACY AS THE POLITICS OF FALLIBILITY

If social democracy is to raise its expectations of political success, it must lower its moral sights. Social democrats need to stop boasting that their ideals are higher or better than Marxist communism's or liberal democracy's. For it is communism's vice that its values are so stratospheric and liberal democracy's virtue that its expectations are so earthbound. Social democracy must get off the ground without soaring too high. Democracy at its best is a politics of fallibility rooted in uncertainty and an inexorable conflict of interests. Applied to social democracy, the law of incomplete realization posits the priority of democracy over socialism. Social democrats need first of all to be democrats pure and simple. Historically, social democracy has come to grief because, in the impatience to remedy the egregious abuses of economic inequality, a tutelary power beyond all limits has been sought, a power capable of liberating the economy and establishing the social conditions for democracy. Believing that democracy is impossible without socialism, socialism has acquiesced to despotism as a means of obtaining the conditions it thinks democracy demands. Despotism turns out, however, to be not only averse to democracy but uninterested in socialism.

Social democrats must take their chances with democracy prior to securing its economic conditions. They must pursue a democratic, if not egalitarian, civil society within which democratic civic and cultural practices are cultivated. A democratic civic culture, Walt Whitman's free American air, John Dewey's "way of life," in turn make political democracy minimally possible. Once democracy is secured in its thin and minimalist version and then reinforced as strong democracy, it can pursue the economic leveling up and social justice that are the condition of its further growth. In the interim, social justice may be less than perfect, may take the form of welfare bureaucracy or progressive income tax or an unsatisfactory regulatory state. Politics first, then economics; a prudent democracy and a limited government, and then, once power is accountable and limited, its use on behalf of justice.

That takes time and means that social democrats must live with a public that will not always seek justice for itself. It scarcely needs to be said in this era of conservatism that democracy cannot guarantee that the people will do what is in their interest as seen by those who have created philosophical archetypes for the common good. But as soon as others propose that they will do for the people what the people refuse to do for themselves, we get, not justice, but tyranny. Too often, social democrats have excoriated the people for their lack of egalitarianism, not only opposing referenda that go the wrong way but attacking the process itself, preferring elites as guardians of the popular good to the people itself. Progressives have preferred reading into California referenda curbing taxation or limiting immigration or rebuking affirmative action a lesson about populist reaction or popular stupidity or common prejudice, rather than reading out of those referenda the understandable anxieties of a public that knows things have gone wrong even if it does not yet know how to set them right.

As Jefferson recognized long ago, if citizens use their power indiscreetly, the remedy is not to take their power from them but to inform their discretion. The task for social democrats, then, is to educate democracy, to help persuade citizens that their interests lie not in dismantling government and liberating the commercial sector in the name of "free markets" but in putting democracy to work in the name of common goods. In order to ask more of us, social democracy needs first to ask less of us—which will still be far more than liberal democracy and capitalism ask of us. A less ambitious social democracy will do more for democracy in the long run, though at the price of less socialism in the short run. But there are no shortcuts: Democracy is the only road to socialism, and patience and humility remain the chief democratic virtues, especially for social democrats.

CHAPTER 4

The Compromised Republic:
Public Purposelessness
in America

THE AMERICAN PUBLIC has always reacted with alarm to the periodic discovery that it is without unifying national purposes. The "crisis in public purpose" reappears every so often, usually in conjunction with such related emergencies as the "leadership crisis," the "energy crisis," the "violence crisis," and the "public apathy crisis."[1] During the tepid 1950s, at the very moment public commentators like Daniel Boorstin, Louis Hartz, and Arthur Schlesinger were celebrating the unique virtues of proceduralism and purposeless consensus, *Life* and *Time* and the *Saturday Evening Post* were lamenting the absence of public goals and sponsoring an ongoing, cover-story "search for national purpose." This national purpose campaign has been revived recently as a result of the deep disaffection with American institutions that has been churned up by the backwash of Vietnam, Watergate, and economic malaise.

Those concerned with the crisis typically address it from a perspective of nostalgia, seeming to suggest that the nation has lost purposes it once had. They argue that America's postwar entanglements in a world immune to American moralism and in domestic quarrels (McCarthy, the Cold War, disarmament, racism) alien to its traditional centrism have sacrificed traditional unity to a new and dangerous spirit of faction. But the perspective of nostalgia presumes answers to what in fact is the most important question raised by the crisis in national purpose: did America ever have truly public purposes that could be lost or forfeited? Is the present crisis a new pathology, or merely the flare-up of what has long been a chronic, if essentially benign, condition?

The hypothesis offered here is that America has never had enduring public purposes and that for a long time this was properly taken to be one of the nation's fundamental strengths; that the present dilemma arises therefore not from a loss of purposes but from changes in the conditions that traditionally made public purposelessness an effective, even necessary feature of the compromises that permitted America to flourish at once as a republic and as an empire—as a constitutionally limited federal state governed by law and as an unlimited unitary state with expanding economic and territorial ambitions. Today's crisis may thus turn out to be yesterday's strength; today's vice, yesterday's virtue. Seen in this perspective, the crisis appears to be tractable: but not by the means suggested in conventional analysis—the "loss of public purpose" interpretation.

I

The American republic was founded at least in part on the political theory of classical republicanism.[2] Although its aims were plural, the motives of its founders complex, and the sources of their rationalizations manifold, the Constitution was conceived and set down in the language of republican thought—a changing but ancient idiom whose history as theory can be traced in various forms through the writings of Rousseau, Montesquieu, Harrington, Machiavelli, and Cicero back to Plato's seminal *Republic* and whose history as praxis has been visible in the living experience of Europe's commercial cities, Switzerland's mountain *Landesgemeinden,* the town republics of Renaissance Italy, as well as Rome's early republic and the *poleis* of ancient Greece. It was an idiom known and used by all of the parties to the American Founding. However little their interests coincided and however much their ideologies collided, Federalists and Anti-Federalists, aristocrats and democrats, mercantilists and agrarians all spoke this common tongue. To some degree they all shared a republican concern for a government of excellence, a citizen body of virtue, a public order defined by fundamental law (the constitution, or *politeia*) and conducive to well-being, and a community of moderation in which the governed would neither be abused nor be permitted to abuse themselves.

The traditional literature of republicanism and the historical practice in which and from which it issued did not, however, treat the republic as an ideal form that could be instituted without regard to condition; the Founders, their practical eyes fixed as much on American conditions as on European political theory, appreciated this. They understood the republican form of government to be as fragile as it was rare, and they knew it could flourish only under very special conditions. Hamilton had noted the tendency of Europe's city republics to "perpetual vibration between the extremes of tyranny and anarchy," dangers that Rousseau and Montesquieu had regarded as inevitable when republics were founded in the absence of the proper conditions.[3] These conditions, it was generally agreed, included: (1) a small-scale society limited in both population and territory; (2) social and cultural homogeneity, to insure a natural consensus on fundamental values; (3) economic self-sufficiency and (relative) autarky—usually specified in terms of a pastoral or commercial (but certainly *not* an industrial) economy; (4) frugality in life-style and manners and austerity in taste conducive to the cultivation of simple, nonmaterial public virtues; (5) rough economic and political equality of citizens; and (6) a distrust of rapid change that would be more accommodating to nature and stasis than to artifice and progress.

The classical literature argued that such conditions were prerequisite to the promotion of a strong sense of commonality, a clear public identity (the citizen as a public person holding a common moral outlook and sharing common interests), and a spirit of self-government that subordinated the private person to the public citizen no less than the private realm to the public life. Conditions conducive to a public spirit were necessarily hostile to hedonistic privatism and contentious self-interest; they thus served to insulate well-conceived republics from the high-tension privatism to which they seemed so vulnerable. Thus, for example, Rousseau insisted that the founding of a democratic republic presupposed

> first, a very small state, where the people can readily be got together where each citizen can with ease know all the rest; secondly, great simplicity of manners, to prevent business from multiplying and raising thorny problems; next, a large measure of equality in rank and fortune, without which equality of rights and authority cannot long subsist; lastly, little or no luxury—for luxury either comes of riches or makes them necessary; it corrupts at once rich and poor, the rich by possession and the poor by covetousness; it sells the country to softness and vanity, and takes away from the state all its citizens to make them slaves one to another and one and all to public opinion.[4]

The Founders of the American Republic, and perhaps even more importantly, those who had to make good on the Founders' blueprints, faced an ironic dilemma: not only were they eclectics drawing on sources other than the republican tradition, *and* ideologues with varying and contrary interests, *and* skeptics of one kind or another about the desirability, feasibility, and degree of democracy in the republican formula; they were also republican lawgivers to a people lacking almost all of the conditions deemed requisite to the founding of a republic. James Winthrop of Massachusetts wrote with incredulity: "the idea of an uncompounded republick, on an average one thousand miles in length, and eight hundred in breadth, and containing six millions of white inhabitants all reduced to the same standards of morals, of habits, and of laws, is in itself an absurdity, and contrary to the whole experience of mankind."[5] Territorially, the new country potentially embraced a continent—a prospect that the Louisiana Purchase made more than merely credible soon after the republic's founding. Patrick Henry looked at that continent and declared that to make it a republic was "a work too great for human wisdom."[6] If its territory outreached the wildest ambitions of Europe's empires, let alone Europe's traditional city-states, its people comprised as heterogeneous a lot as had ever lived under a single national roof. Could a people who barely spoke a single tongue, who answered to different mother cultures and worshiped in different churches, who knew either the hammer or the plow, the loom or the baler, but never both—could they live under a single constitution in a continental republic in what Madison, in *Federalist* No. 14, called an "extended Republic"? Surely, as critics of the Constitution insisted, it was "impossible for one code of laws to suit Georgia and Massachusetts."[7] And even were an extended republic somehow to be founded, America's under-populated land and endless bounty invited growth, expansion, progress, acquisition, and material prosperity—the cardinal sins of republican life against which the Constitutional Convention was repeatedly warned by men like Gouverneur Morris, but which finally seduced even the agrarian democrats and Thomas Jefferson himself (enemy of mercantilism but friend, finally, to expansionism and material growth).[8] Not only was the early American economy heterogeneous and expansionist, but it depended on the two forms least conducive to republican stability: plantation agriculture and mass (manufacturing) industrialism. Moreover, its complexity assured the proliferation of economic orders and competing factions in a fashion completely inimical to the nurturing of a common interest. Quite aside from the two subjugated populations (Black and Indian), differentials among citizens were very great. *Time on the Cross* reports that many urban white workers were poorer than rural black slaves.[9] Sectional interests not only emerged from, but were deeply implicated in, the proceedings of the Constitutional Convention.

In sum, it would be difficult to invent a set of conditions as little conducive to the founding of a democratically tinged republic as the one that described America at the time of its founding. This dilemma presented the Founders and their successors with a virtually unprecedented problem in lawgiving and nation-building: how to serve republican virtue in a land more suited to empire; how to serve empire—economic growth, progress, material well-being, and continental power—without completely surrendering the republican ideal; how, in other words, to take a country whose conditions Montesquieu would have deemed suitable only to empire and Rousseau, to corruption, and give it a constitution of moderation, freedom, and self-government. And to do all of this without falling prey to the inherent deficiencies of either factional democracies ("spectacles of turbulence and contention") or fragmentary republics ("an infinity of little, jealous, clashing, tumultuous commonwealths, the wretched nurseries of unceasing discord").[10]

The constitutional solutions devised to treat with this dilemma were directly responsible for the national purposelessness that has characterized American public life ever since; they enable us to understand both the historical successes and the present failures of purposelessness in our national way of life. Each of these solutions was in part a response to economic and sectional interests, the fruit of a spirit of compromise that itself became integral to the spirit of the new republic; but each also aimed at using the peculiar conditions of America to reinforce in new and novel ways a republican constitution that would normally be undermined by such conditions. The constitutional solution was thus a radical and wholly untested challenge to the traditional wisdom of republican thought, one that turned the nation's early years into an unprecedented historical experiment, and one that could be met only by a people that had, in Madison's bold language, "not suffered a blind veneration for antiquity, for custom, or for names, to overrule the suggestions of their own good sense, the knowledge of their own situation, and the lessons of their own experience"—that had already managed in the Confederation to "rear . . . the fabrics of governments which have no model on the face of the globe."[11] For many, many years, in many, many ways, the experiment achieved a remarkable success. Indeed it was successful enough to make its centralist features tolerable to Jeffersonian decentralists, its sectionalist propensities tolerable to Hamiltonian nationalists, and its increasingly democratic tendencies palatable to both. Only recently have its deficiencies emerged clearly; it is this that has led to what is now seen as the crisis in public purpose.

The formula designed by the Founders was anything but monolithic; it incorporated a variety of institutional innovations and procedural compromises that together created a national pluralism flexible enough to accommodate republican virtue *and* material progress *and* imperial power. The critical institutions included federalism, the representative system, presidential government, and the adversary method as the guiding principle of political procedure and political epistemology. Although they often appear as historical compromises, they were less compromises than surrogates for pristine republican institutions that could not function under America's unique conditions. Thus, for example, it might be said that private property became the surrogate for public norms, self-interest binding men to their public obligations no less surely than shared values once did; that procedural consensus became the surrogate for substantive consensus; that representation replaced participation, as accountability replaced self-government, and autonomy was traded for rights.

More concretely, to take the four institutions cited above, federalism was the compromise power negotiated with scale to permit the development of a national imperium that did not entirely destroy regional autonomy and local self-government. The Articles of Confederation had yielded to state sovereignty and state power a prominence "utterly irreconcilable with the idea of an aggregate sovereignty."[12] National government required a general license to operate; but powers not delegated to it had, in the words of the Tenth Amendment, "to be reserved to the States respectively, or to the people." For purposes of political participation, republican scale, autonomous self-government, and sectional autarky, America was to pass as a nation of semisovereign states. But for purposes of economic development, the security of property and debt, national defense (and imperial offense), and the public weal, it was endowed with all of the centripetal forces of the unitary nation—of, at least *in potentia,* the emerging empire.

Representation was an ingenious device with much the same utility: it used accountability to bridge the widening abyss between participatory self-government and efficient central administration. Like federalism, it permitted a form of self-government (not necessarily democratic) to survive in a land whose scale seemed to preclude self-government. To be self-governed and to be governed by representatives was, to be sure, not the same thing; but even from the skeptical vantage point of later elitist critics of representative democracy like Joseph Schumpeter, it was clear that a people who chose their masters were better off than a people who did not. If the people were to be little trusted—one of the few points upon which the Founders agreed—those who ruled in their name but not by their mandate were to be even less so; this was Jefferson's rather skeptical democratic faith. The representative, then, played two roles. He mediated the divergent interests of heterogeneous constituencies, thereby insuring the "participation" of sectional and other interests in national decision-making.[13] But he also mediated and thus moderated public passions; for, as Madison (sounding remarkably like Burke) had put it, the representative system could "refine and enlarge the public views by passing them through the medium of a chosen body of citizens."[14] Popular control *and* wise government, self-government *and* a national imperium, accountability *and* centripetal efficiency—these were the promises of representative government.

Presidential government was, in one sense, the crowning achievement of the representative system, the One in whom the Many could be safely united: for in the presidency was to be found the source and the symbol of the nation's collective power—the spirit of sovereign nationhood; yet in it too was preserved the right to self-government, initially of the states (through their electors), later of the people themselves—the spirit of sovereign citizenship. The President as Executive Officer and Commander-in-Chief embodied the power of the whole, of The People as a symbolic collectivity. The President as Elected Representative of the semisovereign states, as Chief Tribune, and, later, Party Leader, embodied the power of the parts, of the states and the people as self-governing entities, ruling themselves through their mandated executive representative. The dual accountability of the Presidency—to The People as Nation and to the people as citizens—has remained the source of its strength as a mediator between national power and local citizenship. It is no accident that the mythology of the common man has been more closely associated with the presidency than with any other institution; or that in 1976 Governor Brown of California and Governor Carter of Georgia, like Bryan before them, could lay claim to the presidency in the name of an alienated citizenry as if that office were wholly independent of the governmental bureaucracy against which they railed. Neater solutions to the problem of governmental leadership were to be found in parliamentary or monarchical government, but no more effective solution to the problem of accommodating republican self-government to imperial scale seem conceivable than presidential government.

The adversary method was less an institution than a procedural principle—perhaps *the* procedural principle—that governed the processes in which American institutions manifested themselves. The goal was unity (the republican ideal and the national imperative) through diversity (the democratic ideal and the sectional imperative). It seemed clear that no stubborn search for singular truths or monolithic standards or objective goals or agreed-upon powers could wring from the economic and social heterogeneity of America substantive consensus on anything. The adversary method in effect polarized the *pluribus* of E *pluribus unum* in order to secure a more moderate, centrist *unum*. It transformed market relations into political relations, requiring of every political transaction a buyer and a seller, a purveyor and a client, a complainant and a respondent, an obligation and an interest. Only where there were two sides could there be a reasonable outcome; only where contraries were aired could unity be anticipated.

America has thus been a land of Noah where everything durable comes in twos: the two-house Congress, the two-seat-per-state Senate, the two-sided trial (by prosecutor and defense, not by judge and jury), and, in time, the two-party system and the two-authority legal system (where the Legislature *and* the Supreme Court vie in the conflicting voices of the written Constitution and a Higher Law for the right to give ultimate laws to the nation).[15] And where the system did not create polar opposites, it nonetheless generated adversaries—separating and casting into opposition the major governmental powers (executive, legislative, and judicial), institutionalizing military service rivalries, encouraging the growth of an unofficial representative system (of lobbyists, interest groups, voluntary associations) to challenge, balance, and complement the official representative system, and generally nourishing an understanding of the polity as a public realm within which private forces are encouraged to seek their own advantage—the polity, in short, as a "pluralist pressure system." The faith has always been that from the clash of opposites, of contraries, of extremes, of poles, will come not the victory of any one but the mediation and accommodation of them all. The American version of truth and unity, if there was to be one, could never be forged from some ideal form. It would, as Jefferson knew, have to be hammered out on the anvil of debate.

The adversary method also played a secondary role as the functional equivalent of horizontal federalism: in polarizing authority it divided power; in pluralizing truth it separated powers. Making truth a function of debate, it put force at odds with itself. As Madison had argued in the *Federalist Papers,* "Ambition must be made to counteract ambition . . . [for] in framing a government which is to be administered by men over men . . . you must first enable the government to control the governed; and in the next place oblige it to control itself."[16]

In each of these institutions, then, central power and local control, administrative efficiency and regional autonomy, effective leadership and citizen participation, national planning and individual interest, were assiduously mediated—power (read planning, progress, efficiency, expansion, and prosperity) forever being balanced off against citizenship (read participation, excellence, fellowship, responsibility, and civic virtue). The theory of classical republicanism had been confounded: for a republic (a rather odd sort of republic, but a republic nonetheless) had been devised that would accommodate both democracy (a rather odd sort of democracy, but democracy nonetheless) and imperialism (a rather odd sort of imperialism, but imperialism nonetheless); and if the ancient conditions did not obtain, then the rules had been successfully altered to accommodate the American conditions that did obtain. American exceptionalism—the refusal to follow the historical patterns of the political culture to which America was heir—was thus built into the institutions by which the republic was fashioned; indeed, it was crucial to the initial successes of the experiment.

Despite all the Founders' quarrels, their economic differences, and their varying sympathies toward federalism and democracy, the early successes of the republic they contrived were truly extraordinary. By the time of his First Inaugural, Jefferson could thus say, "We are all republicans—we are all federalists." All of them shared, in Hofstadter's portrait, "a belief in the rights of property, the philosophy of economic individualism, the value of competition."[17] On these private and procedural purposes they constructed a public government that worked. It worked as a safeguard to republican individualism and it worked as a facilitator of imperial dominion. It satisfied the demands of unity by exploiting the energies of heterogeneity. It was short on participation but commensurately long on accountability. It substituted contractees and clients for citizens but thereby guaranteed that private interests would play the part of absent public goals. It trusted in invisible hands to guide the pursuit of private wealth in publicly useful directions—and succeeded if only because there was so very much wealth. It protected equilibrium from the destabilizing effects of progress by leaving economic growth and prosperity in largely private hands—which, however, were permitted informally to grasp the public scepter. That is to say, its mercantilism was supervisory and paternal, only rarely direct or interventionist.

In all of this it absolutely depended on a studied obliviousness to public purposes and public interests as defined by traditional republican formulas. To insist on discovering public goods was only to generate faction and occlude those private interests that alone, pitted against each other, promised the semblance of consensus. In short, the system turned necessity into a virtue and placed public purposelessness at the very core of its value structure. This was the meaning of proceduralism, of the adversary method, of pluralism, and of the agreement to disagree. If public goals were occasionally to foist themselves on the nation—a gift of the Four Horsemen as it were—they could be gratefully accepted. But war, plague, famine, and death were sometime events, without the compelling moral power or the permanence to provide more than a temporary, reactive unity.

Purposelessness was not, then, a residual cost of implementing a republic under adverse circumstances but the guiding principle of its success. If some inspired corporate mogul was later to suggest that "what's good for General Motors is good for America," it was less a tribute to myopic self-interest than to the American ideal, which insisted quite precisely that private interests *were* the only public interests America could afford to pursue. If Jay Gould quipped, "In Republican counties I'm for the Republicans and in Democratic counties I'm for the Democrats, but everywhere I'm for the Erie Railroad,"[18] he was only saying with a grin what political scientist David Truman later said with a poker face: in the study and practice of American politics, "we do not need to account for a totally inclusive interest, because one does not exist."[19]

What began as necessity and soon turned to virtue had by the middle of this century become an awesome American ideal—the finest product of American exceptionalism. Daniel Boorstin thus suggested in the 1950s that the "genius of American politics" (see his book of the same name) lay precisely in its refusal to define itself in terms of a public ideology or a politicized national interest. Louis Hartz, Arthur Schlesinger, and others wrote about the peculiarities of the American system that give to our heterogeneity and unideologized privatism the stamp of centrism and consensus.[20] An American center was possible because America lacked the usual political spectrum by which a center was measured; consensus was built around the agreement to agree on nothing substantive, to hold no exclusively public values of the kind defined by traditional republican theories or modern collectivist ideologies. In a land where the center will not hold, the new wisdom had it, it is the illusion of a public center that is most likely to loose mere anarchy upon the world. The republic worked because it never tried to contrive a center; and thus, by eliciting the assent of the citizenry to this value default, acquired a center after all—in the acquiescence of the people to purposelessness.

II

What, then, are the consequences of this historical vision for the present crisis? Traditional public purposes cannot have been lost or forfeited, for their absence turns out to have been the key to the success of America's republican experiment. But the conditions to which the experiment was addressed and on which its success depended have changed—changed radically, profoundly, irreversibly. When the Constitution was first fashioned, America stood at the threshold of a century of growth, material prosperity, and burgeoning national power. Heterogeneity provided room to operate, privatism was an invitation to speculation and growth (personal gain publicly legitimized), continental power was an unexploited promise as seductive as the frontier seemed endless, inequality appeared to be a remediable condition which, even unremediated, nurtured ambition and (upward) mobility. The threshold has long since been crossed, however, and the American people stand today at the back door of their vast mansion, all its rooms traversed, all its secret passages discovered, attic and basement alike despoiled of resources. With the land settled, the wealth squandered, the self-sufficiency traded away for luxury, and the endless abundance quite abruptly rendered finite, the peculiar compromises between republican ideals and American conditions that have been the genius of American politics have lost their legitimacy. Open spaces, empty jobs, and unmade fortunes are the conditions that made inequality tolerable to the least advantaged in America's compromised republic; with hope gone, the compromise is itself compromised, and inequality becomes a permanent, oppressive, intolerable burden. Diversity and private interest were the necessary conditions of capitalist expansion in America; but now, in the late stages of capitalist development, in which speculation and entrepreneurship are no longer virtues and in which pointless consumption becomes more salient than expanding production, privatism nourishes alienation and despair, feeding only that scourge faction—the dark side of pluralism so dreaded by the founders. The irresistible force embodied in the endless American frontier has encountered the immovable object embodied in the limits of growth. The American nation, frozen between these awesome pressures, seems in danger of failing both as a republic and an empire—simultaneously, and, ironically, for the same reason: the failure of the institutions that once mediated federal republic and imperial nation to adapt to mutations in the conditions that made them work. Too centralized, bureaucratized, militarized, anesthetized—in a word, too imperial—to remain a republic, we are nonetheless too divided, demoralized, and privatized to flourish as an empire. The nation has become too large to accommodate the American republic at the same moment that the world and its dwindling resources have become too small to accommodate the American empire. Under these changed conditions, the very institutions that once fostered success now catalyze failure. They represent a governmental chemotherapy which, though it long sustained the nation's republican health against the twin cancers of anarchy and tyranny, is now itself imperiling the body politic.

Look, for example, at modern federalism—that once sovereign mediator of efficiency and self-government; today it stands only as a monument to unequal standards, parochialism, and factionalism (as a comparative study of state welfare systems will demonstrate). Too large and bureaucratic to enhance a sense of autonomy and self-government in the citizenry, the states are nonetheless too weak, divided, and inefficient to challenge the greater Leviathan of federal bureaucracy. No longer serving distinctive regional or sectional interests, they often impose arbitrary boundaries on what ought to be integrated areas. How many greater metropolitan regions tend today to cut across traditional state boundaries? Washington, D.C., New York, Kansas City, and Philadelphia are each cut off financially and politically from regions that benefit from their resources; most other major American cities find themselves serving extended suburban communities that have no legal or fiscal obligations to them. Thus do the antiquarian structures of federalism compound the urban crises they ought to be alleviating, serving the purposes neither of effective central government nor of regional self-government.

The representative system has undergone the same pathological metamorphosis—a benign tumor metastasized to become perilous to the body it once served. The danger was always present (which is why it can be considered a tumor, even in its benign stage): Rousseau had been certain that "the moment a people allows itself to be represented, it is no longer free; it no longer exists;" and Patrick Henry had voiced profound misgivings about representation in connection with the federal taxation issue: "I shall be told in this place, that those who are to tax us are our representatives. To this I answer, that there is no real check to prevent their ruining us. There is no actual responsibility. The only semblance of a check is the negative power of not reelecting them. This . . . is but a feeble barrier, when their personal interest, their ambition and avarice, come to be put in contrast with the happiness of the people."[21] The Founders hoped to find in representation a home for the noblesse oblige of an elite; representatives chosen by electors embodying the studied interests of property and wealth would be as much a curb on, as a vehicle of, democracy. But in modern mass democracy it is not wisdom but numbers that rule. Under the guise of mass participation, opinion becomes king and through opinion, the manipulative forces of wealth, power, and demogoguery. A representative system operating in a mass society combines the very worst features of direct democracy (the tyranny of opinion, passion, and ignorance) and of elitism (the tyranny of wealth and power)—something not even the most vociferous critics of mass democracy have fully appreciated (see J. S. Mill, Tocqueville, Ortega y Gasset, or Walter Lippmann). Sheer numbers dilute the input of individual citizens and diminish the salience of rational deliberation at the very moment that they reduce the accountability of representatives to any single citizen. At the Constitutional Convention critics worried that a 30,000 citizen constituency for a member of Congress would be too great;[22] congressional districts are today approaching one-half million. The inevitable consequences are everywhere visible: increased irresponsibility in the representatives, increased apathy in the represented.

The institution of the presidency reflects these invidious changes in the impact of representation all too well. Where once the president embodied the powers both of people and The People (of citizens and nation), he seems more and more frequently in recent years to embody neither. His office has become the forum for private battles publicly waged; his responsibilities to party, region, faction, and interest have outweighed his loyalty to his Tribunate. In this sense Watergate was less a perversion than a rather extravagant caricature of the presidency's current condition: not the imperial but the privatized presidency, not the stewardship of public interests but the protectorate of private interests. Vietnam was less a matter of public than of presidential honor; it was Johnson's own face (and the faces of his foreign policy establishment) that had to be saved, not the nation's. Nor do Gerald Ford or Ronald Reagan or Bill Clinton issue a call for renewed citizen participation in politics when they take the federal government out of the regulation or the welfare business; rather, they merely acknowledge the impotence of the public and its chief representative to deal publicly with the nation's most pressing social and economic problems. The president does not involve people, he only exonerates himself. Thus the irony of a presidency that is at once too powerful, and too weak: too powerful, bureaucratic, and clandestine to be representative or public-minded, but too personal, privatized, and banal to be effective.

American proceduralism seems also to have lost much of its legitimacy. Once a device designed to reconcile Americans to their differences by offering them a way to live with them, the adversary method seems now more often to underscore contradictions and embitter competition. Self-sufficiency and thinking for yourself have become self-alienation and existing by yourself. The self-interested individual becomes the self-serving individual and then the self-consuming individual. The hand that once was to guide his private quest for security and well-being in publicly useful directions is no longer simply invisible: it is incorporeal, insubstantial, nonexistent. And so, as the factionalism that drives Americans apart and tends less and less to leave them with residual public interests intensifies, the need for a sense of shared values in an increasingly factionalized and anomic world grows. Adversaries who no longer find in their disagreements a basis for common norms are transformed from adversaries into enemies. Enemies multiply, find their way into presidential as well as private thinking; and finally that most compelling figure of the American exceptionalist imagination—the pioneering frontiersman—turns from competitive self-sufficiency to hostile vigilantism and in doing so goes from being an individual and a competitor to being an outsider and an adversary; and then, in the final stage, the outsider becomes an alien even to himself, and the modern assassin is born: the outsider par excellence, the adversary born of adversity, the self-serving, sharp-shooting frontiersman run amok because the conditions that once justified his independence and satisfied his needs are gone.

The answer, then, to the question of why America neither has nor has been able to cultivate public purposes is simply that it was not supposed to have them. Exceptional American conditions made the quest for them seem both dangerous and impossible, while exceptional American institutions effected compromises that exploited their absence to the benefit of both republic and empire. This interpretation is dismaying in that it gives to present problems historical dimensions that make them seem intractable; but it is also encouraging: for the very failure of institutions that depended on purposelessness suggests changes in historical conditions that may be conducive to a new, historically unprecedented public-spiritedness. Institutional innovations as appropriate to new circumstances as federalism, representation, and the other compromises of the original Constitution were appropriate to America's founding conditions may even reveal that purposelessness is no longer a necessary feature of the compromised republic—that less compromising steps may finally be in order.

Certainly this kind of approach closes the door completely on solutions that are blind to new conditions or to the developments that occasioned them. It discloses as useless, for example, the nostalgic communitarianism that looks for hope to the retrieval of a lost sense of purpose that, in fact, the nation never enjoyed. Those who seek in the American compromise republic some living facsimile of republican Athens seek the absurd—and perhaps, without knowing it, the perverse. Contemporary America remade to the specifications of ancient Athens would probably come to resemble not Athens but wartime Berlin.

Likewise, those who would rely on the revitalization of the original compromise republic can only be disappointed; for it is the failure of that formula to adapt to new conditions that has created the dilemmas the revitalists wish to address. It would seem that neither constitutional atavism nor republican nostalgia can be of service in the present crisis. What Jefferson understood when the Founding was scarcely a generation old surely holds ten times over two centuries later: "I am certainly not an advocate for frequent and untried changes in laws and institutions . . . but I know also, that laws and institutions must go hand in hand with the progress of the human mind. As that becomes more developed, more enlightened, as new discoveries are made, new truths disclosed, and manners and opinions change with the change of circumstances, institutions must advance also, and keep pace with the times."[23]

If new conditions doom old institutions, they also present new opportunities and invite new ways of thinking. All political thinking today is conditioned by the seeming inevitability of a limited-growth economy, by circumscribed American power, by the compulsory interdependence of an increasingly transnational world, by the emergence of national (and even international) norms as the result of a national (international) technology, economy, and communications network, and by the failure of privatism and material success to answer nonmaterial private needs or serve nonprivate life goals (see my *Jihad versus McWorld*). Yet the result of this conditioning is that political thinking can look critically at the compromises forced on the early republic by the circumstances (now gone) of expansionism, heterogeneity, and material abundance of the founding era. Institutions responsive to the new conditions must, to be sure, still contend with problems of scale, bureaucracy, efficiency, and dominion unknown to earlier lawgivers and only conjectured by the Founders; but with the passing of unlimited growth and unchecked privatism as desiderata of the lawgiver, many innovations become possible. Some of them—although this is hardly the place to spell them out in institutional detail—challenge the current utility and perhaps even the spirit of the compromises so critical to the success of the early republic.

Federalism, for example, seems today largely irrelevant to the needs of the sectional interests it was intended to serve—at least in their contemporary manifestations. The units—greater metropolitan areas—most in need of integrated structures and autonomous self-government actually have the least. A greater New York that encompassed the suburban regions to which taxable wealth has fled might be able to solve many of its fiscal and political crises by itself. The middle-class and corporate exodus would become academic, for a relevant regionalism would compel those who utilized the resources and services of a great city to pay for them—regardless of residence. At the same time, mass transportation could be rationalized and encouraged (imagine a city with the powers of the Port Authority of New York), while the welfare burden would be more equitably distributed. Federalism remains a viable compromise: but only if it is based on periodic redistricting in accordance with crucial demographic and economic developments.

Redistricting would also give an important impetus to participatory government and thus leaven the increasingly meaningless system of representation with a degree of real political activity. But participation would also require other forms of institutional innovation. It could mean the introduction of the old communal tradition of Common Work—which requires of citizens participation not only in the deliberation and decision-making processes but also in the implementation of public policy decisions; thus, the decision to permit urban homesteading (the takeover by tenants, for a nominal sum, of landlord-abandoned inner-city housing—a policy already initiated on an experimental basis in Baltimore, New York, and elsewhere) would be decided by referendum and require the participation of the citizenry in implementing it.[24] Policies and building permits cannot remake a city; engaged, working citizens can.

The use of the referendum might also be extended, although this would probably mean, if it were to be effective, the extension of public deliberation and discussion as well as of public voting. Public-access television channels could be of use here. Indeed, technology is a potential ally of very great promise in any campaign to extend citizen participation in various phases of the public-policy process.[25] The aim would be to prevent representation from paralyzing direct participation—to transform politics from a spectator sport in which, accountability notwithstanding, the responsibility rests with the governors, into a participatory sport in which, inefficiency notwithstanding, responsibility is assumed by the governed.

These kinds of institutional innovations—and they are only suggestive in the tentative forms in which they are offered here—point toward an even more critical kind of innovation: a change in attitude. Although conditions have changed, Americans still respond to the public world in terms of the attitudes they take to be suitable to those (now vanished) conditions of the Founding. Though they acknowledge the poverty of privatism, they think privatistically; though they understand the insufficiency of frontiersmanship and vigilantism, they react violently and respond vengefully; though they have learned the risks of material ambition, they crave wealth and luxury; though they have lost faith in the myth of self-sufficiency and the rhetoric of independence, they distrust cooperation and regard interdependence as a weakness. Attitudes lag behind changes in conditions, and institutions lag still further behind attitudes. Nevertheless, the successes, first apparent in the mid-seventies, of politicians dedicated to public philosophies of restraint, austerity, citizen responsibility, and (even) asceticism suggest that the public may be ready to exchange privatism for a sense of common purpose, uncertain luxury for a stable moderation. Faced with the prospects of unlimited growth, America once made a virtue of necessity and modified republican institutions to meet the demands of expansion and empire; faced with the prospect of limited growth, perhaps eventually even zero growth, it now has the chance to make a necessity of virtue and readapt its institutions to meet the demands of contraction and interdependence. The new pressures of ecology, transnationalism, and resource scarcity in combination with the apparent bankruptcy of privatism, materialism, and economic individualism—the pathologies and the ambivalent promises of our modernity—create conditions more inviting to the generation of public purposes and a public spirit than any America has ever known. Abundance is the natural soil of competitive individualism; scarcity, the soil of mutualism. Cooperation springs from a sense of common limits, and limits of one kind or another are the key to America's new conditions. To this extent, the problem of public purposelessness is the product of conditions which, if understood and exploited, suggest and nurture their own remedy.

For two centuries in this new Atlantis of America, man and nature have been pitted in a contest that—Marxists, mercantilists, and free marketeers all agreed—could be resolved only through the total subjugation of nature. Private men put aside public purposes to wage a private war on economic necessity: carrying private banners, they fought in the name of private freedom for explicitly private interests. But the Baconian dream of emancipation through mastery was lost, even as it was realized; nature yielded somewhat, but, as the limits of growth suggest, less than expected. Moreover, the emancipation wrung from nature turns out to have produced more alienation than independence, more rootlessness than self-realization, more solitude than freedom. Genuine freedom, some contemporary Americans must begin to suspect, may possibly turn out to be an aspect of man's relationship *with* nature, of his capacity to live within its laws, of his willingness to accommodate himself to forces that cannot be subdued. The republican polity has always rested on notions of accommodation to nature and mutuality among men. If Baconian hubris has truly run its course in America, the time may finally be ripe for a burgeoning of republican ideals that until this moment have been foreign to the American enterprise in its compromised form.

Not that this will happen by itself. Our dilemma invites easier, more authoritarian solutions.[26] Fascism treats the ills of public alienation without placing burdens of choice and responsibility on the public; anarchy permits privatism to self-destruct. Visionary demagogues may find it more profitable to impose "common" values on a dispirited American people than to give them the institutional resources to discover their own. Public purposes publicly arrived at require hard work and carry with them the mixed blessing of continuous self-government; it asks much less of the people to contrive public myths, public ideologies, and public dogmas from the private interests of aspiring authoritarians; and, of course, it saves them from the burdens of self-government. Democracy in its republican form is, after all, a rare and fragile form of government.

But, history shows, America is a rare and not so fragile nation—forever exhibiting its exceptionalism in new and startling ways. It found the way in its compromised republic to reconcile republic and empire; now it must compromise the compromises and find a way to preserve the republic in a strange new world of finitude, boundaries, and interdependence. If it can again improve the formula, it may once more confound the great tradition out of which it arises by proving that a flexible, well-made, republic responsive to changing American conditions can survive the most pernicious of its modern enemies: modernity itself.

NOTES

I am grateful to my colleague Wilson Carey McWilliams, whose critical republican spirit played a part both in occasioning and motivating this essay.

1. I have treated the leadership crisis in a different but related fashion in my "Command Performance," *Harper's Magazine,* April 1975 (see chapter 8, below).

2. See, for example, J. G. A. Pocock, *The Machiavellian Moment: Florentine Political Thought and the Atlantic Republican Tradition* (Princeton: Princeton University Press, 1975); Bernard Bailyn, *The Ideological Origins of the American Revolution* (Cambridge: Harvard University Press, Belknap Press, 1967); and Cecelia M. Kenyon, "Men of Little Faith: The Anti-Federalists on the Nature of Representative Government," *William and Mary Quarterly,* 3d ser. 12 (1955).

3. Alexander Hamilton, *The Federalist,* No. 9 (New York: Modern Library, n.d.), p. 47. All subsequent references are to this edition.

4. Jean-Jacques Rousseau, *The Social Contract,* Book 3, chap. 4. See also the "Dedication" to the Republic of Geneva, in *The Discourse on the Origins of Inequality.*

5. *Agrippa* Letters in Paul L. Ford, *Essays on the Constitution of the United States* (Brooklyn, N.Y.: 1892), p. 65.

6. In Jonathan Elliot, *The Debates in the Several State Conventions on the Adoption of the Federal Constitution,* 2d ed., 5 vols. (Philadelphia, 1896), 3:164.

7. *Agrippa* Letters, in Ford, *Essays,* p. 64.

8. Gouverneur Morris thus warned the Convention in Philadelphia: "Wealth tends to corrupt the mind and to nourish its love of power, and to stimulate it to oppression. History proves this to be the spirit of the opulent." Cited by Richard Hofstadter, *The American Political Tradition* (New York: Vintage, 1974), p. 10.

9. R. W. Fogel and S. L. Engerman, *Time on the Cross: The Economics of American Negro Slavery* (Boston: Little, Brown, 1974), 2 vols., vol. 1, chap. 2.

10. James Madison, *The Federalist,* No. 10, p. 58; Alexander Hamilton, *The Federalist,* No. 9, pp. 49–50.

11. Madison, *The Federalist,* No. 14, p. 79.

12. Madison to Randolph (1787), *The Writings of James Madison,* ed. Gaillard Hunt, 9 vols. (New York: 1900–1910), 2:336–40. The debate about the sovereignty and power of the states that divided nationalists and decentralists in the Constitutional Convention was not settled by the Constitution, as the Tenth Amendment makes clear.

13. Richard Henry Lee had thus suggested in his *Letters of a Federal Farmer* a system redolent of functional representation; e.g., "a fair representation, therefore, should be so regulated, that every order of men in the community, according to the common course of elections, can have a fair share in it—in order to allow professional men, merchants, traders, farmers, mechanics, etc. to bring a just proportion of their best informed men respectively into the legislature" (in P. L. Ford, *Pamphlets on the Constitution of the United States* [Brooklyn, N.Y.: 1888], p. 288).

14. Madison, *The Federalist,* No. 10, p. 59.

15. Judicial review thus challenged the positivist conception of law as a function of the sovereign will advanced by the Legislature with a conception rooted in natural reason's discovery of a higher law. For a seminal discussion, see Edward S. Corwin, "The Progress of Constitutional Theory between the Declaration of Independence and the Meeting of the Philadelphia Convention," *American Historical Review* 30 (1925).

16. Madison, *The Federalist,* No. 51, pp. 335–41.

17. Hofstadter, *American Political Tradition,* p. xxxvii.

18. Cited in D. W. Brogan, *Politics in America* (New York: Anchor Books, 1960), p. 222.

19. David Truman, *The Governmental Process* (New York: Knopf, 1957), p. 51.

20. The most influential and important of these consensus works was Louis Hartz's *The Liberal Tradition in America* (New York: Harcourt Brace, 1955), which argued that America's exceptionalism was to be found in its uprootedness from the European feudal past and its consequent emancipation from reactive leftist ideology.

21. Rousseau, *Social Contract,* Book 3, chap. 15; Patrick Henry, cited in Elliot, *Debates,* 3:167.

22. See Kenyon, "Men of Little Faith."

23. Cited by Hofstadter, *American Political Tradition,* p. 55.

24. Common Work has roots in the old Germanic feudal usage of *Gemeinarbeit.* Its modern utility is suggested by its reintroduction into village life in contemporary Switzerland. For a full account see my *The Death of Communal Liberty: A History of Freedom in a Swiss Mountain Canton* (Princeton: Princeton University Press, 1974), pp. 176–79 et passim.

25. The popular discussion of the uses of television communications and electronic technology to expedite mass participation in deliberation and decisionmaking has been much more widespread in journalism and the media (see McLuhan), than in serious social and political thought. Modern republicans have also tended too often to be technological Luddites; but if technology can have an alien-

ating impact on men and women, it nonetheless is a remarkable facilitator of communications, and communications are at the heart of a republican polity.

26. That the present American condition is as inviting or more inviting to fascism than to republican innovation may be seen from this remarkable passage by Fritz Stern describing the nineteenth-century German precursors of Nazism in terms alarmingly appropriate to alienated Americans circa 1976: "Theirs was a resentment of loneliness; their one desire was for a new faith, a new community of believers. . . . [T]hey denounced every aspect of the capitalistic society, and its putative materialism. They railed against the emptiness of life in an urban, commercial civilization. . . . [T]hey attacked the press as corrupt, the political parties as agents of national dissension, and the new rulers as ineffectual mediocrities" (*The Politics of Cultural Despair* [New York: Doubleday, 1965]).

CHAPTER 5

The Rights of We the People Are
All the Rights There Are

There can be no right
without a consciousness of common interest
on the part of members of society.
(*Thomas Hill Green*)

Liberty may be endangered
by the abuses of liberty
as well as by the abuse of power.
(*James Madison*)

IN DEBATING the controversial relationship between rights and democracy, a supposedly telling distinction is often postulated between the views of the Founders and today's views. For my purposes here, this is a distinction without a difference. For although current controversies suggest that the intentions and texts and principles of the Founders can be easily identified and distinguished from our own interpretations of them, it is my view that interpretation must always infect, nourish, condition, and redefine what are taken to be the Founder's views. Their views are irrevocably lost to us as pristine authoritative sources of immutable principle. And insofar as we can divine them, their intentions are as varied and antagonistic as those of their modern interpreters. To the degree that the Founders had intentions, these were to draft a constitution sufficiently flexible and ambiguous to allow for ongoing reinterpretation and adaptation. The Constitution itself was widely understood to be an experiment which, in John Marshall's words, was "intended to endure for ages to come and to be adapted to the crises of human affairs."

Whether we are Supreme Court Justices, scholars, or even the Attorney General of the United States, we must finally rely on interpretation: our own views as buttressed and justified by competing interpretations of the words, intentions, and principles of the Founders. In fact, the Founders rather resemble the great political theorists, and their legislative products resemble the great books, in that they are rich, dialogical, ambiguous, and paradox-strewn political icons subject to diverse and contested subsequent understanding.

This is by no means to say that interpretation is purely subjective or arbitrary, any more than political and philosophical discourse are subjective or arbitrary. But it is to say that political discourse is not scientific discourse. Rights are not like triangles or the Second Law of Thermodynamics: the issue is not truth and error but at best right opinion, intersubjective agreement, and common ground. This is the framework for all discussions of the Founding, and is the setting for my remarks on rights and citizenship here. These remarks aim only at discourse—at political persuasion. They presume however that discourse is a more reliable guide to politics than Truth, and that political theory as a quest for Truth issues more often in dogmatism than in understanding.

WE THE PEOPLE

The People of the United States ordained and established their Constitution to form a more perfect union, to establish justice, to insure domestic tranquility, to provide for the common defense, and to promote the general welfare. However, the Preamble to the Constitution concludes, they also established a government in order to "secure the blessings of liberty."

This final phrase echoes the Declaration of Independence and anticipates the Bill of Rights, recalling to the young nation the contractarian origins of America in a philosophy of natural rights. And although the Federal Constitution employs the word *right* only once (in I.8.8), numerous state constitutions and the Declaration itself avow that it is solely to secure their unalienable rights that men institute governments, which must thus derive their just powers from the consent of the governed. Federalists and Anti-Federalists alike agreed that government is preceded by and founded upon right, which becomes its central rationalizing principle and the measure by which all of its institutions, acts, and laws are legitimated.

The rights upon which the American Constitution was founded were natural inasmuch as, like all rights, they were "deduced from the nature (i.e., the needs and the capacities) of men as such, whether of men as they now are or men as they are thought capable of becoming."[1] Yet if rights were thought to attach to men as such, they could be exercised only by citizens: by men living together in a polity capable of enforcing the mutual recognition of those rights. If government was founded to secure the rights of natural men and the blessings of natural liberty, it was only insofar as natural men became citizens that these precious rights and liberties (the right *to* liberty) could be actualized. Men may "have" rights in some abstract generic sense as a consequence of what they are theorized to be in isolation and solitude, but their rights acquire political significance and recognizable power only in the context of social relations. Rights may, as Ronald Dworkin says, trump other claims, but only in the poker game called politics, and only insofar as the rules of the game recognize their priority. In other words, it is only as a citizenry that "We the People"—by "securing" the right to liberty—give it meaning.[2]

Yet where the Declaration and the Preamble to the Constitution, and later, the Bill of Rights, are explicit about the rights to liberty on which all government rests, they remain remarkably silent about citizenship and the character of the citizenry upon whom rights depend. Who exactly "We the People" are is one of the unspoken puzzles of the Founding, the solution for which occupied Congress and Court for the subsequent century and a half. The entire social contract tradition is marked by universalistic rhetoric ("*all* men are born free and equal," government depends upon the consent of *The* Governed) that fails to specify concretely the actual qualifications for citizenship. Locke's general language is universal, but we are left to suspect that citizenship may be reserved to, if not exclusively the propertied, then only the rational and industrious, who are neither "contentious" nor "quarrelsome."[3]

In the American tradition, the rhetoric is also formal and universalistic: "all men are created equal," reads the Declaration; "We the People" begins the Constitutional Preamble. Yet the category seems to be empty: its contents are passed over in silence. The Articles of Confederation (Article 4) at least specify that "the free inhabitants of each of these States, paupers, vagabonds, and fugitives from justice excepted, shall be entitled to the privileges and immunities of free citizens in the several states," thereby expressly excluding slaves as well as a certain economic underclass from citizenship. Neither Negroes nor women are mentioned however, and since there were free blacks in several states, they would seem to have qualified for citizenship under the Articles. Women, though not eligible to vote, presumably also enjoyed such partial rights as the individual states afforded them.

The Constitution, on the other hand, offers no explicit account of citizenship at all. In Article I, section 8 it includes among the powers delegated to Congress the right to "establish a uniform law of naturalization," and in Article II, section I it delimits the requirements for eligibility to run for the Presidency in language distinguishing natural-born and naturalized citizens. Slavery is treated with a discretion that leaves it unmentioned by name, though alluded to in a number of places—not least in the unsatisfactory three-fifths compromise that made representation in the House and direct taxation apportionable by adding to (in each state) "the whole number of free persons, including those bound to service for a term of years, and excluding Indians not taxed, three fifths of all other persons" (Article I, section 2).[4]

By treating slaves as an embarrassing residual category, the Founders expressed their own ambivalence about slavery and their reluctance to strong-arm the South, leaving it to their successors to interpret their intentions. In the Dred Scott decision in 1857, Justice Taney took it upon himself to do just that: "Negroes," he wrote, "were not intended to be included under the word 'citizen' in the Constitution, and can therefore claim none of the rights and privileges which that instrument provides for and secures to citizens of the United States." This applies to all Negroes, whether "emancipated or not." Herbert Storing and others have been at pains to demonstrate that Taney's decision was a "gross calumny on the Founders."[5] Yet in their intentional vagueness and misdirection, the Founders invited such calumnies, which were surely apposite to at least some of them.

Indeed, it required the Fourteenth and Fifteenth Amendments (and the Civil War that produced them) to clarify the Constitution in a fashion that included Negroes as full citizens. Women had to wait another fifty years for a similar clarification, at least with respect to their voting rights. The Fifteenth Amendment was drafted in particularistic language meant to address the Negro question directly: "the rights of citizens of the United States to vote shall not be denied or abridged by the United States or any State on account of race, color, or previous condition of servitude." It was intended to protect the right to vote of those already counted as citizens under the Fourteenth Amendment. But the Fourteenth itself resorts again to the universalistic language of the Declaration, assuming this time—at least with respect to males—the literal meaning of the words: "All persons born or naturalized in the United States and subject to the jurisdiction thereof are citizens of the United States and of the States wherein they reside." Surprisingly, this is the first explicit conferral of citizenship. By encompassing *all* persons (even in the Constitution, Negroes were persons, that is to say, "other persons"), it offers a general description of citizenship. Only a half century later is the "all" extended to include women fully (in particularistic language that mimics the Fifteenth rather than the Fourteenth Amendment).[6] In both the Fifteenth and the Nineteenth Amendments, the particularistic prohibition against "denying" the vote on the basis of race or gender has the flavor of a "clarification." Oh yes, the Amendments seem to read, the framers really meant "all persons" when they wrote the Declaration, and there is no reason to think that men of color or women of every color are other than persons for all relevant purposes of citizenship.

The fundamental question about the relationship of rights and citizenship raised by the American tradition and the theory of natural rights on which it is founded is then this: are we to believe that our forebears regarded Indians, women, and Negroes, to varying degrees, as noncitizens because they were not fully persons and thus incapable of having rights attached to them as persons? That (as the language of the Constitution might suggest) "other persons" actually signified "other *than* persons"?

And that what was required was not the conferral of citizenship on Negro persons (as the Fifteenth Amendment suggests) but the conferral of personhood on Negroes (as the Fourteenth Amendment suggests)? Or are we to concur with such admirers of the Founders' handiwork as Herbert Storing, and allow that the personhood of Negroes and women was never in doubt, and that only the conferral of full political citizenship (as per the Fifteenth and Nineteenth Amendments) was wanting? More generally, what is the relationship between natural rights and citizenship? How are we to specify the character and conditions of citizenship in regimes founded on naturalistic metaphors and a conception of natural man that purports to be universalistic? Does the right to liberty mean the right *of* the free; or does it mean the right of all men to *be* free? Does the right to property mean the right *of* the propertied, or the right of all to acquire and hold property? Do rights confer citizenship, as the theory would seem to insist? Or does citizenship confer rights, as the historical practice seems to demonstrate?

It is the aim of this essay to explore these connections. As will be apparent, it is my view that social contract theory and its attendant notion of natural rights are essentially metaphoric in character: a powerful rhetorical and polemical device—a new abstract language for advancing concrete political claims—that once helped to emancipate England from the tyranny both of its kings and of religious persecution, and America from the tyranny of England, but a device which simultaneously conceded the real dependency of rights on citizenship—a lesson learned the hard way by Negroes, women, and others who, persons or not, enjoyed only degrees of political servitude until they acquired full citizenship. Women may have been somewhat better off than Negroes initially in that their status at law under state statutes gave them at least some of the attributes of citizens. But history after the Civil War suggests women became—at least in formal legal terms—even worse off than Negroes, since the judiciary argued repeatedly after that time that the Fourteenth Amendment could not be construed to overrule state statutes barring women from the polls and from political office. In short, the deference to state statutes which prior to the Civil War slightly advantaged women, after the War seriously disadvantaged them.

History and theory alike seem to show then that the road from rights leads to citizenship, and the road from citizenship back to rights. In what follows, I hope to traverse this road in both directions.

FROM RIGHTS TO CITIZENSHIP

Immigrants to the New Eden may have been escaping religious and political persecution in the old world, but they brought with them the Enlightenment political philosophy of natural rights that was its finest product. When, in the Declaration of Independence, Jefferson posited as self-evident truths "that all men are created equal, that they are endowed by their Creator with certain unalienable rights"—which included life, liberty, and happiness—he assumed familiarity with and acceptance of English and French natural rights thinking. Indeed, such thinking had already infused state constitutions and such documents as the Virginia Declaration of Rights. Thus, standard texts like that of Corwin and Peltason repeat that "the bill of rights did not *confer* rights but merely *protected* those already granted by the natural law."[7]

Some Anti-Federalists regarded natural rights as so powerful that even in the absence of a Bill of Rights individuals might be able to "take advantage of a natural right founded on reason" and "plead it and produce Locke, Sydney, or Montesquieu as authority."[8] Herbert Storing speculates that without a Bill, the courts still would have developed a "common law of individual rights" that served the same purpose.[9] Among Federalists, much the same logic prevailed, though in the name of a different strategy. They justified their opposition to a Bill of Rights not by belittling rights, but by belittling the need to incorporate rights explicitly into what was already an explicitly rights-based Constitution.

"Why," queries Hamilton in *Federalist* number 84, "declare that things shall not be done which there is no power to do?" Since, he reasons, the very Preamble to the Constitution makes it clear that the People ordain and establish their Constitution to secure the blessings of liberty, surely the People already possess "a better recognition of popular rights, than volumes of those aphorisms which make the principal figure in several of our State Bills of Rights, and which would sound much better in a treatise of ethics than in a constitution of rights."[10]

Federalists and Anti-Federalists were united in their distrust of government and their belief that rights represented the ultimate safeguard against tyranny. For the Federalists, tyranny lay in untutored public opinion and in rampant majorities, which could be best counterbalanced by constitutional mechanisms such as the separation of powers and the device of representation. To them, the Constitution itself was a bill of rights that needed no appended declarations to exhibit its devotion to the rights of men. Indeed, such appendages might weaken the commitment to rights by leading the skeptical to believe that only those rights that were explicitly enumerated were actually protected. To the Anti-Federalists, centralized government was the adversary, to be hemmed in by constraints and restrictions that were necessarily extrinsic to the Constitution. Thus, while Madison—once he converted to the cause of a Bill of Rights—fought in the first Congress to integrate its provisions into the Constitution itself, the Anti-Federalists argued for its inclusion in the style of a number of state constitutions, as a principled Preamble that would both set and limit the terms of the following document. Neither side prevailed, and the compromise placing the Bill outside of but after the main body of the Constitution suited no one very well. But the Bill of Rights did explicitly subordinate government to liberty, making it not merely liberty's servant, but its offspring.

American practice seemed in a certain sense to confirm natural rights theory. Rights grounded in something other than mere law or command were required in order to give them a moral force that secures them from the abuse of centralized governments and tyrannical majorities. Free and equal by nature, men possess, in the abstract, rights to those attributes which constitute their humanity. As a contrivance of human volition to secure that humanity, government is always instrumental with respect to rights, which are the source of all political legitimacy.

This understanding of Rights was of course hardly engendered *in vacuo*. It was critical to the ideology of resistance that developed in the Sixteenth and Seventeenth Centuries as a response to ecclesiastical and secular absolutism. Human volition was too weak and temporal a force to challenge, let alone trump, the mandate of kings and bishops. Rights deemed to be "discovered" in "nature" acquired the power of the new physical laws of nature, and gave mere men an ally in their struggle for emancipation. God might be the author of governments but not because he mandates the rule of kings, but rather because he endows men with rights by nature and then gives them the reason to contract with one another to secure those rights. Natural rights theory in effect steals God away from the cause of the divine right of kings and, by casting Him as the Creator of nature and the rights nature confers on men, makes Him the ally of popular government.

The doctrine of natural rights served then as the first philosophical foundation for a politics of emancipation from arbitrary government and resistance to illegitimate rule. Legitimacy found a standard in nature accessible to human reason, and government became a contrivance of reason, accessible to human will. In the new formula, however, there was an inadvertent coupling of power with tyranny and of liberty with anarchy that affected the practice of rights in subsequent generations—not least of all, in the New World. The rights upon which government was made to depend appeared not only as prior to government but as inimical to it. The new natural standard of legitimacy was so pure that it tended to cast as illegitimate not just arbitrary government but *all* government. These incipient anarchist tendencies of liberal rights theory infected much of what passed as liberal practice in the following centuries.[11] What served the politics of emancipation and resistance well did not necessarily serve the politics of constructing a commonwealth at all. When facing tyranny, the motto "the government which governs least governs best" may make sense, but when facing the tasks of constitution-making it can—as the Federalists learned—be an obstacle to prudent government. What served the resistance to capricious English rule in 1776 did not serve the creation of self-government in 1789. Historians have often commented on the turning away of America from revolutionary rhetoric between 1776 and 1789 as if nothing other than reaction were involved.[12] But while buildings can be razed they cannot be raised with bulldozers, and 1789 was less a Thermidor than the victory of political architecture over political anarchy—of political liberty over political liberation.

In fact, the evolution of American political thinking from 1776 to 1789 responds to a profound dilemma—a singular inadequacy—of rights theory. For those rights that resistance ideology insisted had to be adversary to government were shown by political realism also to be the products of government. To be emancipatory rights had to be grounded in nature, but to be of political significance they had to be grounded in social relations. Where liberation theory cast rights as the parent of government, realism cast them as its offspring.

Jeremy Bentham offered the political realist critique of natural rights theory in characteristically extravagant language: "Rights," he inveighed, "is the child of law: from real laws come real rights, but from imaginary laws, from 'laws of nature,' come imaginary rights . . . natural rights is simple nonsense, natural and imprescriptible rights rhetorical nonsense, nonsense on stilts."[13] The Federalists used rights rhetoric, but their concern was with effective government, which, they appeared to believe, secured rights by facilitating the rule of law. They accepted Hobbes' dictum that the greatest liberty was to be found where the laws were silent, and did not need the Tenth Amendment to persuade them that the government established by their Constitution had only those powers explicitly delegated to it. Nonetheless, when a Federalist like Hamilton tells the people of New York (in *Federalist* number 84) that "the constitution is itself in every rational sense, and to every useful purpose, a Bill of Rights," he means not simply that it confers only delegated powers on the government, but that it secures rights by writing them into the very structures of popular sovereignty. Is it not plain, he asks, that what advocates of a Bill of Rights demand is already "done in the most ample and precise manner in the [Constitution's] plan of the convention"? And if it is "another object of a bill of rights to define certain immunities and modes of proceedings, which are relative to personal and private concerns," this too is "attended to in a variety of cases in the same plan."

The Anti-Federalists worried that too much government would submerge the liberties in whose name government was constituted. But the Federalists worried in turn that too much liberty, too great a focus on radical rights, would submerge the government on which liberty ultimately depended for its security. "Liberty may be endangered by the abuses of liberty as well as by the abuses of power," wrote Madison in *Federalist* number 63.[14] Edmund Pendleton was more explicit still: "There is no quarrel between government and liberty," he writes. "The war is between government and licentiousness, faction, turbulence, and other violations of the rules of society, to preserve liberty."[15] The Rights tradition, evolving as a response to absolutism, had come to identify government with the suppression of liberty. But the Federalists suspected that anomie was a still greater enemy of freedom and that isonomy and the rule of law, in overcoming anomie, would nourish freedom.

Even such modern critics of positivism as Ronald Dworkin—who allows that "it makes sense to say that a man has a fundamental right against the government, in the strong sense, like free speech, if that right is necessary to protect his dignity"— nevertheless acknowledge that rights are not "a gift of God, or an ancient ritual, or a noble sport," but rather "a complex and troublesome practice that makes government's job of securing the general benefit more expensive."[16] Since securing the general benefit enhances the security of freedom, the Federalists may be excused for wondering whether an overly zealous concern for rights might not ultimately undermine liberty.

Bentham exposes only a mild deficiency of natural rights theory when he portrays its fictitious derivation from a non-empirical version of nature. More fundamentally, rights are compromised in the very characteristic that purportedly makes them significant: their supposed immunity to relativism. For if rights are attached to a certain conception of human nature and thus human need, what counts as a right becomes all too easily as variable as human nature and human need. Almost all of the very considerable modern controversy that surrounds the issue of human rights derives from debate and disagreement over what is to count as essentially human and what is to count as a genuine human need: wants? desires? the requisites of survival? of growth? of flourishing? As Rousseau saw long ago and D. D. Raphael has noticed recently, "in general, material and moral progress produces a continuous expansion of needs . . . [and] what is thought to be a luxury today may be regarded as a necessity tomorrow."[17] Most modern social progressives, arguing that "people now are vulnerable to kinds of threats and need forms of protection that were inconceivable in the eighteenth century," include subsistence rights, rights to employment and education, and even the right to a paid vacation in their international human rights agendas.[18]

These claims are worthy of notice here because in recalling the contestable character of needs and wants, they exhibit the intrinsic contestability of all rights claims deriving from a conception of human nature and human need. It is the putative universality of rights that gives them their potency in challenging governments; yet in practice, their universality yields to the particularism of specific conceptions of need that change over time. In rooting themselves in concrete human nature, they lose the abstract universality that is their claim to attention.

There is a further dilemma, even more troubling than the one precipitated by the relativism of needs. In order to ground right in a moral and metaphysical imperative beyond the pale of those positive laws for which right is to be the legitimating measure, the naturalistic tradition had to push it beyond the pale of human will and thus, in political terms, of popular sovereignty. Although originally rights were a legitimate device of popular government against absolutism, popular government itself in time became the danger to which rights became the response, so that to secure rights became for advocates of natural rights theory to bridle the very autonomy (in its mutualist manifestations) that rights had once helped to establish. Rights had, ironically, to be defended against political autonomy—the will to self-determination of a united people—that many regarded as their finest expression. Liberty exercised becomes the enemy of liberty—or so it would seem.

On the other hand, positivists went too far in the other direction. Applying Hobbes with one-eyed diligence, they subsumed rights entirely to human will, to the laws yielded by sovereign command, and thereby appeared to rob rights of all of their radical or subversive force. If rights are merely random claims recognized by the sovereign, then they have no status as legitimators of sovereign will. Only a standard prior to sovereignty can be utilized to measure sovereignty. Rights issuing out of human volition are too weakly engendered to bring tyrants to heel or keep an impulsive people from running amok.

Here then is the most poignant dilemma of rights: rooted in nature and the nature of man, they are secured from tyrannical public opinion, from sovereign miscreants, and from the willfulness of those who pretend to be their authors; yet rooted in nature they reinforce the fiction that we do not or should not govern ourselves in common, and they nourish the illusion that we can preserve our liberties only by refraining from exercising our liberty. Too malleable and evanescent as poor creatures of the law, rights are too deterministic and rigid as reflections of universal nature. Thus it was that the Federalists, though in their rhetoric they acknowledged the priority of rights to law, in their practice did all they could to subsume rights to their Constitution by incorporating them into its structural provisions. Thus it was that the Anti-Federalists aspired not merely to attach a Bill of Rights to the Constitution as a caveat and a constraint on the powers of the sovereign people, but to "abridge" where they could such powers as were delegated to the people's government.[19]

The political tangle into which the quarrel between naturalists and positivists—as well as between Anti-Federalists and Federalists—propels us can be mediated by consulting the language of rights usage. Even the most zealous naturalists acknowledge that rights need to be secured or recognized or enforced in order to acquire operational force in the real world. As John Dunn has observed, Americans "possessed their rights by historical and political inheritance as a product of—at a minimum—almost two hundred years of constitutional history. And that history offers no license for viewing their possession of these rights as in any sense prior to the claims of political authority."[20] If rights exist by nature, it is only *in potentia*. As claims, which is what they are as long as they are merely asserted in nature by individual persons, they do not yet possess the normative character that gives them the status of legitimizers.[21] They acquire legitimacy only when they are recognized.

T. H. Green addresses the implications of what it means to recognize rights in a fashion that lays bare their essentially social character: "There can be no right without a consciousness of common interest on the part of members of a society. Without this there might be certain powers on the part of individuals, but no recognition of these powers . . . and without this recognition or claim to recognition there can be no right."[22] In still more elemental terms, one can say that recognition entails the mutuality of a common language, common conventions, and common consciousness—minimally, what is understood as sociability or civility—and perhaps even political relations defined by law. Against others, solitary persons can advance only claims. Citizens alone possess rights which, in Green's words "attach to the individual . . . only as a member of a society of free agents."[23] When Green argues that "a right held against society, in distinction to a right to be treated as a member of society, is a contradiction in terms," he may be saying in philosophical terms very much the same thing as Edmund Pendleton is saying in political terms when he says "there is no quarrel between government and liberty."[24]

Rights attach and pertain to citizens rather than abstract persons, whose evolving natures and needs generate evolving *claims* that become rights only inasmuch as they succeed in eliciting the mutual recognition of citizens bound together by common interests, and thus a common political community. To recognize a right is to confer it. The ordaining of government transforms claims into rights. To become a citizen is to engage in acts of common consciousness that entail the mutual acknowledgment of individuality and personhood that we call rights. The Constitution could be considered to be in and of itself a Bill of Rights because in breathing air into the American polity it gave life to rights. The "we" of "We the People" entailed a prior mutuality and common understanding that issued in those rights upon which, in turn, the legitimacy of the People's well-ordained government was thought to depend. If rights were prior to government, mutuality was prior to rights.

Thus, for example, it can be argued that the resistance ideology of Seventeenth Century commonwealthmen was the invention not of solitary individuals asserting natural rights, but of partisans already bound together by doctrine, convention, and common cause— by ties with a history dating back to the Magna Carta and beyond. The rights in the name of which they rebelled were the by-product rather than the premise of their civil association.

The source of legitimacy that endows claims with the status of rights would seem then to be civility rather than solitude, human convention rather than nature, artifice rather than God-given human character. Right precedes the formal structures of the Constitution and may therefore be thought to constrain and condition those structures, but they are in turn preceded by the informal structures of the social polity, which ultimately may be thought to constrain and condition right. We contrive through common consciousness the "natural" rights with which we affect to constrain the political artifacts of common consciousness. There is no harm in this magnificent illusion as long as the pretense of the lexical priority of rights is not permitted to manacle the political arms of the people whose sleight of hand accomplished the trick in the first place.

If the tyranny of unchecked majorities constitutes one of the gravest of those "abuses of power" against which Madison warned in *Federalist* number 63, rights absolutism rooted in metaphysical naturalism constitutes the gravest of those other equally malignant "abuses of liberty" about which he worries in the same place. Rights not only lead to citizenship, which is the condition of their recognition and which thus not only secures but entails them; they also attach exclusively to citizens, who enjoy them as a result of their civic membership in a polity constituted by common consciousness and common recognition.

Recent controversies in which members of the Reagan Administration such as Attorney-General Meese and members of the Supreme Court were embroiled revolve precisely around this issue. Meese argued for a kind of textual absolutism that construes the Constitution, as mediated by the intentions of its Framers (whatever those are), as immutable dicta that at one and the same time are unambiguous in their commands and prohibitions *and* beyond the interpretive powers of the Court or the people. Justice Brennan and others deny that such self-evident dicta are to be found in what is in any case an antiquarian tradition that *must* be interpreted if it is to be made pertinent to the changed circumstances of our own radically altered world.[25] (One might argue that if this is the case, it is the legislative and not the judicial branch that ought to adapt the old, intentionally flexible, constitutional tradition to the new circumstances; but that is another matter.)

The analysis thus far suggests a resolution to the Constitution's ambiguity about the place of certain outsiders (Negroes, Indians, women) in its scheme of rights. It makes little difference whether such individuals were regarded as human beings or persons. As long as they did not count as citizens they were without significant rights. For whatever the metaphysical origins of rights, it was understood well enough in practice that they attached to and could only be enjoyed by full citizens. All men might be born free and equal, and all women too for that matter, but such universalistic rhetoric was empty and could not change the simple political reality that until all men, black, white and red alike, and until all women too, acquired citizenship, their personhood or membership in the human race even if granted was a meaningless abstraction. Membership in the human race did not confer citizenship, but citizenship did confer human rights. Better to be a naturalized cat or dog than a Negro or a female born free and equal but without the full prerogatives of citizenship. It took the particularistic language of the Fifteenth and the Nineteenth Amendments to concretize the rights of citizenship conferred in the Fourteenth Amendment. It was not by being admitted into the human race but into full political citizenship and its prerogatives that the two outcast classes acquired rights.

By the same token, the futility of much of what passes today as human rights talk and international rights talk is due less to tyranny and injustice than to the absence of a common international citizenship, a common international polity, or a common international framework of recognition. There can be no human rights until what we call humanity ceases to be a philosophical abstraction or the holographic projection of a Kantian imagination, and becomes a genuine, identifiable People—a "We" woven together by invisible threads of common understanding, shared convention, acknowledged commonality, and mutual recognition. We would like world government to arise naturally out of the logic of human rights; but in reality the logic of human rights will fall into place only when world government has found a practice.

Rights lead then to citizenship; they are entailed by citizenship, they are the essence of citizenship—its finest product. Does the road from citizenship to rights traverse the same territory? That question requires that we examine citizenship itself, initially without regard to the problem of rights.

THE ROAD FROM CITIZENSHIP TO RIGHTS

We have become accustomed to thinking of politics as a spectator sport and of citizenship as a passive, watchdog function that is exercised only episodically in the election of those who actually govern in the name of "We the People." Obviously, if citizenship entails only the periodic accountability of voting, it will be a weak source of legitimacy and thus a questionable foundation for rights.

By focusing on the network of mutual consciousness and mutual interests that constitutes the real meaning of civility, T. H. Green's analysis suggests a richer and more subtle account of citizenship. In his analysis, it comprises attitudes as well as actions, and it exhibits itself in a capacity for public thinking and public judgment that is wholly at odds with the capacities of individuals or private persons to act on their own behalf. Citizenship in this sense is defined by what may be called "we" modes of looking at the world that have much in common with what Rousseau understood as the General Will. Citizens are individuals who have reconceived their identities in a public language; private persons who have reconceptualized their interests in a rhetoric of public goods; strangers who have come to recognize in others facsimiles of themselves as a result of common belonging to common communities.

As isolated individuals, as manifestations of gender, as religious sectarians, as creatures of intelligence, as physical beings, we are anything but equal. I am bigger, she is brighter, he is more devout, we are quicker, they have more staying power. It is only as citizens that we acquire equality. Jefferson's "all men are born equal" expresses an aspiration—a longed-for norm. In truth, all men are *born* unequal, but are given the opportunity of equality through membership in a democratic polity. By nature, some are weak, some strong, some white, some black, some male, some female, some stupid, some clever, some industrious, some lazy, some accommodating, some contentious. All are free by nature but only insofar as their natural power allows. None has rights—not because, as Hobbes had it, right is a pure creation of positive law—but because right depends on a system of mutual recognition that the abstract solitariness of man's natural condition precludes. Liberties become rights when individuals become citizens. Citizenship is the device by which natural inequalities and God-given differences are overstepped and artificial categories of likeness are invented to promote a fragile but essential equality. It is the We-ness of community that confers and extends the notion of right intuited by nature but given life only by arduous artifice.

Here the linkage between rights and legitimacy alluded to above is fully visible. What legitimates the actions of a citizenry deliberating in common—the so-called General Will—is that will's generality, its inclusiveness, and its encompassing of separate wills in a single, unified will. This will identifies those who participate in it as occupying common ground—as equals at least with respect to their shared interest. It is then this we-ness, this commonality of a will, that legitimates it.

The arguments of the social contract tradition, anxious to ground right in nature and legitimacy, in something beyond positive law, construe men as rights-bearing by nature. But as we have seen, while there may be natural liberty and natural power, there cannot be natural right in the same sense. For right is a product of power legitimized, and legitimacy is conferred by mutual consent—that is to say, citizenship. There is something suspiciously oxymoronic about the phrase individual rights, for to posit a right is to imagine a world of artificial kith and kin who recognize themselves as alike in their claim to liberty (if nothing else). As a *me,* I can make claims; but only as part of a *we* can I possess and acknowledge rights. Citizenship is, among other things, a kind of self-redefinition in which, with respect to the polity, we rethink who we are and what is good for us. Empathy and imagination are the psychological faculties necessary for identification with the Other, and it is these same faculties that underlie the acknowledgment of rights.

Now if citizenship is understood in the wan terms favored by some advocates of liberal representative democracy, empathy, imagination, the confluence of interests, and the pursuit of a common good can play only the slightest of roles. Elsewhere, I have developed an extended argument in favor of "strong democracy" as the only viable form of democratic government: not government by all the people all of the time over all public matters, but government by all of the people some of the time over some public matters.[26] Critics of this and other versions of participatory government have often cited the antipathy of direct democracy to rights as one of its chief defects. But the argument here suggests rather the opposite: that a form of strong democracy focusing on mutualism, active pursuit of common goods, and creative common action—because it nourishes empathy and imagination—is more likely to be hospitable to rights than a form of thin democracy that waters down citizenship and encourages passive accountability, mutual suspicion, and adversarial bargaining. The linkage between the preservation of rights and democracy is suggested in Madison's initial conviction that self-government is the only true guarantor of individual liberty. As Storing sums it up: "The basic justification for the absence of a bill of rights was that the main business of a free people is to establish and conduct good government: that is where the security of freedom must be sought . . . [T]he rhetoric of bills of rights might serve as a delusive substitute for the hard tasks of self-government.[27]

The quarrel I have with Madison and such current critics of rights as Walter Berns and Herbert Storing is that the kind of self-government that accommodates and succors rights requires a great deal more democracy than they are willing to contemplate. Self-government means ongoing civic participation by a citizenry enfranchised in more than name and engaged in more than voting. Madison correctly envisions the dependency of rights on the devices of the Constitution, yet devotes most of his energy to transforming those devices into checks on popular government. Walter Berns argues that virtue serves liberty better than abstract rights can serve it, but then becomes queasy at the thought of conferring on a citizenry an exercise of power sufficient to cultivate its civic virtue.[28] Herbert Storing and Nathan Tarcov wisely demonstrate that the Constitution omits the conferring of rights on Negroes and women but does not commit the sin of reading them out of the human race by nature; yet they do not notice that Negroes and women are thereby deprived of rights as effectively as if they had been declared non-persons and read out of the race.[29]

There is a good deal of interesting historical evidence in favor of the claim that where notions of citizenship have been most firmly entrenched, the need to devise extrinsic guarantees of rights have been least often felt. Neither the ancient Greek republics nor participatory democracies like the Swiss Confederation or the Raetian Republic had significant records of rights abuse in spite of the absence of declarations of rights. The United States, on the other hand, experienced an unsettling number of rights abuses from the Alien and Sedition Acts of the late Eighteenth Century to Lincoln's suspension of habeas corpus during the Civil War—and this in spite of an explicit Bill of Rights. Indeed, although intended to protect States and individuals from the abuses of a centralized Federal Government, the Bill of Rights in fact was never used for this purpose in the Nineteenth Century (the first case was *Gitlow vs. New York* in 1925). Nor would any such use have been conceivable in the absence of the broad language (equal protection and due process) of the Fourteenth Amendment—in other words, until after the Civil War. As Tocqueville had observed, the real spirit of liberty had to be regarded as local, depending upon an engaged citizenry rather than an abstract declaration.[30]

Intolerance, manipulated opinion, factionalism, privatism, and the abuse of liberty we call licentiousness are the real enemies of right. Participatory self-government—active citizenship nourished by civic virtue—is calculated to diminish the force of such enemies, and is thus a friend to rights. In eras of intolerance and the abuse of liberty, it is not to our rights but to our democracy that we need to look. When, as seems to be happening in this era of prosperity and privatism, we cease to respect each other as citizens, when the differences spawned by our private identities overwhelm the equality engendered by our civic identities, when civic virtue is displaced by wholly private interests, it is then that our rights become most precarious. These rights belong not to individuals but to citizens: To "We the People." This is why it can be argued, as I have done here, that the rights of "We the People" are all the rights there are.

NOTES

1. C. B. MacPherson, "Natural Rights in Hobbes and Locke," in *Political Theory and the Rights of Man,* ed. D. D. Raphael (Bloomington: Indiana University Press, 1967), p. 14.

2. Walter Berns writes: "Commanding nothing, for these are not laws in the sense of commands that must be obeyed, the laws of nature (for Hobbes, for Locke, and for the Americans of 1776) point to government as the way to secure natural rights, government that derives its 'just powers from the consent of the governed.'" "The Constitution as a Bill of Rights," in *How Does the Constitution Secure Rights,* ed. Robert A. Goldwin and William A. Schambra (Washington, D.C.: American Enterprise Institute, 1985), p. 57.

3. Locke distinguishes the "industrious and the rational" to whom God gives the world and the "quarrelsome and contentious" who, it would seem, are entitled neither to property nor to citizenship. John Locke, *Second Treatise of Civil Government,* chapter 5 (On Property).

4. Article I, section 9 of the Constitution bars the Federal Government from prohibiting the importation of slaves for at least 20 years; Article IV, section 2 upholds the right of property in slaves, and compels return of fugitive slaves to their home states. Other than these two articles, only the three-fifths compromise (Article I, section 2) counting slaves as three-fifths of a person for purposes of representation and taxation directly addresses slavery in the Constitution.

5. Arguing that slavery is extrinsic to the Constitution, Herbert Storing writes: "Slavery is the creature, Southern as well as Northern judges said again and again, of positive law only; it has no support in natural law or in transcendent principles of justice." "Slavery and the Moral Foundation of the Republic," in *The Moral Foundation of the American Republic,* ed. Robert H. Horwitz (Charlottesville: University of Virginia Press, 1977), p. 218. My argument follows Storing to a point, but draws very different conclusions.

6. The Nineteenth Amendment, ratified in January 1919, reads, "The rights of citizens of the United States to vote, shall not be denied or abridged by the United States or by any state on account of sex." The provision does not assert that *all* humans can vote, or that *all* humans are citizens, only that women who are citizens cannot be barred from voting.

7. Edward S. Corwin and Jack W. Peltason, *Understanding the Constitution* (New York: Holt, Rinehart and Winston, Inc., 1976), p. 176, emphasis in original. For a useful discussion of the evolution of rights language in Revolutionary America, see Daniel T. Rodgers, *Contested Truths* (New York: Basic Books, 1987).

8. Herbert J. Storing, "The Constitution and the Bill of Rights," in Goldwin and Schambra, *How Does the Constitution Secure Rights,* p. 26.

9. Essay by "A Farmer," *Maryland Gazette,* February 15, 1788.

10. *The Federalist Papers,* #84 (Alexander Hamilton).

11. The more extreme Anti-Federalists possessed an almost anarchist fear of governmental authority; thus, in 1788, Samuel Chase wrote to John Lamb: "A delegation of rights alone will be of no essential service. Some of the powers must be abridged, or public liberty will be endangered and, in time, destroyed." Issac Leake, *Memoir of the Life and Times of General John Lamb* (Albany, N.Y.: J. Munsell, 1850), p. 310. I have explored the anarchist tendencies of liberalism at some length in Part I of my *Strong Democracy: Participatory Politics for a New Age* (Berkeley: University of California Press, 1984).

12. Crane Brinton comes closest to identifying the constitutional era as a Thermidor in relation to the preceding revolutionary era (in his *The Anatomy of*

Revolution), but historians generally have divided the two eras and labeled them radical and nation-building (or conservative or reconstitutive).

13. Jeremy Bentham, *Anarchical Fallacies.*

14. Madison was discussing the six year term for the Senate here and, once again, arguing against those turbulent and contentious factions that are the bane of *Federalist,* #10.

15. *Debates in the Several State Conventions on the Adoption of the Federal Constitution,* ed. Jonathan Elliot, vol. 3, p. 37.

16. Ronald Dworkin, *Taking Rights Seriously* (Cambridge: Harvard University Press, 1977), pp. 198–99.

17. D. D. Raphael, "Human Rights, Old and New," in *Political Theory and the Rights of Man,* p. 65.

18. Henry Shue, "Subsistence Rights," in Goldwin and Schambra, *How Does the Constitution Secure Rights,* pp. 74–75. Those who have argued for the expansion of rights to encompass economic needs like subsistence and employment include C. B. Macpherson, D. D. Raphael, and Christian Bay. Most modern rights documents include economic as well as civic rights, although it is not clear that such rights are anywhere adjudicated or enforced.

19. See note 11 above.

20. John Dunn, *Political Theory* (Cambridge: Cambridge University Press, 1984), p. 11. It may be useful to recall here that Rousseau, that consumate rights theorist, understood rightful authority as *conventional* rather than natural (cf. *The Social Contract,* Bk. 1, Chap. 4).

21. "A right is a claim," writes Bernard Mayo; and although it is a "justifiable" claim, its justifiability derives from mutual undertakings that are part of a social context. Mayo, "What Are Human Rights," in *Political Theory and the Rights of Man,* p. 75.

22. Thomas Hill Green, *Lectures on the Principles of Political Obligation* (London: Longmans, 1941), paragraph 31, p. 48.

23. Green, paragraph 138, p. 143. Green is not arguing that the state creates rights, but he is suggesting that it "gives fuller reality to rights already existing," and that these exist by virtue of prior social relations (paragraph 133, p. 138).

24. Green, paragraph 99, pp. 109–10.

25. Edwin Meese et al., *The Great Debate: Interpreting Our Constitution* (Washington, D.C.: Federalist Society, 1986).

26. In *Strong Democracy,* I have distinguished strong democracy both from representative democracy, and a virulent parody of direct democracy that I have called unitary democracy.

27. H. J. Storing, in Goldwin and Schambra, *How Does the Constitution Secure Rights,* p. 34.

28. See Walter Berns, *Freedom, Virtue, and the First Amendment* (New York: Henry Regnery, 1965).

29. Tarcov argues, "the political arrangements of the constitution excluded enslaved Blacks and autonomous Indians [he does not mention women], rather than Blacks or Indians as such." "American Constitutionalism and Individual Rights," in Goldwin and Schambra, *How Does the Constitution Secure Rights,* p. 113.

Herbert Storing cites Frederick Douglass to similar effect: "I hold that the Federal Government was never, in its essence, anything but an anti-slavery government. Abolish slavery tomorrow, and not a sentence or syllable of the Constitution need be altered . . . If in its origin slavery had any relation to the government, it was only as the scaffolding to the magnificent structure, to be removed as soon as the building was completed." Douglass, cited by H. J. Storing in "Slavery and the Moral Foundations," p. 221.

There are two problems with this approach as a resolution to the question of rights: first, it is belied by history; it took 75 years and a civil war to make the Constitution do for Negroes (and 150 years for women) what Douglass and Storing want to argue it meant, "in essence," to do in the first place. Second, the Constitution *is* a scaffold and not an essence. It contains a practice, but its provisions are all so much scaffolding. What the scaffolding omits to do, is not done. If rights depend on the conferring of citizenship, then the Fifteenth and Nineteenth Amendments are no mere rectifications of oversight, but fundamental alterations in the character of American citizenship.

30. See Alexis de Tocqueville, *Democracy in America,* and J. J. Rousseau, *The Social Contract,* Bks. 3 and 4.

CHAPTER 6

Have Rights Gone Wrong?
The Reconstruction
of Rights

IF THERE IS a single theme upon which Americans agree, it is that ours is a regime rooted in rights. Rights are how we enter our political conversation: the chips with which we bargain, the collateral in the social contract. They are the ground of both rebellion and legitimacy, of our inclinations to anarchism and our proclivities toward community.

Without coaching, any American will cry out:

"I know my rights!" or
"You got no right!" or
"What about my rights?" or
"Read him his rights!"

Corporations mimic individuals in their devotion to rights as barriers against the public regulation of private profit. The Philip Morris Company recently paid the National Archives $600,000 to associate itself with the Bill of Rights, presumably to promote its view of advertising as a First Amendment right essential to selling tobacco in an age of democratic public health advocacy. Rights are how Americans have always advanced their interests, whether as individual or corporate persons. Some might say (I will do so below) that there is even an element of obsession in the American devotion to rights, that we sometimes risk a rights absolutism as unbalanced in its political effects as the fabled "tyranny of the majority" against which rights are often deployed as the primary defense.

Yet there are good reasons for the focus on rights. The naked self comes to the bargaining table weak and puny; the language of rights clothes it. The naked self extends hardly beyond that bundle of desires and aversions that constitute its raw, prelegitimate wants. Rights carve out a space for it to operate in—call it autonomy or dignity or, in its material incarnation, property. Wants become needs and needs acquire a moral mantle that, as rights claims, cannot be ignored. The hungry man wants to eat; the ravenous man needs to eat; the starving man has a right to eat. Rights turn the facts of want into powerful claims—powerful, at least, in civil societies that consider rights rhetoric legitimate.

Even the naked self is perforce a social self, whose claims on others imply reciprocity as well as equality. If, as this suggests, democracy is the form of governance especially suited to the language of rights, it is ironic and troubling to find the language of rights often deployed in a fashion adversarial to democracy. Perhaps this is because democracy is often understood as the rule of the majority, and rights are understood more and more as the private possessions of individuals and thus as necessarily antagonistic to majoritarian democracy. But, as I will suggest, this is to misunderstand both rights and democracy.

THE ROOTS OF RIGHTS

America has always been a civil society hospitable to rights. It borrowed its earliest norms from diverse roots: from Puritanism, with its egalitarian version of the rights of a Christian; from the English Dissent tradition, which conceived of rights as a bastion against illegitimate monarchic authority; and from classical republicanism (James Harrington or Montesquieu, for example), where rights were linked to civic virtue and constitutional government. Even in colonial times, American institutions treated government as an artificial contrivance which had to be created; a collectivity to be sure but one instrumental to the religious and secular interests of individuals; one that saw government as originating in consensus and in a contract between all those who were to be citizens or subjects. The Mayflower Compact for example, though scarcely a document concerned with natural rights, saw the Pilgrims "covenant and combine" themselves "together into a civil body politick, for [their] better order and preservation."

But just how democratic was this society, hospitable as it was to rights, or how democratic could it become? The question offers one way of considering whether rights and democracy can cohabit or perhaps even reinforce one another.

On the face of things, and in keeping with the eighteenth-century view, the answer would seem to be not very democratic, at least not at the outset. In the great Founders' debate, both Federalists concerned with strong central government and the sovereignty of the whole over the parts, and Anti-Federalists concerned with the relative autonomy of the states and the sovereignty of the parts over the whole, shared one thing: they both understood the Constitution as a tool of rights. Federalists saw in its governmental powers the explicit political expression of rights; Anti-Federalists saw in its provisions a set of rights limiting governmental power.

Historically, these standpoints were both complementary and in tension in just the same way as the social contract theories of Thomas Hobbes and John Locke were complementary and in tension. Hobbes sought to protect individual liberty and security *through* strong government; Locke wanted to protect liberty and property *against* strong government. In the Federalist case, there is a Hobbesian faith in strong contract-based government as a guarantor of rights; in the Anti-Federalist case, there is a Lockean distrust of strong government which understands rights as constraints on government. Both positions conceive of government as an artificial means whose primary object is the preservation of rights that are anterior to politics—that exist in a "natural" or "higher" pre-political form.

Returning to our question, then, the terms of the Federalist/Anti-Federalist debate would suggest that the American rights tradition in both its Federalist and Anti-Federalist forms had a primarily anti-democratic bias. For the Federalists, the issue was how to insulate the power in which rights were expressed and by which liberty and property were to be safeguarded from popular majorities and private opinion. Madison warned against "an infinity of little jealous clashing commonwealths, the wretched nurseries of unceasing discord" and essayed to design a constitution that would supply republican remedies to treat republican vices (among which democracy was paramount!). These included indirect election of representatives and an expanded compass for civil society; by multiplying the number of factions and groups, their capacity for divisiveness might be attenuated.

For the Anti-Federalists, the aim was to limit government *tout court*. Despite the democratic spirit of the strategy favored by Jefferson calling for the devolution of power, the object remained to check and limit central power as the exercise of a unitary popular sovereignty. Here the Bill of Rights figured as a studied obstacle to centrally organized popular power. Locke had worried about how "polecats and foxes" (ordinary men, quarrelsome and contentious) might protect themselves from the sovereign lion brought in to police their disputes. The Federalists wanted to keep the "people" from riding the lion, believing that only the best men could subdue its power and divert it to their virtuous ends; the Anti-Federalists were less concerned with the rider, hoping rather to imprison the lion itself in a cage of rights. Neither had much trust in the people from whom popular government took its legitimacy. Hamilton is said to have expressly calumnized the people as a great beast, "howling masses" not fit to govern.

Thus, it is hardly a surprise that the Founders managed to create a form of government in many ways antipathetical to any real institutional expression of the popular sovereignty that was its paper premise. Moreover, they wrote a constitution whose letter was self-consciously distrustful of democracy. Popular sovereignty could not for them mean popular rule. The abstract status of sovereign permitted "we the people" to establish a government, but did not license it to participate in the government it had brought forth.

The word "equality" failed to make an appearance in the Constitution's language, and almost every device of government contemplated was aimed not at embodying but at checking popular power. The real democrats (Sam Adams, Patrick Henry, Tom Paine, Jefferson himself) were not present at the Philadelphia Creation, and radical democratic models calling for a unicameral legislature and universal white male suffrage of the kind represented by the Pennsylvania Constitution were given short shrift.

Jefferson had written of the Virginia Constitution: "Try by this as a tally every provision of our constitution and see if it hangs directly on the will of the people."[1] By this measure, the federal Constitution failed—and thus, for the suspicious Founders, succeeded. As Patrick Henry had dryly remarked, as far as he could see the people gave them (the Founders) no power to use its name. Such incipient tendencies to popular government as "democrats, mobocrats and all the other rats," as the slogan had it, might have insinuated into the Constitution were unlikely to survive that document's institutional arrangements. These included the separation of powers with its immobilizing checks and balances, federalism as a forced vertical separation of powers enhanced by the Tenth Amendment, the indirect election of senators and the President which interposed a filter between the people and their servants, judicial review as a check on popular legislation (and in time a warrant for judicial legislation), and the division of popular will into two parts equal and opposed—one represented by the House of Representatives, the other by the presidency.

The two expressly democratic instruments—the House of Representatives and the Amendment Article—were hedged in with restrictions. Limitations on suffrage (standards were a matter for the states to decide at their own discretion within the loose confines of republicanism) left it, in Henry Lee's scathing indictment, "a mere shred or rag of representation." The powers to amend the Constitution detailed in Article V were popular sovereignty's most potent constitutional instrument. But they were made sufficiently complicated and unwieldy to turn the amendment provision into a last and improbable recourse of what would have to be, if they really were going to use it, a wildly dissatisfied and endlessly energetic people. Sixteen amendments in two hundred years (I count the Bill of Rights as part of the original Constitution) does not suggest a very democratic instrument or a very engaged popular sovereign.

And yet the letter of the Constitution and the intentions of the Framers are only part of the story. America's spirit of democracy is older than the republic. Equality had its ardent advocates then as now, and even where it was contradicted by the Constitution's letter, the democratic spirit found its way into the tenor and the logic of the Constitution. This spirit arises not in opposition to rights but from the political context that gives rights meaning and force.

There is a simple but powerful relationship between rights and democracy: universal rights logically require equality. Rights, as political philosophers say, "entail" the equality of those who claim them; and democracy is the politics of equality. Without democracy, rights are empty words, dependent for their realization on the goodwill of despots. Rights in their own turn promote and promise emancipation, suffrage, and empowerment. Even Madison recognized that rights without supporting political institutions were so many "parchment barriers" to tyranny (one reason for his early opposition to a separate Bill of Rights). Late in his life (in 1821), like so many Americans who had once feared the people as a rabble, he had come to take a less harsh view of democracy. He would not perhaps have agreed with Louis Hartz that "the majority in America has forever been a puppy dog tethered to a lion's leash," but on the question of the enfranchising of the propertyless, he came to acknowledge, "Under every view of the subject, it seems indispensable that the Mass of Citizens should not be without a voice, in making the laws which they are to obey, in choosing the Magistrates, who are to administer them, and if the only alternative be between an equal and universal right of suffrage for each branch of the government and a containment of the entire right to a part of the citizens, it is better that those having the greater interest at stake namely that of property and persons both, should be deprived of half their share in government; then that those having the lesser interest, that of personal rights only, should be deprived of the whole."[2]

Madison's use of the language of "an equal and universal right of suffrage" just thirty years after a Founding consecrated to limiting both popular suffrage and popular access to government seems startling, but rights language permitted no other evolution. If popular government and laws understood as self-prescribed limitations on private behavior are the real guarantors of liberty, if natural rights are secure only when political rights are guaranteed by popular government, then the right to suffrage turns out to be the keystone of all other rights—a principle increasingly recognized in the real democratic politics of the early nineteenth century and one eventually written explicitly into the Constitution with the Thirteenth, Fourteenth, and Fifteenth Amendments.

I mean here to advance both a logical claim and a historical claim. I want to say rights can be shown theoretically to entail equality and democracy. And at the same time, I want to argue that the actual history of rights talk in America unfolds as an increasingly progressive and democratic story. Philosophically, rights claims are always and necessarily equality claims as well. To say "I have a right" is to posit that I am the equal of others and at the same time to recognize the equality of the persons to whom, on whom, against whom the claim is made. No master ever said to a slave: "Give me my right!" for rights can be acknowledged only by equals. Likewise, the slave who proclaims "I have the right to be free" says in the same breath "I am your equal," and hence "you are my equal." In a certain sense, in speaking of equal rights one speaks redundantly: rights are equalizers. Individuals may use rights to insulate themselves from others, to wall in their privacy, but their rights claims depend entirely on the proposition that as claimants they are the equal of all others, that no one living in a free and democratic society is privileged because of who they happen to be by virtue of race, gender, religion, and so forth.

More than anything else, this is why a constitution rooted in rights cannot systematically exclude whole classes of persons from citizenship without becoming inherently incoherent and thus unstable. Even where it is anti-democratic in its institutional provisions, it will incline to democratization, tend over time toward greater inclusiveness. This is exactly what happened to the American polity in the course of the nineteenth century. That the Constitution included provisions implicitly recognizing slavery (the three-fifths compromise for example) was a shameful comment on the Founders and perhaps on their motives. Nonetheless, such provisions sat like undigested gruel on the Constitution's rights-lined stomach and were in time regurgitated. This resulted not simply from pressures brought to bear from the outside, but arose from the inherently universalizing character of all rights talk, which pushes against artificial boundaries of every kind and makes inequalities increasingly indigestible.

If rights imply citizenship and citizenship appears as a right—the right to liberty, the right to self-legislation, the right to be included in a civic polity founded on "popular" (that-means-me!) sovereignty—the idea of the citizen will always have an aggressive, liberating, even imperial character, pushing to extend its compass to the very periphery of the universal. In Rome, early modern Europe, and America, it has been expansive in its logic and liberating in its politics. Today as rights continue to press outward, reaching the very edge of our species boundary, we can even speak of "animal rights" or "fetal rights" and still seem to be extending rather than perverting what it means for beings to have rights.

Rights are also linked logically to democracy and equality as a consequence of their essentially social character. Rousseau had already observed in *The Social Contract* that though all justice comes from God, "if we knew how to receive it from on high, we would need neither government nor laws. There is without a doubt a universal justice emanating from reason alone; but to be acknowledged among us, this justice must be reciprocal. . . . [T]here must be conventions and laws to combine rights with duties and to bring justice back to its object." In a classical nineteenth-century idealist argument, the English political philosopher T. H. Green elaborates Rousseau's argument by insisting "there can be no right without a consciousness of common interest on the part of members of a society. Without this there might be certain powers on the part of individuals, but no recognition of these powers . . . and without this recognition or claim to recognition there can be no right."[3] Recognition entails the mutuality of a common language, common conventions, and common consciousness: in other words, civility. Citizens alone possess rights, for as Green said, rights "attach to the individual . . . only as a member of a society." Tocqueville is, of course, right to remind us that citizens united as a majority are still capable of abusing the rights of citizens taken one by one. But Green's rejoinder is that the tyranny of the majority may be more a reflection on the inadequacies of democratic processes than the absence of rights.

DEMOCRACY AS THE REALM OF RIGHTS

Now if rights entail equality and require a civic context of mutual recognition to be effective, the regime form most compatible with rights is neither decentralized, limited government on the model of the Anti-Federalists, nor screened and filtered representative government on the republican model of the Federalists, but quite simply democracy—defined by universal suffrage and collective self-legislation. For democracy is the rule of equality. Limited government is indifferent to who rules so long as the rulers are constrained. Republican government elicits the consent and accountability but not the participation and judgment of the people, which is why Jefferson sometimes called representative government elective aristocracy. Rights do best, however, where those who claim them are one and the same with those upon whom the claims fall—where sovereign and subject are united in one person: the citizen. Without citizenship and participation, rights can become a charade. Without responsibility, rights may not always be enforceable. Without empowerment, rights can seem like decorative fictions. A constitution is, after all, a piece of paper, and "parchment barriers" are never much use against lead and steel and chains and guns, although they can be a significant trip-wire against majority assaults on minorities, something the Founders obviously appreciated.

In what may be the world's most effusively rights-oriented constitution, a famous document not only guarantees citizens "freedom of speech," "freedom of the press," "freedom of assembly," and "freedom of street processions and demonstrations," but also guarantees judges who will be constitutionally "independent and subject only to the law," "separation of church from state," as well as the "right to education," "the right to work," "the right to rest and leisure," "the right to maintenance in old age and also in case of sickness or disability," and, as if these were not enough, equal rights to women "in all spheres of economic, government, cultural, political and other public activity," and finally, guaranteeing what comes before, universal elections in which all citizens have the right to vote, "irrespective of race or nationality, sex, religion, education, domicile, social origin, property status or past activities." This unprecedented fortress of human liberty was the Constitution (Fundamental Law) of the Soviet Union, a nation in which rights have truly been paper parapets from which no defense of liberties can be undertaken.

As Madison observed in questioning the value of a Bill of Rights detached from the Constitution, "Repeated violations of . . . parchment barriers have been committed by overbearing majorities in every state. . . . Whenever there is an interest and power to do wrong, wrong will generally be done and not less readily by a powerful and interested party than by a powerful and interested prince."[4]

Philosophical argument finds persuasive historical expression in the American setting. Successful popular movements aimed at the emancipation of slaves, the enfranchisement of women, and the remediation of the condition of the native American Indian tribes, as well as the empowerment of the poor, the working class, and others cast aside by the American market, have all had in common a devotion to the language of rights. Indeed, the single most important strategic decision faced by those who felt left out of the American way of life has been whether to mobilize against or in the name of the American Founding, understood as the Declaration of Independence, the Constitution, and the Bill of Rights. Movements that have made war on the Constitution, holding that its rights promise no salvation to the powerless, have on the whole failed. Movements that have insisted that the Founding can and must make good on the promise implicit in its universalizing rights rhetoric have succeeded.

In their explicit mimicry of the Founder's language and the citation of great rights jurists like Blackstone, the bold women at Seneca Falls in 1848 captured the logic of "entailment" with their own militant rights claims. "We hold these truths to be self-evident," they asserted, "that all men and women are created equal."[5] And although the radical abolitionists at times seemed to declare war on America itself, one of their most fiery leaders understood the entailments of the American tradition well enough. William Lloyd Garrison burned a copy of the Constitution in Framingham on July 4, 1854, but he nevertheless declared in *The Liberator,* in his *To the Public,* and in impassioned speeches delivered throughout the North, that he "assented to the 'self-evident truth' maintained in the American Declaration of Independence, 'that all men are created equal, and endowed by their Creator with certain inalienable rights—among which are life, liberty and the pursuit of happiness.'" On this foundation, he concluded, he would "strenuously contend for the immediate enfranchisement of our slave population."[6]

Some might say these radicals were trying to drive a wedge between the Declaration and the Constitution, but when John Brown went looking for legitimacy he found it in the Preamble to the Constitution as well as in the Declaration. When he offered the People of the United States a "Provisional Constitution," its preamble read: "Whereas slavery, throughout its entire existence in the United States, is none other than a most barbarous, unprovoked, and unjustifiable war of one portion of its citizens upon another portion . . . in utter disregard and violation of those eternal and self-evident truths set forth in our Declaration of Independence, therefore we, citizens of the United States, and the oppressed people (deprived of Rights by Justice Taney) . . . do ordain and establish for ourselves the following Provisional Constitution and ordinances, the better to protect our person, property, lives and liberties, and to govern our action."[7]

From this perspective, the Civil War and Reconstruction Amendments ending slavery and involuntary servitude and guaranteeing universal male suffrage, due process, and the equal protection of the laws to all citizens were not a reversal of America's constitutional history but the culminating event in the history of the Constitution's rights commitments as they manifested themselves in the practical politics and civic life of the nation. Justice Taney's decision in *Dred Scott* was, by the same token, the last gasp of those trying to stem the floodtide on which rights were sweeping through history. Taney's problem was how to construct rights whose thrust was ineluctably universalizing in narrow, self-limiting terms appropriate to his prejudices. He had to show that "we the people," synonymous with "citizens," could somehow be construed to exclude the Negro race. His decision tortuously avoids the entailments of the idea of citizenship and instead turns on the "historical fact" that Negroes "were at that time considered as a subordinate and inferior class of beings." Taney takes care to avoid a careful examination of what such crucial terms as "person," "citizen," and "right" might entail. For it was precisely against those entailments that he was rather desperately trying to construct an argument.

Even at the time of the Founding there had been powerful opposition to slavery as an embarrassment to the language of the Declaration and the Constitution's Preamble. John Adams and John Jay were vigorously eloquent in their opposition to it (although not at the Convention), and there were a number of statesmen who would sympathize with George Mason's refusal to sign the Constitution because its twenty-year extension of the slave trade was "disgraceful to mankind."

Madison had acknowledged "moral equality of blacks" and in *Federalist*

No. 54 had allowed that Negroes did "partake" of qualities belonging to persons as well as to property and were thus protected in "life and limb, against the violence of all others." The slave, Madison said elsewhere, "is no less evidently regarded by the law as a member of the society, not as part of irrational creation; as a moral person, not as a mere article of property."[8] It was not so much the moral argument but the logic of what it meant to be a person that is captured by Madison, and it was this logic that created the problems for the hapless Taney.

ARE RIGHTS ERODING DEMOCRACY?

In our century, the powerful alliance between rights and political emancipation, between the claim to be a person and the right to be a citizen, seems in danger of coming unstuck. Increasingly, rights have retreated into the private space won for them by their civic entailments, allowing us to forget that they are secured by and only have meaning for citizens. The communities rights once created are now too often pictured as the enemies of right and the political institutions by which we secure rights are made over into external and alien adversaries—as if they had nothing to do with us. The sense of rights as a claim for political participation, and participation and civic responsibility as the foundation of rights, has yielded to peculiarly privatized notions of rights as indisputable possessions of individuals who acquire them by birth or membership in some special subgroup, and must do nothing to enforce them. Such rights exist and are deemed efficacious as long as they are noisily promulgated.

There are multiple reasons for the new take on rights, many of which have little to do with the logic of rights itself and for which rights advocates cannot be blamed. The erosion of viable notions of the public and of a common good and the growth of interest-group liberalism in which private factions and their rights come to count as the only political entities worthy of attention has undermined citizenship and the public rights associated with it. Under conditions of privatization, consumerism, radical individualism, and cultural separatism, rights cease to be regarded as a civic identity to be posited and won, and are instead conceived as a natural identity to be discovered, worn, and enjoyed.

As a consequence, young people are more likely to use rights to make a case about what government owes them than to point to what they themselves might owe to the democratic government that is the guarantor of their rights ("Ask not what your country can do for you . . ."). Thus, for example, they may exclaim that the government has "no right" to conscript them into the army, as if it were not their government, as if there could be a democratic government in the absence of their willingness and responsibility to service it—quite literally to constitute it. Many young persons in fact do engage in community service or enlist in the armed services or participate in demonstrations and protests, but as often as not these activities are either seen as "voluntary" (it is a "volunteer army") or as a manifestation of rights and prerogatives held against government and the polity. Civic duties and social responsibilities simply do not come into it.[9]

The changing climate of politics is evident in the vanishing of volunteer fire departments for want of volunteers, and in the growing ungovernability of municipalities that cannot afford liability insurance against disgruntled inhabitants who conceive themselves as dissatisfied clients rather than as responsible citizens. Fire protection comes to be viewed as a service provided by government to residents rather than a service by, for, and of citizens. Where "Our Town" becomes Their Town, rights can become a knife that severs the bonds of citizens rather than the glue that holds them together. The right to sue is a precious resource against abusive authority; yet democratic responsibility is also a powerful guarantee against abuse. We need both. The litigious citizen expresses his rights as an individual but may be overlooking his responsibilities to the community being sued.

The precarious balance between individual and community which rights properly understood can mediate is upset, and rights are introduced on only one side of the scales, leaving the community hard pressed to advance the public good. Legal philosophers like to say that rights are trumps, which is a poignant way of underscoring the crucial subjugation of democratic government to the liberties of citizens. But there is also a sense in which, as Rousseau once wrote, citizens are trumps: "There can be no patriotism without liberty," Rousseau observes in his *The Government of Poland*, "no liberty without virtue, no virtue without citizens; create citizens and you will have everything you need; without them you will have nothing but debased slaves from the rulers of the state on downwards."

Rights, after all, belong to individuals as citizens, and citizens belong to communities that therefore also have rights. There is no reason not to use the power of rights as legitimizers of claims in order to advance community goods. Tenants organizing against drug traffickers, victims organizing to secure their rights in a criminal justice system disposed (quite properly) to pay special attention to the rights of criminal defendants, and mothers organizing against drunk drivers (MADD) offer compelling examples of the power of rights-thinking on behalf of the community at large.

The American Civil Liberties Union has been an ardent and valuable advocate of the rights of individuals in our democracy. Yet the ACLU's conception of rights has occasionally veered toward a denial of community that may reflect the breakdown of our sense of common civic purposes as a nation. In recent years, in addition to its healthy concerns with the sanctity of political speech and the right of assembly (both of which are important to the polity and the public good), the ACLU has dug itself into a foxhole from which it can engage in a firefight with democracy. The ACLU has opposed airport security examinations, decried sobriety checkpoints (recently declared constitutional by the Supreme Court in a 6–3 decision), argued against the voluntary fingerprinting of children in areas subject to kidnapping. By making privacy over into a supertrump card in a deck of individual rights that, with respect both to public goods and community rights, is already trump to start with, it places at risk the balance between individual and community that is the prize achievement of the history of rights in America.

In the case of the *Michigan Department of State Police v. Sitz,* a leading argument held that sobriety checkpoints abridged the constitutional rights of Michigan motorists by causing them "fright and surprise" in the course of ninety-second stops that were tantamount to "subjective intrusion upon liberty interests." The liberty interests of other drivers as potential victims of drunken driving usually thought of as belonging to the rights of the community, or the responsibility of the body politic, were not weighed and found wanting; they were ignored. This is a growing problem in a society where the idea of civic community has lost its resonance and interest groups such as the National Rifle Association use rights as a foil for their special pleading.

This unbalancing of the rights equation feeds into the historical mistrust some Americans still feel toward popular government. It threatens to disenfranchise the very citizenry rights were once deployed to empower. The new strategy links a Federalist distrust of popular rule with a form of judicial activism that permits courts not merely to enforce rights but to legislate in their name whenever the "people" are deemed sufficiently deluded or insufficiently energetic. It is not at all clear that rights enforced on an obstinate citizen body rendered passive-aggressive (quiescent but angry) by an encroaching court are really made more secure over the long haul. But it certainly is clear that a "democratic" government that will not permit its citizens to govern themselves when it comes to rights will soon be without either rights or democracy.

It was, of course, an original Federalist strategy aimed at curbing democracy that produced judicial review as a limit on popular legislation. In the Madisonian approach to the balance of power, the judiciary has remained a key instrument in preventing majorities from getting out of hand. Yet as Louis Hartz noticed, the majority has not really gotten out of hand very often in America. Tolerance notwithstanding, at least since *Brown v. Board of Education* (1954), impatient democrats seeking to secure rights that majorities sometimes neglected have allied themselves with courts willing to act as surrogate legislators where the people are found wanting. The "filtration" of the public mind favored by the Founders thus has found a modern incarnation in the not so democratic practices of judicial government.

In the recent Supreme Court case upholding a lower court decision concerning Kansas City (Missouri) school desegregation, the majority ruled in favor of a judicial intervention whose final outcome was the raising of taxes. The case is complicated, and the Missouri court did not itself directly levy taxes, but Justice Anthony Kennedy issued a sobering caution about the logic of the judiciary acting as legislative surrogate when he wrote in dissent: "It is not surprising that imposition of taxes by a [judicial] authority so insulated from public communication or control can lead to deep feelings of frustration, powerlessness and anger on the part of taxpaying citizens." Frustration, powerlessness, and anger have become the currency in which many Americans have paid for the usurping of their political authority in the name of their political rights. Americans need their rights, but they need also to understand the responsibilities their rights entail. If seen solely as private things to be secured by judges rather than public things (*res publica*) to be secured by citizens, rights atrophy.

Democracies do not always do justice. Frequently they do injustice. Yet the remedy for this, as Jefferson noted a long time ago, is not to disempower citizens who have been indiscreet, but to inform their discretion, which may sometimes mean extending rather than circumscribing their power. For power teaches responsibility and responsibility limits power. Like experienced legislators, publics can and do become more discreet and competent over time. The ravages done by Proposition 13 (which initiated the tax revolt in 1978, limiting state expenditures) have gradually educated the people of California into an appreciation of their civic responsibilities. In the spring of 1990, quite on their own, and without the mandate of a court, they approved a referendum raising taxes. What America most needs just now are not more interventionist courts but more interventionist schools; not lessons in the rights of private persons but lessons in the responsibilities of public citizens; not a new view of the Bill of Rights, but a new view of the Constitution as the democratic source of all rights.

Madison might have had a better understanding of rights than the advocates of a separate Bill of Amendments when he argued for including rights in the substantive text of the constitution. For by placing them there, where they would be read in context rather than isolating them in a document that might make them seem a natural possession of passive private persons, their civic and social nature as part and parcel of the fabric of democratic republicanism might have been crystal clear.

On this two hundredth birthday of the Bill of Rights, we need to learn for ourselves what the first seventy-five years of American history, culminating in the Civil War, taught our ancestors in a still young America: that rights stand with, not against, democracy and if the two do not progress together, they do not progress at all.

NOTES

1. Thomas Jefferson, cited in Richard K. Matthews, *The Radical Politics of Thomas Jefferson* (Kansas City: University of Kansas Press, 1984), 78.

2. James Madison (1821), "Note to Speech on the Right to Suffrage," in Saul K. Padover, *The Complete Madison* (New York: Harper, 1953), 40.

3. Thomas Hill Green, *Lectures on the Principles of Political Obligation* (London: Longmans, 1941).

4. Madison, *The Tree of Liberty: A Documentary History of Rebellion and Political Crime in America,* edited by Nicholas N. Kittrie and Eldon D. Wedlock, Jr. (Baltimore: Johns Hopkins University Press, 1986).

5. See "The Declaration of Sentiments and Resolutions of the First Women's Rights Conference," in Elizabeth Stanton, Susan B. Anthony, and Matilda Joslyn Gage, eds., *History of Woman Suffrage* (New York: Fowler & Wells, 1881) 170–73.

6. William Lloyd Garrison, in Wendell Garrison and Francis Jackson Garrison, *William Lloyd Garrison, 1805–1879* (New York: Arno Press, 1969), 408.

7. Louis Ruchames, *John Brown: The Making of a Revolutionary* (New York: Grosset & Dunlop, 1969), 119–20.

8. James Madison to Frances Wright, Sept. 1, 1825, from James Madison, *Letters and Other Writings,* vol. 3, 495.

9. For a provocative symposium on a "bill of duties" in which this commentator participated, see *Harper's,* February 1991.

Part II

AMERICAN PRACTICE:
LEADERSHIP, CITIZENSHIP,
AND CENSORSHIP

CHAPTER 7

Neither Leaders nor Followers:
Citizenship under
Strong Democracy

Strong leaders make a weak people.
(*Emiliano Zapata*)

Some say pity the "country that has no heroes";
I say "pity the country that needs heroes."
(*Bertolt Brecht*)

AT THE HEART of democratic theory lies a profound dilemma that has afflicted democratic practice at least since the eighteenth century. Democracy requires both effective leadership and vigorous citizenship; yet the conditions and consequences of leadership often seem to undermine civic vigor. Although it cries out for both, democracy must customarily make do either with strong leadership or with strong citizens. For the most part, depending on devices of representation in large-scale societies, democracy in the West has settled for strong leaders and correspondingly weak citizens.

Thus, for example, in championing the cause of American democracy, James MacGregor Burns has been an eloquent advocate of strong leadership. In his magisterial study of strong leadership (*Leadership*), he has focused on the special qualities required of great leaders. In his work on the crisis of American democracy (*The Deadlock of Democracy*, for example), he has drawn our attention to representative institutions—parties and legislatures and their centrality to the democratic process. He has distinguished between "transforming" and "transactional" leadership in an attempt to develop a useful political taxonomy of the concept. In short, he has offered us a sustained and brilliant examination of democracy, which, however, is couched almost entirely in the language of representation and leadership. He is hardly alone in this.

Arthur M. Schlesinger, Jr., introduces a concluding essay on democracy and leadership in his *Cycles of American History*[1] by noting that leadership is what makes the world go round. Democracy, he argues, rises or falls on the quality of its leaders rather than its citizens. In practice, political scientists and pundits from Walter Lippmann and Irving Babbitt to Richard Strout and Samuel Huntington have understood every crisis in the American system to be a case of a crisis in leadership, a crisis of too much rather than too little civic participation by a people. Thus when he was "TRB," the celebrated columnist for the *New Republic,* Strout offered this paean to the founders: "Two hundred years ago a little republic on the edge of the wilderness produced so many great leaders . . . it had only three million people—we have two hundred million—we should have sixty Franklins at least." Yet would sixty Franklins really be able to rescue a nation peopled by 200 million abject and incompetent political subjects who preferred private gain to public service?

Woodrow Wilson's stewardship of daring has in fact set the standard for strong presidential leadership in the twentieth century. It asks little of Americans but focuses anxiously on what Americans might ask of their president. "This is not a day of triumph," Wilson intoned in his first inaugural address. "It is a day of dedication. Here muster not the forces of party, but the forces of humanity. Men's hearts wait upon us; men's lives hang in the balance; men's hopes call on us to say what we will do. Who shall live up to the great trust? Who dares fail to try?"

This stewardship of daring has become the hallmark of our presidential politics. In 1940, after several terms of the bracing but caution-inducing leadership of Franklin Delano Roosevelt, Harold Laski was still crying out in his *The American Presidency*[2] for leadership and more leadership. "Power is also opportunity," he wrote, "and to face danger with confidence is the price of its fulfillment." Twenty years further down the road, Richard Neustadt was still arguing in his *Presidential Power*[3] that power used was power enhanced, that presidents became powerful not by conserving and husbanding their power for a rainy day as if it were in a jar in the cupboard but by employing it with energy and zeal, knowing that it reproduced itself as it was expended. John F. Kennedy was received as a glittering knight on a white horse who might restore America to itself. Although he told Americans to ask what they could do for their government rather than what it might do for them, his presidency has been discussed exclusively in terms of what he did (or, as the revisionists argue, did not do) for his country. Arthur Schlesinger, Jr., is only the most prominent among a host of historians who celebrate his leadership and decry the notion that an active citizenry might do without—even prosper in the absence of—such a forceful and charismatic presence.

Nowadays we continue to bemoan not the absence of civic competence but the absence of leaders and the fear to lead that characterized presidents in the 1970s. Ronald Reagan, although more popular than genuinely powerful as a president, is universally celebrated for returning dignity and force to the office of the presidency. The irony is of course that a politician who has made war on the powers of the federal government and represents a philosophy that distrusts political leadership has become the most effective leader the nation has seen since Kennedy or perhaps even Roosevelt (both of whom President Reagan admires and emulates, though it is their legacy he means to dismantle). Finally, then, the critic of the imperial bureaucracy that is today's federal government turns out to be the man who has restored the luster of the imperial presidency.

The argument I wish to make here is that strong leaders have on the whole made Americans weak citizens; that representative institutions have conformed to Michels' iron law of oligarchy and distanced the citizenry from the government to which representation is meant to tie it. As a consequence, when faced by crisis—when leadership has failed them—the American people have turned not to themselves or the civic resourcefulness of their fellow citizens, but to a futile and self-exonerating quest for new and better leaders. Presidents such as Jimmy Carter, who have made prudent noises about the limits of leadership and about the responsibilities a people must assume for their own destiny, have been ridiculed and turned out of office. Democrats who offer to assume full responsibility for the welfare of Americans, who insist they will do it all for their constituents, and Republicans who insist they will get government off the backs of the people by liquidating government altogether are making the same argument—and have been rewarded accordingly by a politically lazy people. The struggle to improve the quality of democracy has thus become a search for leadership, a quest for excellence, a hunt for better delegates, more effective representatives, wiser surrogates, more grandiloquent mouthpieces. Civic responsibility has in turn ceased to mean self-government and come to mean electing governors to govern in the public stead. Democracy means simply to enlist, to choose, to elect, and to reward (or to punish) representatives—and, of course, to keep them accountable via future elections.

It is not simply that Americans have gone astray in substituting leadership for citizenship. It is that the very virtues that make for leadership have attenuated the skills and capacities that constitute citizenship. A too responsible leadership can make for an irresponsible citizenry; an overly vigorous executive can reduce citizens to passive observers whose main public activity is applause. Public officials displaying an omnicompetent mastery of their public responsibilities unburden private men and women of their public responsibilities and leave them with a feeling of civic incompetence or civic indifference. Incompetence is what makes otherwise enfranchised citizens powerless in a democracy.

Thus, legislators and executives who arrogate to themselves the responsibilities of political judgment, the adjudication of public interets, and the bargaining and exchange of public goods in the name of the public interest leave citizens only with the responsibility to articulate and fight for private interests. Modern political science has in fact ascribed to the public at large only functions of private interest interaction, leaving it to representatives to force from these private interests such minimal common ends as a pluralistic democracy may be said to possess.

In the same fashion, knowledgeable leadership—prudent bureaucrats, fiscal experts, foreign policy professionals, defense specialists, and so forth—relieve citizens of the need to understand their public world, domestic or foreign. To call an issue technical is to excuse the general public from responsibility for it, even though almost all public policy rests on issues of a technical nature, even though their technicality is well within the grasp of intelligent lay politicians and bureaucrats and thus, presumably, of intelligent lay citizens. Expressions such as "the experts know better," and "they must know what they are doing" point to a vocabulary of exoneration by which the modern citizen eschews competence to govern his world. Yet again and again we see effective politicians rendering prudent judgments about complex matters on the basis of general value positions. President Reagan is certainly not a careful student of the technical sides of the policy issues he faces, but this makes him no less effective a judge of crucial political issues. For civic competence, whether in leaders or citizens, is finally a matter of good political judgment and the application to particular cases of general value systems, not of technical expertise. Advocates of strong leadership pretend otherwise, but in fact good citizens require no more expertise than presidents and senators, and need not be economists or nuclear scientists to reach intelligent positions on trade policy or arms negotiations. Minimally, it might be said that a citizen need be no more technically knowledgeable than Ronald Reagan to be effective—for surely we need not ask more of citizens than of presidents.

In traditional political theory, we customarily speak of the act of sovereign authorization by which a people empower a sovereign to govern in its name. The trouble with representative institutions is that they often turn the act of sovereign authorization into an act of civic deauthorization. They do not authorize but transfer authority, depriving the authorizing people of its own generic sovereignty and thus of its right to rule. A people that empowers leaders to govern for it can end by disenfranchising itself. As one nineteenth-century French critic of representation put it, the equality with which voters enter the polling booth disappears into the ballot box along with their vote. Electoral activity reduces citizens to alienated spectators—at best, watchdogs with residual and wholly passive functions of securing the accountability of those to whom they have turned over their sovereignty. Under the representative system, leaders turn electors into followers; and the correct posture for followers is deference. Democracy becomes a system that defines how elites are chosen—in Joseph

Schumpeter's classical definition, elective oligarchy, in which the subjugated public from time to time selects the elites who otherwise govern it. Democratic politics thus becomes a matter of what leaders do, something that citizens watch rather than something they do. Civic spectacles like the party nominating conventions are little different than such spectator sports as the Super Bowl—watched but not participated in by a lazy and privatized public. Indeed, were it not to do an injury to the English language, one would be tempted nowadays to refer to Americans collectively as "the Privates" rather than "the Public."

"Lead or follow or get the hell out of the way," reads a popular corporate desk sign. It goes to the heart of what is wrong with contemporary approaches to leadership under democracy. The pair to which the term leader belongs is not leader-follower as the aphorism suggests, but leader-citizen. Leader-follower leaves no room for the mutuality and sense of collective responsibility implicit in the idea of citizenship. The citizen is a self-sufficient and autonomous being, who is nonetheless defined by engagement in a self-governing community. Strong leaders can impair autonomy, and thus mutuality and self-government. An old saw made popular by President Ford has it that a government powerful enough to give us everything we want is a government powerful enough to take away everything we have. We might paraphrase Ford by suggesting that a leader strong enough to do everything we would like done for us is strong enough to deprive us of the capacity to do anything at all for ourselves.

Leaders lead—both for good and ill, lead us aright and lead us astray. As Garry Wills has noticed in his study of the Kennedy Presidency (*The Kennedy Imprisonment*),[4] "we do the most damage under the presidents we love most." A great leader leaves behind gaping holes when he retires or dies. The people are apt to cry "What will we do without him?" and doubt whether they can go on. What is really only a departure is experienced as a loss and an incapacitation. When a courageous officer leading a charge is shot from his horse and the troops retreat in panic and disarray, it is a sign of awe-inspiring and thus awful leadership. The test of democratic leadership is found in its passing. If the death of Roosevelt and the assassination of Kennedy demoralized America more than they energized it, if their passing left Americans wistful and uncertain rather than focused and decisive, then—however effective their leadership in the short run—we must judge their stewardships corrupting to democracy in the long run.

Lao-tse had a prescription for leadership which the Western democracies are unlikely to be able to live up to. "A leader is best," he advised, "when people barely know he exists. Not so good when people obey and acclaim him, worse when they despise him . . . but of a good leader, who talks little, when his work is done, his aim fulfilled, they will say 'we did this ourselves?'" Our leaders cultivate and flaunt their charisma (which is how they get elected in the media age) and are either much acclaimed or much despised for it. Leaders who talk little and scarcely exist for their constituents are unlikely candidates for office in a modern representative democracy where power is won by packaging and imagery.

Yet the aim of genuinely democratic leadership must not be merely to create the illusion of a people noisily taking the credit for what the leadership has in reality quietly achieved on its own, but to create genuine civic engagement and civic competence. Strong democratic leadership is leadership that leaves a citizenry more capable when the leader departs than before he arrives. It is leadership that can boast: "Now that he is gone, we can do this ourselves."

The question is whether such leadership is possible. Conventional leadership operates successfully by creating loyal followers rather than self-sufficient citizens. Are there leaders who arrive on foot rather than astride magnificent white horses? who modestly catalyze a people to self-government rather than governing on their behalf? who are scarcely noticed, let alone missed when they go? Are there delegates who facilitate popular sovereignty instead of stealing the sovereign's mantle? H. G. Wells recommended to his auditors leaders who could "guide us as far as they can and then vanish." Without invisible guides, without vanishing leaders, democracy seems fated to degenerate into the kind of cynical oligarchy elite theorists such as Pareto, Mosca, and Schumpeter have insisted it will always be.

There are, I will argue, three kinds of leadership that are compatible with strong democracy: they are what I will call founding leadership, moral leadership, and facilitating (or enabling) leadership. While leadership in its current manifestation under representative democracy bears little resemblance to any of the three, suggestive models for each can be found elsewhere in modern society.

Both founding and moral leadership can be regarded as apolitical or extrapolitical forms of leadership. Both kinds of leader guide by inspiration, moving others to political engagement without themselves being politically engaged. The founding leader may institute a constitution or a movement or a political cause, but if he conforms to classical republican strictures about the limited role of the Great Legislator, he will permit his duties to extend only to the creation of a framework or an ideology or a point of view within which others will engage actively in politics. The founder is an empowerer.

A telling example is the democratic constitution, which is almost always the product of a process less democratic than that which it institutes. Whether forged by progressive elites or by the vanguard of the populace in rebellion against tyranny, it is always the creation of a few who believe in the rule of the many. As mentors of revolutionary mobs, founding leaders often fail to vanish. Regarding themselves as indispensable to the proper working of the constitutions they have devised, they stay on and on, until their personal rule has displaced the democratic designs called for by their political blueprints. Wise democratic founders, on the other hand, recognize that until they disappear their constitutions will fail to realize the democratic aspirations with which they are conceived. Our own prudent founding fathers lingered—if not too long, more than long enough. With the likes of Washington, Jefferson, and Madison hovering over their handiwork, it was difficult for the young country to free itself from its creators and give to the citizenry an opportunity to take responsibility for self-government (as happened in time with the rise of political parties from the presidency of Van Buren onwards).

The leaders of the social movements that grew up at the end of the century—Populists and Progressives—had a firmer sense of the dangers they themselves presented to their comrades. Eugene Debs was painfully aware of the dangers that a too-competent leadership could pose to a popular movement. To his adoring would-be followers he issued this warning:

> Too long have the workers of the world waited for some Moses to lead them out of bondage. He has not come; he will not come. I would not lead you out if I could; for if you could be led out, you could be led back again.

Debs is a model of what can be called extrapolitical moral leadership. Like founding leadership, moral leadership sets an example and creates a moral zeal for engagement and self-responsibility. Because it is aimed at democracy, it refuses to act in place of those it would inspire. The step from moral catalyst to moral surrogate is a tiny one, and the moral leader must exert extraordinary self-control. Martin Luther King, on the whole, did. Did the Reverend Jesse Jackson? He took the tiny step (and has been imitated by preachers from the other side of the political spectrum in recent years). As a candidate, he lost much of his moral luster and at the same time aroused expectations in his followers that, when Jackson was unable to win, could only engender hopelessness and cynicism. In moving from the moral to the political domain, Pat Robertson is likely to lose his moral influence without acquiring a corresponding political clout. Political leaders require a moral rhetoric rooted in a moral vision—but these visions are best borrowed from nonpolitical moral leaders.

Unhappily, we prefer to turn our preachers into politicians. We presumably elect astronauts, athletes, movie stars, and other celebrities to office because they possess what we do not: having achieved money, power, status—the appearance of mastery over their worlds—they possess what we covet. Their success may serve only to underscore our own inadequacies; they persuade us that, superior to us as football players or film actors, they must also be superior to us as civic players and political actors. Even when they radiate high principle, they cause us to live in their shadow, small, mean, and impotent.

Jesse Jackson is in many ways able to speak more forcefully to the American people from outside the political arena than from within it. Robert Kennedy probably induced more political action out of office than in. The West German Green Party confronted similar dilemmas in leadership. Born as a popular, extrapolitical movement rooted in extensive grass-roots participation, the Greens subsequently won unexpected political victories that propelled them into potential leadership positions as coalition partners of the Social Democrats—in state government in Hesse and elsewhere. Having achieved a preeminence that permits them to actually affect policy outcomes and assume political offices at the state, and potentially national, leadership levels, they are faced with the loss of that moral integrity that was the key to their success as an extrapolitical social movement. Their victory entitles them to become parliamentarians, representatives, and thus surrogates from the movements they wished originally to inspire to direct action. In succeeding, they supersede and pacify their followers. Thus, the peculiar irony of effective leadership—to succeed is to fail.

The ancient Greeks had some understanding of this contradiction, and developed tactics to combat not tyrannical but merely successful leadership. Magistries rotated among citizens chosen at random; generals were selected from among common citizens (Sophocles was a general); leaders who crossed the threshold leading from mere efficacy to greatness could find themselves exiled ("ostracized" by special ballot) from office and city—all for having led, not badly, but too well. Plato argued that only the wise could rule, and that until philosophers became kings, there would be no justice. His democratic critics in Athens worried that the wise might rule too well, that their wisdom might reduce the people to stupidity. Without competent citizens, they reasoned, there could be neither democracy nor lasting justice. It was no succor to them that the Guardian class might make adept and modest rulers: the more adept, the more likely they were to be acknowledged and acquiesced to.

We affect to be much more democratic than ever the Athenians could claim to be—with only one-fifth of their populace included in the citizen body—yet we have abandoned their caution about great men and seek out celebrities to govern us, measuring their leadership by the extent to which we are eclipsed by their glory. In times of crisis, we deify leaders whom we ought to have good reason to mistrust. For it is during crises that leadership has a way of spinning out of control. The British were alert enough to dismiss their great wartime Prime Minister the moment the war, thanks to that great leader, was over. We Americans have displayed a like prudence in preferring subtler, more self-effacing heroes like Eisenhower and Reagan to firebrands like General MacArthur and Jesse Jackson, although we also permit ourselves to be seduced by shining knights in the Kennedy mold. For a long time, liberal critics of majority tyranny have tried to persuade us that an overzealous people is the foremost peril of modern democracy; but the overzealous leader who becomes a citizen-surrogate and a citizen-usurper is no less a threat. It was once said that in a monarchy there was only a single citizen—the king himself. In our representative democracy, it sometimes seems that the only true citizens are politicians.

Our discussion of founding and moral leadership does little to dispel the dilemma, however. The kinds of moral and founding leaders a genuine democracy can permit must, I have argued, remain outside of the political process. They can inspire political leaders but they must not become political leaders. They may catalyze democracy but, as powerful figures, they make dubious democrats. The question then remains, is there a form of political leadership compatible with strong citizen-based democracy? The third model of leadership noted above—facilitating or enabling leadership—embodies a kind of leadership that is not only fully compatible with democracy but formulated to strengthen it by reenforcing citizenship.

Facilitating leadership empowers people. It functions modestly to enhance the quality and intensity of civic participation, and simultaneously guards the rights of all citizens to equal participation. Inverting the customary relationship between vigorous leaders and passive, watchdog followers, the facilitating leader subordinates himself to his constituents, making himself the vigilant watchdog of his community's civic activity and the guarantor of equitable participation. He holds the people accountable to standards of civic engagement and mutual respect. He holds but does not exercise power. Rather, he facilitates its exercise by those to whom it rightfully belongs. He assures equity among participants without throwing himself into the political balance. He resembles more the teacher than the administrator, the judge than the legislator, the therapist than the surgeon, the moderator than the chairman. Indeed, we may define facilitating leadership by the qualities attached to role models of this sort.

Take the teacher—a person who is poised to have a profound impact on students. As mentor, propagandist, indoctrinator, socializer, shaper of character, he can mold disciples and assure himself abject followers—clones who will learn not how to think but how to think as he thinks. Yet the measure of the great teacher is not discipleship, but critical self-sufficiency and the ability to think independently. The teacher who has discharged the liberal pedagogic function properly is the teacher who has become superfluous. The student who has been well taught is the student who no longer needs the teacher, who can argue with him as an equal and who demonstrates his debt to the teacher's skills by displaying his independence from the teacher's beliefs. The successful tutor boasts "I am superfluous! I will not be missed." The facilitating political leader must be capable of just this boast.

The judge in a jury trial plays an analogous role. She must instruct the jury in the substance of the law, preserve decorum in the courtroom, and guarantee that evidence is fairly presented, that witnesses are properly interrogated, and that the cases for plaintiff and defendant are judiciously argued. Yet the judge who has done her job well will secure conditions under which a jury can reach an independent verdict of which they can say "it is truly our decision; it is the people's verdict" and not some manipulated reflection of the judge's covert will. Like the teacher, the judge must be a facilitator who enables a jury to undertake its vital duties fairly and effectively. A thoughtful and just jury verdict attests to a competent and democratic judge, who glories not in her own but the jury's wisdom.

The vitality of the jury system suggests how hypocritical the attacks on democracy are that question the people's capacity to acquire sufficient technical knowledge and expertise to deliberate, adjudicate, legislate, or govern. The judge takes responsibility for instruction in the technicalities of the law, but leaves it to the jury to apply the law under factual circumstances of which it is the sole interpreter. The role of citizens in a referendum on trade quotas or tariffs is similar. Their task is not, for example, to develop statistics on trade or explanations of the mechanisms by which embargoes operate; it is to pass on the overall desirability—in light of what facilitating leaders tell them about quotas, embargoes, and other pertinent conditions—of trade restrictions *tout court*. They may have to pass judgment on broad theories of economics (the claim that free trade enhances domestic economic productivity, or that quotas in one nation are necessary when other nations pursue national industrial policies, etc.), but they need not be economists or international lawyers; at least not any more than jurists who pass judgment on theories of insanity or criminal intent have to be psychologists or professors of criminal law in order to reach fair verdicts on homicide cases. Juries need prudent and caring judges, and citizens need fair and caring leaders, but such leadership ought to enhance their own activity rather than replace it.

This points to one of the central misconceptions of a great deal of modern democratic theory: it too often confuses expertise and political judgment. The wise citizen, like the wise president, need not master the full technical details of every issue up for decision. It is his duty to offer general principles for the application of policy. President Reagan is no master of data, but he understands that he can give policy its direction without entering into the world of detail in which his advisors are necessarily mired. He may thus propound the general goal of a world free of nuclear weapons and ask for an insurance policy against cheating (SDI). Questions of a technical nature are pertinent: Is SDI a realistic insurance policy? can it work? how much out-of-laboratory testing will it require, and when? does an insurance policy in a world with no weapons become an invitation to a nuclear first strike in a world with some weapons? Yet these are questions his experts can answer for him, without denying him his overall principle or preventing him from negotiating one-on-one with the Russian leader (as he did at the Iceland nonsummit). "Yes," Richard Perle, the President's arms control advisor, can tell his leader, "SDI with some nuclear weapons still in place could be thought of as an incentive to a first strike; so if you want a nuclear weapon-free world *and* SDI you will have to get the first one first, and then develop the other." Or Senator Sam Nunn of the Armed Services Committee may even suggest that the paradoxes of SDI are such that it is incompatible with an acceptable disarmament program. But such advisors and technical experts cannot say: "Therefore you can no longer be for nuclear disarmament."

What is true for presidents is true for citizens called upon to make policy decisions. In the case, for example, of safety standards for genetic engineering, they need not be able to arbitrate between the technical claims of competing molecular biologists about how risky gene-altering laboratory experiments are. All they need do is reach a judgment about how much risk they are willing to tolerate, given the uncertainty of the experts, the potential dangers of experimentation, and the possible medical benefits that will accrue to such research. Their decision will take this form: "Given the lack of consensus among the 'experts,' and the fact that all agree there is at least some risk of grave consequences that could have a runaway effect, and given that the benefits are not altogether certain, we believe that no genetically altered agents ought to be licensed by the government for at least two years." As with so many other decisions, this one is a judgment on the acceptability of risks, the allocation of resources, and the desirability of broad principles. Such decisions are the mainstay of politics, and are debated by legislators, statesmen, and leaders regularly. There is no reason why citizens, when well informed and well led, cannot debate and reach decisions of this kind as effectively as their leaders. Indeed, this ought to be the principal aim of facilitating leadership.

A second model for the facilitating leader is the therapist or, more accurately, the group therapist. On first glance, this may seem to be a rather farfetched example. Yet the therapist is above all an enabler whose success is measured by the degree to which his patients become self-sufficient life actors, able to function without him. The therapist restores men and women to good health, and his success is marked by the termination of his involvement. The patient does the hard labor, while the therapist only provides the conditions under which that labor is possible. He is an aid to a process in which the patient's own activity is crucial. In a successful therapy, the therapist is passive ("nondirective") and the patient is active. Many therapists will argue that the patient's will to get well is the single indispensable factor in a therapy and that the therapist does little more than witness and reenforce that will. Not "physician heal thyself," but "patient heal thyself" is an apt motto for the patient and, it seems, the citizen.

Our political doctors have created a society of dependent hypochondriacs who think themselves capable of being healthy only when they are under the doctor's care. Accepting uncritically Plato's analogy of rulership and technical skill, they regard the ruler's competence as a tribute to their own incompetence. No wonder they remain permanently incapacitated, while their political doctors come to bear an odd resemblance to witches. The witch doctor, of course, aspires not to cure but to subjugate the bewitched. If there are analogs in politics to abusive therapists who profit from their patients' incapacities and toil to enhance rather than diminish their dependency, there are also analogs in politics to corrupt judges who exploit their special knowledge of the law and their authority in the courtroom to wring premeditated verdicts from juries that are autonomous only in name. There are also political versions of the teachers who prefer disciples to critics among their students, and who use their brilliance to intimidate rather than emancipate their best pupils.

Each of these models of enabling leadership is then subject to abuse; each opens itself to the corruption of an authority that is necessary to the tasks of emancipation. One of the most difficult challenges faced by democratic theory as it grapples with leadership is to forge an emancipatory and egalitarian concept of authority. Traditional social science definitions of authority link it to consent but emphasize the authoritative characteristics that distinguish the leader from his followers. Democrats seek an understanding that measures authority by its potential for catalyzing not merely the consent but the ongoing activity and involvement of those in whom it originates. For authority ultimately suggests an act of *authorization* in which the real authors are those over whom the authorized officials hold sway. Liberals and elitists have focused on authority itself, neglecting the constituent authors to whom the term points. This stresses aspects of authority that are authoritarian (focused on power) rather than authoritative (focused on consent or authorization).

Yet despite the authoritarian tendencies of our discussions of authority, most observers are liberals in their assessment of the ideal or proper role of teacher, judge, and therapist in the moral development of democratic citizens: to nourish self-sufficiency, self-responsibility, and independence; to encourage active engagement in the world; to foster the growth of autonomous will. Subjects of a nation and members of a people (or *gens*) are born; but citizens are created artificially afterwards. This is perhaps why democracy is so rare and fragile a form of government, and why it demands a special kind of authority and a special breed of leaders with which representative government does not sufficiently acquaint us.

To this point in the argument, our three examples are drawn from non-political analogies that instruct only by inference. But there is one example of enabling leadership that does not depend on analogy, since it is inherently political: the example of the town moderator. The moderator is splendidly named, for his function is precisely to provide the moderating conditions under which citizens can interact, debate, listen to one another, deliberate, and eventually arrive at common decisions that do not radically alienate individuals or minorities of the small, neighborly townships where all must live together. The moderator is not a chairperson or a presiding officer who directs a meeting in accordance with his own agenda or acts as *primus inter pares* to weld together a committee into a functioning unit. On the contrary, he remains an outsider to the actual proceedings, listening, watching, and intervening only to assure equity, to guarantee fairness, and to secure the orderliness and moderation of the meeting. A well-moderated meeting will not notice its moderator; it will know only that its business is conducted and that participants are satisfied whether they emerge as winners or losers. In fact, the consensus that emerges should preempt terms like winner and loser altogether in favor of the common belief that good sense and the common good have prevailed. Nor will consensual decisions conceal some covert and manipulating will possessed by the moderator. Nonetheless, that there *are* such decisions in the face of real debate over conflicting interests will be his victory.

The moderator's skills are as much skills of listening as talking. Like the wise teacher, the moderator will impart to his constituents something of his own artfulness. For listening is equity's best ally in participatory meetings where garrulousness is always unequally distributed. Leaders typically speak well, and skillfulness in speech divides communities into the eloquent and the mute. Citizens typically listen well, and the capacity to hear unites communities through an art all can master. To be a citizen is not merely to express but to receive opinions, not merely to articulate one's own interests but to empathize with the interests of others. In representative societies, talk is vertically structured: leaders talk *to* citizens, though citizens rarely talk to or among one another. There is little lateral interaction.

Too often in representative democracies, speech means only talk *by* leaders. The institutions that are most valued are those that most benefit talkers: thus, the parliament or talk-assembly, which places a premium on the eloquent articulation of interests, or the representative political party that becomes a mouthpiece for otherwise inarticulate constituencies. However, it is far easier for representatives to speak on our behalf than to listen on our behalf. There are many human activities where representation is inappropriate: the World Series, a church communion, a sing-along, for example. Or politics.

The moderator does not pretend to represent anyone; he neither speaks nor acts for the town. He is rather a scrupulous listener. His task is to ensure that participants in the political process listen as well as they talk, or that the usual talkers are made to listen, and the usual listeners get a chance to talk. "I will listen" means to the moderator not to scan an adversary's position for weaknesses or potential trade-offs, nor even to permit every speaker his or her moment on the floor. Rather it means to encourage each to put himself in place of the other, to empathize with the other, to discover in the babble of voices a consensus that is audible only to the scrupulous auditor. The effective moderator wishes to transform all the He's and She's who come into the meeting with their own interests into a single We with a common interest. He will insist that every citizen be heard, but by that he will mean not only that all can speak but that all must listen.

Good listeners are not necessarily charismatic leaders, but they turn out to be excellent neighbors and trustworthy citizens. Where talking focuses on inequalities in the capacity to speak with clarity or eloquence, listening is a mutualistic art that by its very practice enhances equality—the equality of silence. The empathetic listener becomes more like his interlocutor as a consequence of sensitive listening. Indeed, one measure of healthy political talk is the amount of silence it permits, for silence is the precious medium in which reflection is nurtured and empathy can grow. In listening there is no cacophony, in silence no competition. The adept moderator will cultivate silence with the same assiduousness the adept leader cultivates eloquence. He will not be able to turn political discourse into a Quaker meeting, but the lesson of Quaker meetings for the attainment of concord and public good will not be lost on him.

If we are to have facilitating leaders on the model of the sensitive and modest moderator, we obviously require participatory institutions organized around his talents. Great Communicators do well in our great political talkshops and flourish in the kind of electoral politics where television is a dominant instrument. Citizens, on the other hand, do well where their energies are enlisted on behalf of direct political responsibility and where they can deliberate, interact, and legislate together. In Switzerland, where citizens are more valued than leaders, the presidency rotates among a seven-person Executive Council (whose members are often not known to the average citizen), and legislative duties are parceled out equally between the Federal Legislature and the people—voting, up to six or seven times year, in national and local referenda. Citizenship in the Alps still begins and ends with village and town residence and is expressed in yearlong political and civic activity at the local and cantonal levels. The Swiss worry about their democracy too, but their anxieties are aroused by the defects of their citizens rather than the shortcomings of their leaders.

If these remarks on leadership carry conviction, then Americans concerned with democracy and with the nature of democratic leadership need to shift their focus away from heads of state and towards the body politic that is the citizenry. Citizens are neither leaders nor followers: they embody a form of civic activity that precludes such radical forms of polarization. Our current weak form of democracy, relying on representation and preoccupied with leadership, permits us to choose who governs us but does not allow us to be self-governing. It makes our rulers accountable to the people but does not make the people citizens. Instead, it turns them into passive spectators, sometime watchdogs and grasping clients of leaders who are cynical bureaucrats and expert manipulators of popular prejudice. As the chasm between leaders and followers grows wider, democracy grows frailer.

The remedy is not better leaders but better citizens; and we can become better citizens only if we reinvigorate the tradition of strong democracy that focuses on citizenship and civic competence. This calls for participation as well as accountability; for civic duty as well as individual rights. It demands that we add the constructive use of public judgment and power to the already well-established protection of private rights and interests. I have called this tradition *strong democracy,* to distinguish it from its "thin" representative cousin.

To reorient democracy away from leadership and representation and towards stronger forms of citizenship and participation, we need to foster institutional and practical experimentation with participatory institutions — many of which are already in place at the state and local level. These institutions, which I have elaborated in some detail in my *Strong Democracy: Participatory Politics for a New Age,*[5] would include the following:

- A nationwide system of neighborhood assemblies of approximately 5,000 citizens that would meet weekly and permit discussion and eventually voting on issues of local, regional, and national significance. These forums could be linked together by regional television networks and provide the setting for less parochial inter-regional debates as well. Their aim would be to enhance lateral communication among citizens and lessen the importance of national leaders.
- A communications cooperative that would oversee and regulate civic uses of new telecommunication technologies and distribute free civic information through a civic videotex service; the aim here would be more informed, self-sufficient, and thus competent citizens, less in need of expert leadership.
- Selective use of a lottery system of election, like the system used for jury

service, but modeled on the lottery representation device used to fill a majority of political offices in ancient Athens. This system would be employed to fill some local and regional political offices — on school boards, local finance committees, or zoning boards, for example — and to select a limited number of delegates at large to state assemblies. By permitting citizens to actually serve in public office, and making every citizen a potential public servant, the chasm between leaders and followers would be significantly narrowed.

- Local "common-work" volunteer programs. These could include sweat equity projects, housing renovation, urban neighborhood farms, crime-watch programs, service to sick and elderly shut-ins, and rural reconstruction; by involving citizens in the actual work of democracy, the distinction between "us" and "them" would be reduced, and the responsibility of neighbors for the welfare of their own neighborhoods would be enhanced.
- A program of universal citizen service, including but not limited to a military option for all women and men between 18 and 26 for a two-year period. Citizen service restores the linkage between rights and duties and gives the young an introduction to citizenship rooted in participation and responsibility rather than mere voting.

These and other similar measures (spelled out in *Strong Democracy*) together create a powerful program of civic reorientation. They would not reconstitute America as a direct democracy—which is government by all of the people all of the time in all public affairs; but they would constitute the country as a strong democracy, which is government by all of the people some of the time in some public affairs. And they would reenforce an understanding of citizenship that permits citizens to give as well as to take, to serve as well as to be served, to cooperate as well as to contest, to act as well as to vote. Above all, it would demonstrate that democracy thrives neither when it possesses powerful leaders, nor when it breeds loyal followers, but only when it creates competent citizens who—in governing themselves—follow their own lead. We will know we have succeeded in our democratic aspirations not when we have found great leaders, but when we can boast that we no longer need great leaders.

NOTES

1. Boston: Houghton Mifflin Company, 1987.
2. Reprint; New Brunswick, N.J.: Transaction Books, 1980, with a new introduction by James MacGregor Burns.
3. New York: John Wiley, 1961.
4. Boston: Little, Brown and Company, 1982.
5. Berkeley: University of California Press, 1984.

CHAPTER 8

Command Performance:
Where Have All
the Leaders Gone?

OUR LEADERS are mostly dead, and leadership is in bad repute. Some of them have been killed off; others have been tainted with a megalomania perverse even by the standards of politicians. Some have been driven from office; still others have withdrawn to pursue destinies more usually associated with adolescent dropping out—self-realization, poetry, religion, the vague, pastoral idyll of self-sufficiency. "Leaders," wrote H. G. Wells, "should guide us as far as they can and then vanish." Ours have simply vanished. Nixon is gone from the Oval Office, but few would suggest that leadership was ever part of his political baggage. President Ford—exhibitionistically honest—seems more comfortable with the rhetoric than the substance of leadership. If the White House was ever the "center of moral leadership in the nation," as John Kennedy suggested in 1961, Vietnam, Watergate, and the Great Pardon guarantee that it is no more.

Yet the need for both political and moral leadership is deeply felt, and its absence is a subject of incessant media attention. A year-end editorial titled "The Fear to Lead" in the *New York Times* [in December 1974] warned: "The cloud of nonleadership hangs over the nation's key activities like polluted air." TRB, *The New Republic's* senior columnist, devoted his own year-end column to the "leadership shortage": "Two hundred years ago a little republic on the edge of the wilderness suddenly produced Jefferson, Hamilton, Madison, Adams and others like that. It had only three million people. Today we have 200 million. Where are our great men? We should have 60 Franklins at least." *Time* magazine actually went looking for the sixty missing Franklins last summer in a cover story on leadership. The search was in vain; *Time* was eventually forced to spread its publicity largesse over several hundred worthy, if mostly, faceless, Americans—mostly lawyers, administrators, and the predictable complement of pop athletes, aspiring politicos, and media gurus—who, far from being faceless, have known faces rather than known views, powerful images rather than powerful beliefs, and strong recognition potential rather than strong leadership potential.

At the university level, faculties have found themselves squeezed between student demands for relevance and administration strictures on efficiency, and have surrendered what little authority they once enjoyed. One group still follows the example of Charles Reich (*The Greening of America*), and goes looking for standards among the students it ought to be guiding; another withdraws into the protective obscurity of specialization, immunizing itself to relevance and efficiency alike; still another tacitly acknowledges the academic corporation and the student constituency it "services" by embracing unionization, hoping that the closed shop will somehow make up for the loss of the ivory tower.

Worse still, much therapy today celebrates group values and makes instant gratification of emotional needs its chief aim—the pleasure principle now as ever treating men, women, and children as perfectly equal animals. Through the therapeutic lens, leadership is most often seen as a pathological function of repressive behavior patterns and bad head trips. Individuality is functional misanthropy masquerading as eccentricity, while reasoned explanations and appeals to moral standards are avoidance techniques by which visceral realities are evaded. In the depressurized world of adaptive interpersonal relations, there is no room for authority and leadership, or for the standards they imply. The efficient therapist is an emotional facilitator, rarely a leader.

Radical movements have suffered the same misperceptions. Associating leadership with the institutions they oppose, they have spent more time combating discipline and internal structure than they have combating injustice, as if the values they cherished and the aims they fought for did not require moral leadership for their realization. The student movement of the Sixties often seemed more wary of Leninism than of capitalism, and often mimicked laissez-faire liberalism in its hostility to organization and planning.

Parents have also grown loath to regard themselves as leaders, not only because they fear that their own lives are exemplary mainly of confusion, but because families, too, have developed an egalitarian rhetoric to rationalize their disintegration. Brotherhood and sisterhood are the only familial relations that retain a public legitimacy. This is perhaps less a question of children insisting they are adults than of adults insisting they are children. That fraternity implies paternity is a genealogical subtlety best forgotten in a period when it is fashionable to deny the distinction between apprentice and master, student and teacher, novice and elder, the growing and the grown.

Even the movie protagonists are immobilized by the creeping *Gleichschaltung* that requires they be no better or stronger or more virtuous than their "enemies." They appear unheroic, if endearing; ineffective, if amusing; jaded, if well intentioned; cynical, if faintly honorable—scarcely able to cope, much less to lead.

If this rhetorical distrust of leadership corresponded to a genuine emergence of equality in our society, some might welcome it as a sign of the coming of age of American democracy. But the absence of leaders is more often a symptom of decay in representative democracy than a harbinger of its maturity. Leadership is precisely what distinguishes a representative democracy and permits a collection of self-interested private persons and special interests to act as a civic entity on behalf of public purposes. Leadership is not a surrogate for participation in a representative democracy, it is its necessary condition. Without facilitating leaders, a citizenry is unlikely to remain active; without active citizens, responsive leaders are unlikely to emerge, and leaders who do emerge are unlikely to remain responsive.

It is, in fact, the distinctive feature of democratic leadership that it defies the traditional Carlylean choice: it is produced neither by great men (although it can create great men), nor by great challenges (although it can be catalyzed by great challenges). It arises, rather, out of great purposes—a delicate consensus tenable only when the polity is able to define common goals. To put it another way, democratic leaders are *authoritative* but not *authoritarian* figures: they lead a people by following it. Potentially, they may be as corruptible as authoritarians, but they are accountable. Accountability—the specter of electoral defeat or even recall—compels them to be followers, facilitators, enablers.

Walter Lippman wrote many years ago, "Leaders are the custodians of a nation's ideals, of the beliefs it cherishes, of its permanent hopes, of the faith which makes a nation out of a mere aggregation of individuals." Tyrants are *authoritarian* leaders, and are in part responsible for the bad odor of leadership among democrats. Custodians only of their own interests, they inculcate consensus by propaganda, maintain it by fear, and defy it when it stands in their way by a seductive terror called charisma. They lead without following, "represent" without embodying, and tell without asking. In democratic systems, *authoritative* leaders also pursue unity. But they are incapable of defying a consensus reached by citizens, and they inculcate it only by discovering it, maintain it only by respecting it. Authoritarian rule rests finally on coercion, however well disguised; authoritative rule rests on consensus, however tacitly expressed.

For the past thirty years we have witnessed a gradual but sure erosion of America's common purpose and national consensus. There are today no leaders, only heads of factions; there is no leadership of ideas, only a competition of ideologies; there is no consensus, only an unstable balance of opposing interests. Adversaries are soon construed as enemies, assassins have their work cut out for them, and finally the prosecution-persecution of enemies is elevated into Presidential business. Some may say that there was never that commonality of ideals, hopes, and faith that Lippman wrote of, only a consensus among oppressors. But today we seem to lack even the standards by which we once judged our hypocrisies. The leaders no longer seem certain of what they ought to expect of themselves, and we in turn no longer expect anything at all of our leaders. It is an occasion of deep national gratitude when a President is willing to be honest. Chappaquiddick did not, despite its implications, disqualify Edward Kennedy from elective office, and the Argentine Firecracker sex scandal did not prevent Wilbur Mills from being reelected to Congress.

Our dilemma, then, is not an absence of leaders but a paucity of values that might sustain leaders; not a failure of leadership but a failure of follower-ship, a failure of popular will from which leadership might draw strength. Accountability entails responsibility. The failure of democratic leaders is also the failure of the people to whom they are accountable. In the land of the blind, the one-eyed is not king, he is tyrant. In the absence of strong, citizen-supported democratic leadership, the deepening of our national crises can only bring anarchy or tyranny—most probably the first followed by the second, as in the Weimar Republic. In the long run, the polity abhors anarchy as nature abhors a vacuum: it will generally prefer despotism to chaos. The tyrants to come will be efficient Nixons, intelligent George Wallaces, capable Klansmen, and virulent Kennedys; they will know well how to use mass resentment to exterminate mass participation, how to transform accumulated bitterness into a program of political persecution, how to use frustration and despair to wall in the open society and entomb its institutions.

A variety of forces currently militates against the delicate reconstruction of the national consensus needed to restore authoritative leadership. Three of these are paramount. First is the force of interdependence, which gives an appearance of anonymous determinism to the world, a view that is absolutely devastating to human action. Second is the power of the media to confuse standards and confound image with leadership. Third is the power of violence—assassination—to distort the landscape of leadership in irremediable ways.

Perception of the world as anonymous and deterministic has had a paralyzing effect on citizens and leaders alike; both the powerful and the penniless seem to be pawns of complex forces beyond control or understanding. Large cities are deemed ungovernable—ungovernable by responsible, elected mayors, by political machines, by anyone at all. The economy is beyond predictability—even for the experts. President Ford is able to assemble "the nation's best economic minds," but they cannot agree on what is wrong or on what might make it right. Even war and peace seem to be beyond the control of the leaders, depending on internal developments in foreign nations that are no longer responsive to American pressure or opinion.

At the core of these difficulties is ecology—ecology understood as the seamless interdependence of geography, economics, geology, politics, and culture in a world made one (but hardly whole) by trade, transportation, communications, and energy. Ecology thus defined turns out to mean imperviousness, inaccessibility, unaccountability, irresponsibility. Ecological crisis by its very nature is unmanageable. Change or reform in one component of the system changes every other component of the system, and thus changes the system itself in ways that alter the initial reform, rendering it irrelevant or ineffectual. Each attempt to restore a "natural balance" further unbalances the system as a whole. The interdependence that defines ecosystems thus often seems to put them beyond planning or predictability, and leaves potential reformers—potential leaders—with a sense of impotence. Responsibility has to be fixed before changes can be made. But who (for example) is responsible for our depression-cum-inflation that defies all traditional economics? Congress? The President? National companies? Multinational corporations in control of oil? The sheiks to whom they are beholden? The Palestine Liberation Organization? Israel? Europe (which created Israel)? All of them? Or none of them?

The agonies of this regressive logic seem only to prove that the decisions or nondecisions that affect and sometimes endanger our lives are more and more often the outcome—unplanned, undesired, unexpected—of complex processes involving multiple individuals, corporations, nations, and other systems of power. We may lift off the mask of such national enemies as crime or unemployment or inflation or urban decay, but there is no face to be seen. The systemic adversaries that confront us are without human identity, their invidiousness the product neither of human error nor human malevolence. Governors and governed alike mutter vaguely about the System, the City, the Syndicate, attributing our problems to invisible conspiracies.

Films such as *Chinatown, The Conversation, The Parallax View,* and *Serpico* pay rueful tribute to the growing potency of facelessness—of systems no longer vulnerable to virtue, boldness, or heroism. Richly textured, all-too-human villains, once vanquished in personal combat by a Cagney or a Bogart, are replaced by forces that can hardly be identified, much less overcome. In each of these films the protagonist loses—loses, moreover, to a system rather than to a man, to inexorability rather than to villainy, to shadowed hierarchies of faceless power not even the audience (nor the filmmakers themselves) can comprehend. "There are no more heroes," says a hardboiled cop in the television movie *Birds of Prey*. "The system is the hero now."

Watergate exhibited certain of these same features. Nixon is gone, but the Watergate system lingers, reemerging melodramatically from time to time in banner headlines, as if it had a life of its own. The new President was drawn in by the pardon, the trials stumbled forward with the clumsy momentum of old recriminations and new betrayals, and finally the CIA, the IRS, the entire Executive branch appear to be implicated. Placing the blame, exacting retribution, determining ultimate responsibility seem impossible: there are too many villains—Nixon, the President's men, the White House ethos, the will to win at all costs, the technology of snooping, the Imperial Presidency; complicity extends too far. Citizens, unable to hold leaders responsible, sigh wearily or groan cynically, and turn away. Without clear lines of accountability and an explicit understanding of political cause and effect, neither active citizenship nor democratic leadership is possible.

At the same time, television and instant communications confound standards and trivialize leadership by their preoccupation with fashion and merchandisable novelty. Warhol suggested the time would come when everyone on earth would be famous for fifteen minutes. The media are trying their best. False prophets make the lives of real prophets difficult; fashion leaders do the same for real leaders. For when authority is confounded with media visibility and leadership with public recognition, a Mark Spitz is no longer to be distinguished from a Benjamin Franklin. Celebrity is a key to influence, if not to power; but, like the praying mantis, it consumes the consumer. It stands mischievously by the gates to the citadel of power and destroys those select few it permits to enter. Like children mugging before the new family movie camera, aspirants to public influence engage in competitive antics before the public eye. The winners, at least in the short run, are those who have clowned away their souls and thus can no longer use the power they have won. Who's afraid of Virginia Woolf once she makes the cover of *Time*? Will success spoil Rock Hunter, if he appears once too often on the Johnny Carson show? When the celebrity name becomes a society totem, what is left of the person behind the name?

Norman Mailer's serious interest in politics could be realized only at the expense of seriousness. His mayoralty campaign in New York succeeded, through no fault of his, only as a joke. It thus failed as politics. His campaign to expose governmental conspiracies against the open society, launched at his fiftieth birthday party at the Four Seasons in New York, also failed, even as a joke. The event was universally covered, and was wholly without political significance. To sell his ideas Mailer had to sell himself, and, in selling himself, he sold out his ideas. Thus does celebrity protect power. Novelty and topicality go hand in hand; fashion and trivia serve one another. Like firecrackers, they are noisy, short-lived, and powerless to harm, affect, or change the world. Wisdom goes unheard in a firecracker society where prominence is measured in decibels and significance determined by the roar of the crowd.

Even where leaders do eventually achieve a media-supported reputation, the confusion over standards gives their detractors and their assassins equal time. When cherry bombs are as loud as cannons how are we to identify the real "big guns"? When the report of a single assassin's pistol rings with more decisive finality than the clamor of an electorate's voiced will, can we any longer speak of democratic leadership at all?

The leveling powers of assassination have come to represent a third force operating against the revival of leadership in America. Whenever in recent years leaders have emerged who speak across the boundaries of party, class, and interest, assassins have eliminated them with a private perversity which nonetheless seems to be accommodating a tacit public will. Bridge-builders are not popular when each side is bent on annihilating the other. Where defeated tyrants once executed the messenger who brought them bad tidings, defeated democrats seem more often to execute those who bring good tidings. John Kennedy, Malcolm X, Martin Luther King, Medgar Evers, Robert Kennedy—these, not David Halberstam's liberal functionaries, were the best and the brightest of this generation, men unafraid to lead in defiance of public opinion when they were certain they followed a deeper public interest. Each man had spoken in the name of goals which united races and economic classes, rather than in the name of issues that polarized them. Each had developed the power of persuasion that belongs to authoritative leadership. Each was destroyed by authoritarian subjects who were victimized by the very fear and divisiveness the leader wished to overcome. Where are the leaders? Many of them, quite simply, have been assassinated.

The failure of leadership which endangers our democracy is a failure of national will, a failure of public standards. And these failures are in turn enhanced by the growing amorphousness of the nation's problems; by the witlessness of a communications network concerned too much with fashion and novelty; and by the insidious transformation of the adversary method into a policy of systematic destruction that almost seems to be endorsed by America's embittered factionalism.

Leadership is the unacknowledged premise of almost all relationships in a mature, complex society, and the only important questions are whether that leadership is recognized or denied, whether it is accountable or unaccountable, whether it is public-spirited or self-interested, whether it is facilitating or paralyzing. The alternative is not equality but anarchy.

Nor is there a necessary incompatibility between authoritative leadership and democracy. On the contrary, in complex industrial societies the latter depends on the former to sustain it. It is the best of our leaders, those whose leadership is authoritative, who are damaged by distrust, cynicism, and the impulse to anarchy; the worst, those who are authoritarian, flourish, for they are uninterested in the public's uneasiness but benefit from the frustration and impatience uneasiness spawns. Public censure meant nothing to Nixon; to Willy Brandt, schooled in authoritative leadership, its mere shadow was reason enough to resign. Leaders who follow the led are paralyzed by uncertainties in the public will; authoritarians on the other hand read public uncertainty as a license for self-aggrandizement. It is significant that New Jersey, which cannot agree on how to support higher education or whether to tax income, has a history of corruption among its public servants. In the absence of a clear public interest, politicians are all too willing to pursue clear private interests.

In the long run, then, America must look for the solution to its crisis of leadership in the rediscovery of democratic purposes rather than in the discovery of new leaders. Such purposes may, in fact, be hidden in the very obstacles that impede leadership. Ecological interdependence also compels a new awareness of common dilemmas. That our lives are globally interdependent and that our destinies can no longer be pursued in individual or even national isolation may compromise our sense of power but can only enhance our sense of commonality. If interdependence suggests a basis for unity, the media can be a vehicle for its expression, and aid in nourishing a common sense of the world's common problems.

Assassination in America has fed on quiet homicidal rage born of paranoia and polarization. The selectivity with which targets were chosen and the efficiency with which the killings were carried out support the terrible suspicion that a larger public, against its better instincts, in some way wished these deaths. If this is so, only an amelioration of America's climate of frustration will put an end to assassination. Put in the affirmative, the restoration of even a minimal sense of national purpose would serve as a better deterrent to assassination than a hundredfold increase in the Secret Service.

It is no good for us to go looking for leaders; we must first rediscover citizens. It will not help to indict the faceless system if we are without common purposes that can be used to challenge facelessness and turn systems back into servants. If America is to have leaders, it will have to agree upon goals. If we wish to have leaders to follow, we will have to show them the way.

CHAPTER 9

The Undemocratic Party System: Citizenship in an Elite/Mass Society

> If I could not go to heaven, but with a party,
> I would not go there at all.
> (*Thomas Jefferson, before he became
> president and party leader*)[1]

THE PARTY SYSTEM AND REPRESENTATION

A raging controversy has enveloped the party system in America. The debate has turned on such questions as whether democracy is best served by a regional or a national party system, by a state convention or primary system for presidential nominations, by traditional machine party politics or "democratic" people's party politics, by personality- or issue-oriented political campaigns—in short, by old-style party politics or new style reform party politics.

It is my contention here that the controversy is in one sense fundamentally irrelevant to the issues it affects to raise. The simple fact is that party government and the representative system to which it belongs are both deeply inimical to real democracy and have evolved from the outset, to no small degree by design of the Founders and early practitioners of our political system, in a fashion that has consistently diminished rather than enhanced self-government.

There is without doubt a crisis of sorts afflicting party government. James MacGregor Burns described it years ago as a "deadlock of democracy" in which the congressional and presidential branches of the major parties created a four-party system that paralyzed national leadership and the effective use of power for national policy making.[2] More recently, a venerable pundit has alluded to "the near collapse of the party system,"[3] while the inability of President Carter to treat with a Congress controlled by his own party suggests systemic as well as personal problems for the president as party leader. Meanwhile, but a third of the eligible electorate votes, and a third of those are without any party affiliation.

Yet much of this crisis has been precipitated by the incompatibility of representation itself with full freedom, equality, and social justice. A well-known cautionary adage has it that the voter under representative government is free only on the day the ballot is cast. But even this act is of dubious moment in a system where, although millions share the franchise, it is used only to select the few who exercise every other duty of civic importance in the nation. To exercise the franchise is unfortunately at the same time to renounce it. The representative principle steals from individuals all significant responsibility for their values, beliefs, and actions; ultimately it turns them into passive clients of party bosses (the old elite under the old elite party system) or active pawns of public opinion manipulators and their well-packaged national leaders (the new elite under the new mass party system). In neither case is there any real question of self-government—only a dispiriting choice between direct elite rule or elite rule via the masses, between elite persuasion and mass persuasion, between rule by party hacks and rule by popular demagogues, between backroom politics and editorial page politics.

The vital political idea of citizenship eludes completely the sociological (and hence unpolitical, even antipolitical) terminology of elite and mass. Modern parties, construed in this alienating language, leave no room for citizens understood as self-governing community participants. It is no accident that the mainstream tradition of American social science has concerned itself not with The American Citizen, but only with The American Voter,[4] voters being as far from citizens as spectators are from participants or patients are from the doctors they select to heal them.

The startling and dismaying truth is that those who have entered the debates about the democratic or undemocratic implications of the American party system either do not believe in democracy or do not understand it. Conservative critics of party reform presumably follow in James Madison's footsteps, perceiving in large, democratically controlled, majoritarian parties a clear and present danger to stable and prudent government. To them, party reform must appear as another instance of that "excess of democracy" against which Samuel P. Huntington sounds a tocsin in his bicentennial essay, "The Democratic Distemper."[5] They no more believe in popular rule than did their forebears like Alexander Hamilton who espied in the people only a voracious and dangerous "Beast." Their concern is with prudent rulership not participation, the protection of private rights not the pursuit of public purposes, limited government not active citizenship; hence they view democracy at its best only as a possible means to other primary ends. In Martin Diamond's emphatic description: "*democracy was only a form of government* [for the Founders] *which, like any other form of government, had to prove itself adequately instrumental to the securing of liberty.*"[6] In this framework, the traditional elite party model obviously seems a safer, if less democratic, bet than the reform model.

The reformers appear to be democrats, and they do appeal explicitly to popular sovereignty and accountability in assailing the traditional elite party system. Jefferson was perhaps the first of such reformers, his "supreme achievement as a party leader" having been to "reach out to embrace new voters," giving majority rule "a more popular, egalitarian impetus" and creating a "vigorous, competitive party, under strong leadership."[7] Yet few of his heirs seem to have grasped that within the confines of a representative system which, in Schumpeter's characterization, allows the people only to select among the elites competing to govern them,[8] attempts at democratization tend to diminish the prudence and attenuate the moderateness of rulership without increasing its accountability or enhancing the quality of participation and citizenship. As George Bernard Shaw scoffed, one can "substitute selection by the incompetent many for appointment by the corrupt few," but it is not at all clear that the latter is any more democratic than the former if thoughtful, autonomous, community self-government is to be the measure of democracy. The problem apparently lies not in the insufficiently democratic character of the reformers' wish to democratize, but in the intrinsically undemocratic character of the larger representative system to which both traditional and reform party politics belong.

This system is much less hospitable to the three most cherished values in American political life—freedom, equality, and social justice—than is generally perceived. It is incompatible with freedom because political will is alienable only at the cost of self-government and autonomy, because, as Rousseau warned in *The Social Contract,* "the instant a people allows itself to be represented it loses its freedom,"[9] because freedom and citizenship are correlates, each sustaining and giving life to the other, because women and men who are not directly responsible through common deliberation, common decision, and common action for the policies that determine their common lives are not really free at all—however much they enjoy rights of privacy, property, and individuality.

Representation is incompatible with equality because, in the astute words of the nineteenth-century French Catholic writer Louis Veuillot, "When I vote my equality falls into the box with my ballot—they disappear together";[10] because equality construed exclusively in terms of abstract personhood or legal and electoral equity omits the crucial economic and social determinants that shape its real-life incarnation, because equality without community is not only a fiction that can divide as easily as it unites but, in the form of *Gleichschaltung,* offers the dread specter of a mass society of indistinguishable consumer clones.

Finally, representation is incompatible with social justice because it encroaches on the personal autonomy and self-sufficiency that every moral order demands, because it incapacitates the community as a self-regulating instrument of justice and destroys the possibility of a participatory public in which the idea of public justice might take root.

Freedom, equality, and justice are in fact all *political* values that depend for their conceptual coherence and their practical viability on self-government and citizenship. They cannot be apprehended, let alone practiced, by clients or by pawns; they are not to be found in the lexicon of either elites or masses. They are the special provenance of citizens, and unless some way is discovered to represent citizens without annulling citizenship, all party government—in its traditional and its reformed versions—will continue to obstruct rather than serve them.

CENTRIFUGAL AND CENTRIPETAL TENDENCIES OF ELITE/MASS PARTY ORGANIZATION

It can be said, in defense of the party system, that the device of representation was precisely the solution the Founders offered to the problem of rendering democracy workable in a large-scale republic, a way of addressing the dangers of faction and anarchy without falling prey to the perils of unaccountability and tyranny (whether popular/majoritarian or elite). As Madison had put it, the representative system could "refine and enlarge the public views by passing them through the medium of a chosen body of citizens,"[11] thereby achieving a delicate balance of popular control *and* prudent government, participation *and* effective national administration, accountability *and* centripetal efficiency. Political parties, in turn, as they evolved piecemeal from the administrations of Jefferson and Madison through those of Martin Van Buren and Andrew Jackson, became the chief institutional means through which the representative principle was established in American political life. They were (to appropriate Bagehot's phrase) the buckle linking governmental authority to the people in whom authority had its theoretic origin, linking elite and mass in a continuum that made voters the ultimate yet passive arbiters and the elite the active but dependent governors of the nation's political life.

Parties were rooted in the populace, thereby securing the people from abuse by their governors; but parties were at the same time insulated from the people, thereby securing the government from abuse by the people (manifested as popular prejudice, majority tyranny, and mob caprice). Party government held the promise of a temperate democracy, one which, even when tried by populist and progressive excesses and stretched by mass manipulators or near demagogues (Jackson? Roosevelt? Kennedy?), could mediate the anarchic factions and the tyrannical majorities that would inevitably accompany the growth of American democracy. That at least was the theory, the hope, the faith of our skeptical republican forefathers.

For all this, there is not much in the historical experience of American political parties, and still less in the political theory of party government as argued in the tradition from Edmund Burke to Robert Michels, to demonstrate that parties have made good or can make good on this faith. Quite aside from the fundamental problems representation raises for democracy, parties bring with them their own liabilities both for self-government and for central administration. I contend that parties are afflicted both with radical centripetal (elitist) tendencies and with radical centrifugal (disintegrative or anarchic) tendencies which together undermine their utility as mediating devices between authority and the public and thus their viability as saving compromises in the service of popular democracy.

Both tendencies have long been well-known to critics of political parties, and little is offered here that has not been largely anticipated in early English and American discussions. Yet because both the old guard and the reform movement seem united on the intrinsic merit of the party system and at odds only over the character of that system, a number of the earlier arguments may bear rehearsal.

Perhaps the most searching as well as the most sweeping critique of the centripetal tendencies of party government came at the beginning of this century in Robert Michels's elaboration of the iron law of oligarchy in the context of party. To Michels, the evolution of representative democracy is inherently unstable, following a "parabolic course" that, however promising the democratic beginnings, leads inevitably to oligarchy. Moreover, these "oligarchical and bureaucratic tendencies" are a "matter of technical and practical necessity" since they are an "inevitable product of the very principle of organization."[12] This suggests natural limits to representative democracy of a far more severe kind than usually attributed to pure or participatory democracy. Michels concurs with Rousseau in insisting upon "the logical impossibility of the 'representative' system, whether in parliamentary life or in party delegation."[13] If "the will of the people is not transferable, nor even the will of the single individual," then clearly "the first appearance of professional leadership marks the beginning of the end."[14] Victor Considérant, a forerunner of Michels, offers this striking metaphor: "In delegating its sovereignty, a people abdicate it. Such a people no longer governs itself but is governed. . . . Turning Saturn on his head, the principle of sovereignty ends up being devoured by its daughter, the principle of delegation."[15]

In the particular French Left examples he had before him, Michels was witness to what he saw as the typical democratic attempt to maintain popular sovereignty by "subordinating the delegates altogether to the will of the mass, by tying them hand and foot," as well as to the failure of this attempt. Mandate representation inevitably gives way to specialization, expertise, organization, bureaucracy, and leadership so that, albeit power "issues from the people, it ends by raising itself above the people."[16] Michels's bitter conclusion was this:

Under representative government the difference between democracy and monarchy, which are both rooted in the representative system, is altogether insignificant—a difference not in substance but in form. The sovereign people elects, in place of a king, a number of kinglets. Not possessing sufficient freedom and independence to direct the life of the state, it tamely allows itself to be despoiled of its fundamental right.[17]

Unhappily, this form of criticism, because it is associated with neo-elitist and left-anarchist ideology of a distinctly nineteenth-century variety, has been largely ignored in America. Pareto, Mosca, Michels, Proudhon, Malatesta, and Considérant are hardly fashionable elders of American social and political science. Yet there is much in the history of American party evolution that confirms Michels's tough analysis by exhibiting the centripetal tendencies of party government. For one thing, every attempt at countering party elitism in America has run afoul of the nation's Lockean consensualism. As Louis Hartz and Daniel Boorstin have effectively argued, this consensualism has been a permanent barrier to the kinds of ideological polarization and doctrinal party programs that might otherwise have been used to secure through an obligatory mandate popular control over government. Where parties have upon occasion been rendered more ideological and programmatic, the result has often been intraparty breakdown and electoral failure rather than greater democracy (the Goldwater and McCarthy campaigns are prime examples in recent decades). Even proponents of democratic reform (Donald M. Fraser, for example) acknowledge that the great efforts at democratizing the Democratic party of 1968 through 1972 did more to weaken and fragment than to democratize it; constituencies were polarized and a variety of interests given expression, but the party did not end up with a clear mandate. The Carter presidency has suffered in part because of the incoherence left behind by those heady years.

For the most part, however, party government in America has pretty much followed the Michels script. The requisites of effective leadership and a winning electoral strategy have created party bosses and machine politics at the local level and party hierarchy and presidential hegemony at the national level. Modern life with its demands of specialization, efficiency, and expertise has compounded the difficulties. As Michels astutely foresaw:

It becomes more and more absurd to attempt to "represent" a heteronomous mass in all the innumerable problems which arise out of the increasing differentiation of our political and economic life. To represent, in this sense, comes to mean that the purely individual desire masquerades and is accepted as the will of the mass.[18]

Party government is then prone to centripetal elitism because party government is government by *leaders,* and as Burke rightly understood, while leaders are "faithful watchmen . . . over the rights and privileges of the people," their "duty" is to "give them information, and to receive it from them"; a leader cannot "go to school to them, to learn the principles of law and government."[19] The people are thus at best *voters* when they choose their leaders and *clients* when they are served diligently by them. They are not citizens in either capacity, and cannot be.

Nonetheless, it can fairly be argued that the evolution of American party government has followed a cyclical rather than a parabolic course, that political parties have alternated between elite and popular (or mass) models. Unfortunately, as my brief discussion of reform may suggest, this qualification (if true) does not moderate the centripetal tendencies of party; it only provides an equal centrifugal tendency, equally undermining to stable democracy. The centrifugal tendencies of representative government are most visible during periods of populism, progressivism, and reform when rank-and-file voters are trying to reclaim their parties from ossified elite leadership. Voters insist on being taken seriously, demand that neglected interests be articulated and served, and take control of their party either through programmatic party platforms or institutional and procedural modifications that permit more input into the process of leader selection. But at no point do such changes transform voters into self-governing citizens or permit clients to see themselves as self-responsible agents. Communities are not established, interests are promoted. Consequently, although the intent is to return government to the public at large, such reforms generally return it to this or that particular public—Michels's "purely individual desire masquerading as the will of the mass." The public at large, however, remains even more fragmented and privatized than under elite leadership (where, in deference to the Burkean principle, leaders at least attempt to attune themselves to cross-sectional, national, and occasionally even truly public purposes).

Once again, there is little here that would have surprised Burke or Rousseau or indeed the Founders. The polarizing and tyrannical disposition of popular prejudice (what then went by the name of popular opinion) when given the force of a representative franchise was a constant concern of almost every great political theorist from Montesquieu through John Stuart Mill and Tocqueville. Madison made the problem of faction the centerpiece of his first *Federalist* paper (Number 10), and saw in it the greatest single threat to the stability of republics. He anticipated almost every conceivable abuse of popular party politics of the putatively "democratic" variety when he wrote there: "Men of factious tempers, of local prejudice, or of sinister designs, may, by intrigue, by corruption, or by other means, first obtain the suffrages, and then betray the interests of the people."[20]

Public opinion turns out to be private opinion endowed with public power; in the absence of civic education and a politically experienced citizenry, the public can only be a mouthpiece for those best able, with image, media access, money, or demagoguery, to buy it. In Burke's phrase, what cannot be accomplished openly will be achieved by "insidious art, and perverse industry, and gross misrepresentation."[21] This is no brief against democracy, no cynical censure of the incapacities of the people. It is only a precise portrait of what happens when a disfranchised public in a representative democracy is given the illusion of power during periods of popular reform.

The overall effect is one in which the checking of elite leadership occasions only divisiveness and interest conflict, no true democratization. In his devastating diagnosis of the maladies of what he called four-party government, James MacGregor Burns noted how

> American leaders have had to gain the concurrence not simply of a majority of the voters, but of majorities of different sets of voters organized around leaders in mutually checking and foot-dragging sectors of government. The price of this radical version of checks and balances has been enfeebled policy.[22]

In the end, bridling our leaders does not get us more democracy, just less leadership. It does not make for better citizenship; it only makes for worse government.

The particular reforms initiated by crusading progressives within the Democratic party in 1968 and 1972 were intended to enhance party democracy and secure the control of the public over the representative institutions purporting to serve them. Presidential nominating procedures received particular attention: state delegations to nominating conventions were made more representative through the abolition of unit rule and the widening of the candidate pool; proportional representation was widely discussed as a device of party reform (one is reminded of John Stuart Mill's devotion to the Hare system of proportional representation in his *Representative Government*), and the state primary system was given major impetus in preference to the old elite-controlled nominating convention at the state level. Issues, not leadership, were brought center stage; personalities and platforms rather than political acumen and experience were given star billing.

Yet, for all this, there seems to be broad, bipartisan, cross-sectional consensus on the failure of the reforms—whatever else they might have done or undone—to enhance democracy. Centrifugal forces, to be sure, did and do counter the elitist disposition of party leadership and efficient government, but paralysis rather than participation seems the most frequent outcome. Representative government, while perhaps at least partially cyclic in its movement from elite to mass and back again, seems neither in its centralizing nor in its fragmenting tendencies to serve the interests of community, citizenship, or self-government, and is thus, with respect to real democracy, ineluctably parabolic in its evolution, just as Michels claimed. Moreover, political parties, though designed to mediate authority and citizenry in a "compound" and "extended" republic (Madison), in fact turn out to be among the least satisfactory mediating institutions known to polity or society.

None of this should give much solace to the elitist critics of party reform and popular government. To the extent such critics are not merely venting their hostility to democracy *tout court,* they are generally doing little more than completing the antidemocratic logic of the elite-mass-elite cycle. Institutional authority is preferred to popular authority because it is insulated from popular opinion. Elite leadership is preferred to mass leadership because it promises to be less demagogic and more professional and efficient. State conventions are preferred to primaries for presidential nominations because they maintain traditional political elites in place. At bottom is the deeply cynical view of the people as mass, of voters as—in James Q. Wilson's appalling phrase—"amateur democrats" whose activity is the greatest single threat to efficient republican government.[23] With this view and its attendant appeal to old-fashioned elitist politics, we simply come full circle in the Michels syndrome portrayed above, with all the contradictions of centripetal party elements reemerging.

Centripetal and centrifugal tendencies built into the representative system do then appear to precipitate polar elite/mass forces that are destabilizing to government and subversive of democracy. The party government compromise does not mediate efficient authority and popular sovereignty; it merely embodies and exacerbates their defining incompatibility.

THE STRONG THEORY OF DEMOCRACY
AND THE MAKING OF CITIZENS

If the foregoing analysis is correct, the crisis of party is a crisis of democracy and the crisis of democracy is a crisis of theory as well as practice. That is to say, it suggests a fundamental incoherence in the theory of representative democracy—or as I shall call it here, the "thin" theory of democracy. Representative democracy is a thin theory of democracy because it holds democratic values only provisionally: they are prudential, conditional, or instrumental with respect to other ends (negative freedom, rights, private property, and so forth) that are themselves individualistic and privatistic. No firm belief in the intrinsic worth of citizenship, participation, public goods, community, and self-government can be expected to be nourished by this instrumentalism. Representative democracy can thus never really be too far from Ambrose Bierce's cynical formulation of politics as "the conduct of public affairs for private advantage"; it must always be more concerned to promote individual liberty than to secure public justice, to advance interests (whether mass or elite) than to discover public goods, to keep individuals safely apart (government as the adjudication of conflicting interests through party representation) than to bring them fruitfully together (government as the pursuit of community goods through communal self-government). It is a democracy that defines the crucial ingredient of popular sovereignty as control rather than participation—thus Robert Dahl's well-known construction of democracy as "at a minimum . . . concerned with processes by which ordinary citizens exert a relatively high degree of control over leaders,"[24] or David Easton's "a political system in which power is so distributed that control over the authoritative allocation of values lies in the hands of the mass of the people."[25]

Yet Reinhold Niebuhr lamented many years ago that democracy must have "a more compelling justification and requires a more realistic vindication than is given it by the liberal culture with which it has been associated in modern history."[26] It seems apparent that representative democracy in both its elite and mass party variations has not and will not provide that justification. The apathy and alienation and anomie that are found on the underbelly of America's vaunted freedoms, the rootlessness and anonymity that makes normal familial, kinship, and neighborly relations so problematic, the privatizing, interest-balancing approach characteristic of putatively "public" policy making, the sapping materialism of the nation's economic successes as well as the devastation occasioned by its economic failures, and the paralysis of both presidential and congressional government in the face of a party system that seems equally incapable of mobilizing and engaging citizens or creating and motivating effective leaders all point to the inadequacy of the thin theory of democracy and its supporting representative institutions. Its provisionality ultimately makes representative government a citizen-corroding, community-denying instrument of elite and mass interests. It can know no form of citizenship other than the sometime voter and the hungry client, and can achieve no public purpose other than the self-interested trade-off and the prudent bargain.

Representative democracy is thus always weak democracy and can never yield the pleasures of participation or the fellowship of fraternity, the individual strength of community membership or the mutuality of public goods, and, perhaps most essential, can never comprehend that all-too-human interdependency that underlies all political life.

The "strong" theory of democracy, as I would like to call it,[27] takes Rousseau as its mentor, and concurs with John Dewey in understanding democracy not as "an alternate to other principles of associated life [but as] the idea of community life itself. . . . [It is] a name for a life of free and enriching communion."[28] It begins with the idea that there can be no "amateurs" in politics because there can be no professionals, and insists that sovereignty can neither be alienated nor represented without eventually destroying the autonomy of the individual or people represented.

Representative democracy, as weak democracy, tends to instruct women and men in their rights and offers them tools for selecting and controlling the elites who govern them; strong democracy instructs them in their obligations (inextricably bound up with rights) and teaches them how to govern themselves. Where weak democracy is marked exclusively by the language of right, interest, power, privacy, contract, and representation, strong democracy employs a language of citizenship, community, fraternity, responsibility, obligation, and self-realization as well—not to the exclusion of the first set of terms, but to ground them in the actual conditions of interdependency and sociability that constitute the real social and economic environment of politics.

Michael Oakeshott may think he is portraying only conservative politics when he depicts the political condition as that of sailors on a "boundless and bottomless sea [where] there is neither harbour nor shelter nor floor for anchorage, neither starting-place nor appointed destination [and where] the enterprise is to keep afloat on an even keel";[29] but he is also portraying a politics that *is* an end rather than one that only *has* ends, a politics where the communal spirit kindled by sailing is as important as potential communal destinations—one where, most importantly, such destinations as are discovered or invented represent not the private interests of a manipulating elite or the private passions of a manipulated mass but the deliberate common will of a community of active citizens.

Despite the several virtues of the strong theory of democracy and the many deficiencies of thin or representative democracy, the strong theory remains an ideal which even in the Founders' era could be dismissed as irrelevant (if not insidious) in the context of a burgeoning continental republic at once both extended and compound. What possible bearing can it have on the pressing exigencies of party government in America today? Were the Founders not finally deeply wise (as Edward C. Banfield insists throughout his corpus) in their refusal to base government on direct participation by a people which, if not always as hungry as Hamilton's Beast, was nonetheless never for its own good to be trusted with rulership?

Certainly there seems to be wide consensus among both neo-Burkean conservatives like Robert Nisbet and Samuel Huntington and neo-Marxist radicals like Peter Bachrach[30] that the people, or that false consciousness that parades itself in the people's proletarian garb, are not to be trusted. Radicals fear that ordinary women and men, if given the chance, will cripple government with narrow-minded, unthinking conservatism of the kind exhibited in California's Proposition 13, or will repeal the Bill of Rights in the name of law and order, or will precipitate other outrages equally offensive to (radical) good sense. Conservatives fear that the same women and men, if given the chance, will form into clamoring special interest groups that are already overrepresented in the system and force government into imprudent expenditures for conservation and social welfare or demand nefarious cutbacks in defense spending, or precipitate other outrages equally offensive to (conservative) good sense. This kind of scapegoating at the people's expense is typical of the long campaign representative democracy's advocates have waged against participatory democracy.

The strategy is elementary but not ineffective: give the people all the insignia but none of the tools of citizenship and accuse them of incompetence; throw referenda at them without providing civic education or insulation from money and media and then pillory them for their ill-judgment; inundate them with problem issues the "experts" have not been able to solve (busing, inflation, atomic energy, right-to-work legislation) and then carp at their uncertainty or indecisiveness or simple-mindedness in muddling through to a position.

Yet voters do not become citizens overnight any more than clients become autonomous self-governors in the course of a day. Representative government has had two hundred years in which to commit a thousand errors; direct popular government is rarely given more than a single chance. Certainly there is neither hope for nor point in trying to "convert" from representative to direct democracy or to substitute at the wave of a hand or the waiver of a constitution some strange breed of federalized participatory assembly rule for two-party government. There is more than enough room for a shift of emphasis, however—away from party realignment and electoral reform and toward institutional modification favorable to greater public participation not in the selection of governors but in governing itself. These institutions, nourished by the strong theory of democracy, would have as their purpose the making of citizens as well as the making of public policy, and might include experiments in common legislation and common work as well as in common deliberation and common decision making. I have discussed (in the context of America's political realities) the promise as well as the problems of such institutional changes elsewhere,[31] but I can repeat here that the objective, initially, is a change in emphasis, attitude, and spirit rather than a radical remaking of the American system of government.

John Stuart Mill, no friend of direct democracy though an admirer of proportional representation and a powerful believer in the necessity of civic education and a morally alive citizenry, issued a warning in *On Liberty* that has been widely overlooked by his teeming liberal fans:

> The mischief begins when, instead of calling forth the activity and powers of individuals and bodies, [a government] substitutes its own activity for theirs;

when, instead of informing, advising, and, upon occasion, denouncing, it makes them work in fetters, or bids them stand aside and does their work instead of them. The worth of a State, in the long run, is the worth of the individuals composing it; and a State which postpones the interests of *their* mental expansion and elevation to a little more of administrative skill . . . in the details of business; a State which dwarfs its men, in order that they may be more docile instruments in its hands even for beneficial purposes—will find that with small men no great thing can really be accomplished; and that the perfection of machinery to which it has sacrificed everything will in the end avail it nothing, for want of the vital power which, in order that the machine might work more smoothly, it has preferred to banish.[32]

In America, the "vital power" has been banished by party government; what is worse, the machine refuses to run smoothly for all that! The system has certainly provided that "degree of circumspection and distrust" of which Madison, in *Federalist* Number 55, deemed mankind's "depravity" worthy; but Madison suggested in the same passage that there were also "other qualities in human nature which justify a certain portion of esteem and confidence,"[33] and those have been barely recognized let alone honored and institutionalized in the American party system. Consequently, it may indeed be true that Americans are today *small* women and men incapable of any great thing. Still, great things are required of our nation in the coming years—not least among them, survival as a democracy—and it seems clear enough that if those things are to be achieved, voters and clients will have to become, if not great women and men, at least active, participating citizens in the governance of our public life.

NOTES

1. Jefferson, like so many of the Founders, can easily be cited on every side of an issue. His fondness for rural democracy, ward government, and individual rights must be balanced against the strong party leadership and executive authority he exercised in his presidential years.

2. *The Deadlock of Democracy: Four-Party Politics in America* (Englewood Cliffs, N.J.: Prentice-Hall, 1963), pp. 324–25.

3. Richard Strout ("T.R.B."), *The New Republic,* May 26, 1979.

4. All the classical electoral studies of the 1940s and 1950s focus on the voter rather than the citizen; see, for example, P. Lazarsfeld, B. Berelson, and H. Gaudet, *The People's Choice* (New York: Columbia University Press, 1948); A. Campbell et al., *The Voter Decides* (Evanston, Ill.: Row, Peterson, 1954); and most recently, N. H. Nie et al., *The Changing American Voter* (Cambridge: Harvard University Press, 1979).

5. *The Public Interest,* no. 41 (Fall 1975), pp. 9–38. Huntington's particular biases are evident in these passages: "The effective operation of a democratic politi-

cal system usually requires some measure of apathy and non-involvement on the part of some individuals and groups. . . . Marginal social groups, as in the case of the blacks, are now becoming full participants in the political system. Yet the danger of 'overloading' the political system with demands which extend its functions and undermine its authority still remains." (p. 37)

6. "The Declaration and the Constitution: Liberty, Democracy and the Founders," *The Public Interest*, no. 41 (Fall 1975), p. 47, emphasis in original.

7. Burns, *Deadlock*, pp. 33, 41.

8. Cf. Joseph Schumpeter, *Capitalism, Socialism and Democracy*, 3rd ed. (London: George Allen & Unwin, 1950), pp. 269–83.

9. *Oeuvres complètes* (Paris: Editions Gallimard, 1964), vol. 3, book III, chap. 15, p. 431, my translation.

10. Cited by Robert Michels, *Political Parties: A Sociological Study of the Oligarchical Tendencies of Modern Democracy* (Glencoe, Ill.: Free Press, 1915; reprinted, 1949), p. 39, my translation.

11. *The Federalist*, No. 10 (New York: Modern Library, 1964), p. 61. The representative system is among the institutions discussed in their original constitutional setting in my "The Compromised Republic," in *The Moral Foundations of the American Republic*, ed. R. H. Horwitz (Charlottesville: University of Virginia Press, 1977), pp. 25–26 et passim, reprinted as chapter 4 in this volume.

12. *Political Parties*, p. 33.

13. Ibid.

14. Ibid., pp. 33–34.

15. *La solution, ou le Gouvernement direct du Peuple* (Paris: Librairie Phalanstérie, 1850), pp. 13–15, my translation.

16. *Political Parties*, p. 38.

17. Ibid.

18. Ibid., p. 40.

19. *Burke's Politics: Selected Writings and Speeches of Edmund Burke*, ed. Ross J. S. Hoffman and Paul Levack (New York: Alfred A. Knopf, 1949), p. 219. Of course Burke at this point sounds rather like James I, who insisted likewise he was not to be instructed by the public in "my craft. . . . I must not be taught my office." Cited by Samuel Beer, *Modern British Politics* (London: Faber & Faber, 1965), p. 6.

20. *The Federalist*, p. 59. Madison's definition of faction might also serve as a definition of the modern political party wedded to electoral victory and the "articulation and aggregation of interests": "By a faction I understand a number of citizens, whether amounting to a majority or a minority of the whole, who are united and actuated by some common impulse of passion, or if interest, adverse to the rights of other citizens, or to the permanent and aggregate interests of the community" (p. 54).

21. *Selected Writings*, p. 146.

22. *Deadlock*, p. 324.

23. *The Amateur Democrat* (Chicago: University of Chicago Press, 1962). The phrase has been used more recently by neoconservative critics of democracy.

24. *A Preface to Democratic Theory* (Chicago: University of Chicago Press, 1956), p. 3.

25. *Political Systems* (New York: Alfred A. Knopf, 1953), p. 222.

26. *The Children of Light and the Children of Darkness* (New York: Scribner's, 1944), pp. 5–6.

27. "The Strong Theory of Democracy: A Communitarian Challenge to Liberalism," manuscript.

28. *The Public and Its Problems* (Chicago: Swallow Press, 1954; reprint of 1924 ed.), p. 148.

29. *Rationalism in Politics* (New York: Basic Books, 1962), p. 127.

30. See Peter Bachrach, Testimony before the Subcommittee on the Constitution of the Committee on the judiciary on S. J. Res. 67, 95th Cong., 1st sess., Dec. 13–14, 1977.

It is particularly disheartening to see critics of elitism who spring from the popular Left join the outcry against such populist institutions as the referendum in America. Once again, however, Michels perceived the danger seventy-five years ago when he wrote:

> Where party life is concerned, the socialists for the most part reject . . . practical applications of democracy, using against them conservative arguments such as we are otherwise accustomed to hear only from the opponents of socialism. In articles written by socialist leaders it is ironically asked whether it would be a good thing to hand over the leadership of the party to the ignorant masses simply for love of an abstract democratic principle. (*Political Parties*, p. 336)

31. See my *Political Participation and the Creation of Res Publica*, Poynter Pamphlet (Bloomington, Ind.: Poynter Center, 1977), particularly pp. 13–19; see also my testimony before the Subcommittee on the Constitution of the Committee on the Judiciary on S. J. Res. 67, 95th Cong., 1st sess., Dec. 13–14, 1977.

32. (London: Everyman's Library, n.d.), p. 170.

33. *The Federalist*, p. 365.

CHAPTER 10

One Nation Indivisible or a Compact of Sovereign States? The Two Faces of Federalism

FEDERALISM is neither an institution nor an idea; it is an argument. It is the American argument about nationalism and sectionalism, about order and liberty, about sovereignty and factionalism, and about wisdom and democracy. It is the protean vessel into which Americans have poured their competing ideologies and their diverse theories of power and liberty from the time of the founding to the present day. In this sense, federalism is not an aspect of the U.S. Constitution or even one of the Constitution's founding principles. It is, rather, an argument about what the Constitution is and how it best can be construed to serve liberty.

The United States was born of a revolt against the constraining tyrannies and the reactive tumults of Europe. It was thus infected at its birth with twin fears: the fear of tyranny—absolute despotism and arbitrary authority of the kind manifested by George III—and the fear of anarchy—licentiousness and factionalism of the kind manifested by Daniel Shays and his Massachusetts rebels marching, in the early days of the Republic, on the banks to close them down by force of arms. The Framers were wall-eyed with anxiety, keeping one baleful eye on the specter of Leviathan and the other on what Madison called that "infinity of little, jealous, clashing, tumultuous commonwealths, the wretched nurseries of discord." Federalism was a bulwark constructed against both tyranny and anarchy. By uniting disparate regions and factions into one single union deriving its power directly from the people, the federal solution would protect against the unpropertied rabble and their fractious passions; yet by constituting the union with states with their own distinct histories and their own legislative body (the Senate), the federal solution would check central power and afford a permanent defense against would-be kings and other enemies of republicanism.

The argument of federalism has always been an argument of degree. In principle, all of the founders, federalists and antifederalists alike, were in accord on the justifying political theory of republicanism. Government was to serve liberty (whether construed as self-government or property), and liberty could in turn only be served by moderation, by civic virtue, and by the disciplining of central power by a system of horizontal and vertical separation of powers. But to many, the greatest danger to liberty was presented by central government itself; this required that federalism be understood as a system of vertical checks on power in which the states occupied a unique position. Others insisted that anarchy and factionalism placed liberty in far greater jeopardy; this meant that federalism had to be defined as the consolidation of once disparate powers into a sovereign union possessing sufficient authority to enforce the rights of liberty against the encroachments of state and faction. That America was to be a federal republic was clear to everyone, but the meaning of *federal* became the most persistent and deadly quarrel in the nation's history.

There were friends of liberty on both sides, but there were two sides from the outset. On one side stood those who had rebelled against the Stamp Act and the English prince who had imposed it. In establishing Committees of Correspondence and eventually the Articles of Confederation, they nonetheless were careful to retain their "sovereignty, freedom, and independence and every power, jurisdiction, and right" not expressly delegated to the feeble Continental Congress. This side saw in the Congress only a "league of friendship" rooted in voluntary cooperation among sovereign states, and therefore construed its authority as inferior to that of the states. For this side even the new, more powerful union that emerged from Philadelphia in 1787 remained a "compact of states" that governed at their pleasure and as their agent. These men—free yeomanry, frontiersmen and farmers, debtors without substantial property or mortgagees in hock for their land to the banks—were federalists, but they were federalists who saw in federation a guarantee of local liberties and sectional self-government. Although labeled "antifederalists" by proponents of national union who had appropriated the term *federalist* for themselves, theirs was not an argument against federalism, but an argument for a certain construction of federalism.

On the other side stood those who believed that America could not be secured against foreign tyranny without a strong national government. This side thought that to promote a thriving commerce and nourish a national economy capable of utilizing the resources of a great, untapped continent meant to consolidate power—to consolidate it first and divide it only afterwards. Making property synonymous with liberty, these nationalists insisted that property could not be preserved without order and that order called for centralized power. As bankers and manufacturers, but also as governors and generals—ambitious continentalists as well as critics of slavery—they argued in the language of the Preamble to the Constitution, that it was "we the people," not "we the states," who were to "ordain and establish" the Constitution, whose law was to be "supreme" over "one nation, indivisible." Their nationalist biases were clearly expressed in the method of ratification chosen for the new constitution: the method required the approval of only nine of the thirteen states to come into force and solicited votes not from state legislatures but from specially constituted conventions representing the people. These men were also federalists, but theirs was the federalism of a new nationalism. With Madison, they distrusted the power of the new union they had contrived and so they agreed to hem it in with checks and balances, but it was a government of national power to which they aspired.

The country would have liked to believe that the argument between federalists and antifederalists would not outlive Washington's presidency of national consensus. Jefferson was so bold as to claim in his first inaugural address that "we are all federalists, we are all republicans." But Hamilton's plan for a national bank and a national economy, the Alien and Sedition Laws that seemed to place the newly won Bill of Rights in jeopardy, and John Adams' regal ways as the second president in fact intensified the struggle. And at the very moment in 1800 when Jefferson sought to rise above party and politics, he was being labeled an infidel, a howling atheist, an intellectual voluptuary by folks who, as James MacGregor Burns reports in his *Vineyard of Liberty,* were hiding their Bibles under their Boston beds on inauguration day.

A few years earlier, friends of the antifederalists, like Philadelphia newspaperman Benjamin Bache (a grandson of Franklin who died of the plague shortly after being tried under the Sedition Act), were referring to President Adams as "old, querulous, bald, blind, crippled, toothless Adams," and reminding the nationalists that the Tenth Amendment stated clearly enough that "powers not delegated to the United States by the Constitution, nor prohibited to it by the states, are reserved to the states respectively, or to the people." The nationalists gave as good as they got: the president of Yale College, on Jefferson's accession to power, warned against a country soon to be "government by blockheads and knaves . . . where the ties of marriage are severed . . . and wives and daughters thrown into the stews." Thus did one group of federalists, speaking as advocates of national unity against the rabble of the hinterlands, make war on another group of federalists, speaking as advocates of sectional independence and assailing in turn the monarchical pretentions of the nationalists who seemed so quickly to have forgotten the lessons of 1776.

The quarrel did not abate, but waxed with the new century. In 1819 a clerk in the Baltimore branch of the Bank of the United States decided that he could not pay the state of Maryland a tax it had levied, since the bank was an agent of the national government. Luther Martin, representing Maryland, brought the case before the Supreme Court, arguing that the federal government had no power to incorporate the bank to begin with and that Maryland was, in any case, within its sovereign rights in taxing it.

But in *McCullough* v. *Maryland,* Chief Justice John Marshall preferred Daniel Webster's nationalist cause as he argued it before the bench. Marshall's decision, echoing Webster and looking forward to Lincoln, read in part as follows:

> The government of the Union is emphatically and truly a government of the people. In form and substance it emanates from them, its powers are granted to them, and are to be exercised directly on them. . . . Let the end be legitimate, let it be within the scope of the constitution, and all means are appropriate which are plainly adapted to that end.

The nationalist interpretation of federalism won the battle, but only at the eventual cost of a great fratricidal war. For federal sectionalists continued to rebel against centralism and, in the name of liberty, developed doctrines of state sovereignty, nullification (the right to declare national legislation invalid), and, as an ultimate sanction, secession. In his *Disquisition on Government,* John Calhoun thus attacked the Tariff Acts of 1828 and 1832, arguing not merely that South Carolina has the right to negate and void an Act of Congress, but that

> it is this negative power—the power of preventing or arresting the action of the government, be it called by what term it may, veto, interposition, nullification, check, or balance of power—which in fact forms the constitution. . . . There can be no constitution without the negative power.

Both sides continued to argue in the name of liberty, but practical issues of economic power and the system of slavery superseded the abstract constitutional arguments; indeed, the argument over federalism became a quarrel that threatened the very life of the nation. And so when Jefferson Davis took up arms and, with the compact theory of the Constitution as his bible, set about dismembering the union, Lincoln responded with Hamiltonian nationalist rhetoric:

> The Union is older than any of the states [he declared] and, in fact, it created them as States. . . . The Union and not the states separately produced their independence and their liberty. . . . The Union gave each of them whatever of independence and liberty it has.

The union prevailed and the doctrines of nullification and state sovereignty died, but the argument went on. How far did the powers of the federal government extend? To the busting of private sector monopolies, as Teddy Roosevelt contended against those new converts to sectionalism and states' rights, the barons of oil, steel, and the railways? To problems of employment and social welfare, as Franklin Delano Roosevelt argued against an unconvinced antifederalist Supreme Court? To the enforcement of civil rights, as Presidents Kennedy and Johnson insisted against the outcries of the old Confederacy and more than a few northern cities as well?

To anyone with experience in intergovernmental relations, I hardly need say the argument goes on. Academics pick their own quarrels over the commerce clause, or the due process clause, or the elastic clause, arguing not just about constitutional doctrine but about which levels of government better serve the needs of a modern people. Thus, Michael D. Regan declares that "state governments are structurally inadequate and politically weak even when they are not actually corrupt." He finds himself contradicted by Daniel Eleazar, who writes, "There is no justification for thinking that the states and localities are less able to do the job than the federal government."

The politicians, not content to limit their positions to bickering over efficiency, have also returned to the rhetoric of the Framers' debate—Ronald Reagan announcing a new federalism in his inaugural address, and justifying it by asserting that "the federal government did not create the states; the states created the federal government." And historian Richard Morris rebuking him for purveying such a "hoary myth" and reminding him, as Chief Justice Marshall reminded Luther Martin and President Lincoln reminded Jefferson Davis, that "the United States was created by the people in collectivity, not by the individual states."

History will not settle the argument, however, any more than it will settle the quarrel between the Argentinians and the British over the Falklands, or the Palestinians and the Jews over the West Bank. For history here is itself in hock to ideology; both interpretations of the constitution, centralist and sectionalist, have their precedents, their constitutional features, and their history to call upon. The argument today remains what it was at the time of the founding, an argument over how the needs and liberties of individuals are best served, how a republican government is most safely constructed, how power is best subordinated to the requirements of liberty.

These arguments are finally *political* in character; that is to say, they are premised on fundamental theoretical and practical differences about what liberty is, how it is related to familiar terms like property, independence, and self-government, and how it is best served institutionally. To say the argument is political is not to say that it is irrational or ideological in the narrow sense. The argument against an interventionist national government has, to be sure, been put forth often enough by segregationists, business monopolies, exporters anxious to avoid national tariffs, and others looking more to their interests than to the liberties of the people. But it has also been put forth by liberal advocates of participation and self-government who agree with Jefferson that "making every citizen an acting member of the government, and in the offices nearest and most interesting to him, will attach him by his strongest feelings to the independence of his country, and its republican constitution." And it has been put forth by advocates of localism, who worry with de Tocqueville that

> a central administration is fit only to enervate the nations in which it exists, by incessantly diminishing their local spirit. Although such an administration can bring together at a given moment, on a given point, all the disposable resources of a people, it injures the renewal of those resources. It may ensure a victory in the hour of strife, but it gradually relaxes the sinews of strength. It may help admirably the transient greatness of a man, but not the durable prosperity of a nation.

In light of this history, this grand debate over the meaning of federalism, what are those engaged in the administration of governmental policies who must work in the complex interstices of our federal system to do? Merely consult the historical rhetoric and make up their minds which is the better interpretation? Whether nationalism or localism better serves their interests? Or the liberties of their "clients"? What, for example, is the best instrument of health care policy compatible with the constitutional order? The federal government? And then, which agency—the surgeon general's office? A department of health? State government? Municipal institutions? Are policies best left to politicians and government administrators (at whatever level of government) or to health and welfare professionals whose expertise attunes them to the problems of clients but who also have professional interests that may not coincide with the public interest? What of clients? Does segregating them as a special class defined by the patronage of the health care establishment harm them as citizens and free individuals (as Ivan Illich has argued)? Is the idea of clientage compatible with the idea of citizenship and self-government?

Specific questions such as these may seem to be unrelated to the broader historical and constitutional issues we have been reviewing. But in fact not one of them can be settled internally in a way insulated from a theory of power and liberty. Like it or not, we are all citizens and thus are all politicians in whatever we say and do. Administrators produce and apply political values and norms all the time, if only inadvertently. For this reason, the constitutional and historical background needs to be consulted even by— particularly by—health care or transportation or welfare professionals and administrators. Their neutrality vis-à-vis particular political parties cannot extend to political philosophy and history where, like it or not, they will hold views that affect performance.

What then is the significance of the historical struggle over federalism for the narrower debates over the new federalism? First, we must acknowledge that the rhetorical battle for the Constitution between nationalists (federalists) and localists (antifederalists) has been constantly informed and transformed by history itself. The extraordinary changes our country has undergone since the founding era have changed the character of the debate over federalism—or ought to have changed it, although in fact the rhetoric has changed all too little.

After all, in 1790 America comprised sixteen states strung out along the Eastern Seaboard containing a population of under four million (750,000 were slaves of African origin), 95 percent of whom lived in towns, villages, and rural communities with populations under 2,500. The new Leviathan of national government, feared by some as the seedbed for monarchy and lauded by others as a unifier of the nation, was in reality a slight edifice at best. The President's staff consisted of two clerks and several secretaries; he traveled alone with them and a half dozen servants. His cabinet comprised a secretary of the treasury (who, in Hamilton's case, had to found a bank and produce a new currency before he had anything to be in charge of); a secretary of state, who relied on special missions for his diplomacy well into Jefferson's term; a war secretary (but no navy secretary because there was literally no navy); and an attorney general. The capital, such as it was, was in New York (until Hamilton traded it away to the South in return for support on his federal bank scheme), and, once established in Washington, it was barely habitable in the summer months.

Though the states felt robbed of their sovereignty under the first two nationalist administrations, they in fact continued to control almost all governmental affairs other than those directly related to banking, currency, international commerce, and the treaty power. The federalist argument thus at times seemed more theoretical than practical, particularly after the antifederalists won their victory of a bill of rights. When sectionalist anarchy in the form of the Whiskey Rebellion reared its head in western Pennsylvania, federalists and antifederalists alike came down hard on the rural troublemakers.

As America grew from a seaboard confederation to a continental nation with imperial ambitions; as its economy grew increasingly industrial and urban; as the mobilizing impact of transportation and technology was felt (the railroad, electricity, and the internal combustion engine did more for national union than Hamilton's wildest dreams of union could have done); as populations were uprooted and agriculture lost its paramount place in American economic life; and as municipalities came to occupy a more important place in the life of individuals than states: by the time all of these momentous events had come to pass, federalism and arguments about what it meant had been transformed.

The situation today bears only the slightest resemblance of that of the Framers. There are new Leviathans on our landscape that stalk both the federal and state governments—and the liberties of individuals—namely, the multinational corporations, the media giants, the interregional unions, and the special interest groups purveying private goals in public settings. De Tocqueville's idea of civic activism at the local level has been displaced by apathy or hostility. Race relations have proved intractable to sectional and national solutions, and continue to embitter national life with a nearly undiminished force thirty years after the Civil Rights Act of 1965, forty years after the court struck down the old antifederalist separate-but-equal doctrine, more than a century after the end of the Civil War. Economic and fiscal problems are no more responsive, resisting both the costly adjustments of the market and its supply side partisans *and* the best laid plans of nationalist democrats trying to plan America to prosperity and full employment.

The old states seem almost beside the point when we look at the problems of metropolitan regions like New York, Washington, D.C., Philadelphia, or Kansas City that straddle several states and have become distinctive units of government at least as far as their problems are concerned. The U.S. Conference of Mayors may find itself better understood by the federal Congress than by the governors of the several states. Health professionals may distrust all politicians alike, seeing them as pawns of special interests lacking the capacity of the professionals to gauge the public good in disinterested terms. Bureaucracies may inadvertently come to substitute for public goals instrumental norms generated by their own institutional concerns (survival, patronage, below-the-line budget allocations, retirement benefits, etc.), but then insist on defending those norms as if they were really public goods after all.

The novelty of the modern world and its intractability to government solutions of any kind at any level can inspire in us a kind of vertigo where we feel too dizzy to think big and so content ourselves with thinking little or not thinking at all. But for all the changed circumstances—and they must be recognized and made sense of—the federalism argument remains an argument about power in the service of liberty. It ought then to be of enormous value to examine our New Federalism dilemmas in light of the old federalism debate, asking how our several options serve not a particular ideology, a particular version of good government, a model of public service administration, or a specific public policy, but rather the liberty and self-government of citizens.

Liberty was the single virtue on which federalists and antifederalists agreed; we have been diverted from that question by the enormity of the problems facing our society. If the civic dignity and self-responsibility of free individuals is the final measure of our policies and positions, then we may discover that there *are* answers to the questions of whether or not we should adopt a national health insurance plan, whether or not welfare is a federal responsibility, whether or not race relations can be left to the several states to regulate, whether or not a massive federal bureaucracy is compatible with civic activity at the local level. The answers will not necessarily conform to a single model: the virtues of localism are indisputable with respect to civic education, political participation, and the mobilization of responsible women and men in the name of self-government; the virtues of national uniformity are equally evident in guaranteeing social justice, resisting discrimination, and extending economic equality.

This suggests the argument will continue, and that its continuance will be one sign of the vitality of politics in our times. James Madison noted that America was an unprecedented historical experiment, one in which the people could not afford to suffer "a blind veneration for antiquity, for custom, or for names, to overrule the suggestions of their own good sense, the knowledge of their own situation, and the lessons of their own experience." The experiment got under way catalyzed by a quarrel, and that quarrel has become a crucial component in the flexibility and life of our constitutional system.

In the differences between President Reagan's new federalism and President Johnson's new nationalism (the Great Society) lies a dynamic that moves the entire society. To guarantee the survival of that society, we require only two things: that both sides of the argument adjust to and recognize the changing realities of our rapidly evolving world, and that both sides acknowledge the value of the argument itself. For in the final analysis, history shows that liberty has been best served in our unique system neither by the nationalist nor the sectionalist interpretation of federalism, but by the argument itself. If this is so, we should not fear argument but welcome it—and be glad that our republic still resounds with the clamor of women and men arguing over the meaning of their constitution. That clamor is the life breath of the Republic, the sign that tells us that America, for all of its massive problems, lives on in the glorious discord of its ambiguous founding—one nation, indivisible, and yet also a compact of states—states and nation alike trying to outdo one another in their service to precious liberty.

CHAPTER 11

The Market as Censor in a World of Consumer Totalism

I WANT TO USE the occasion of the inaugural Willard Pedrick Lecture to raise some fundamental questions about the relationship between democracy and community on the one hand and free expression and the arts on the other. I will not try to survey the extant literature or to offer a novel classificatory scheme. Laying further categories on the table can only lead to a kind of conceptual overload. Rather than rehearse this kind of analysis, I want to problematize the set of questions that are usually the context for the problem of censorship, and suggest that how we pose these questions may affect the kinds of answers we are able to give. The problematizing I will engage in raises issues important not only for theorists but also for citizens. That is to say, the sharply divided choices that face us when we consider the range of application of the First Amendment are not merely technical and professional but normative and practical. They create difficulties for civic life as well as for political philosophy.

I begin with the premise that the debate in this arena has been unduly constrained by an overly—some might even say imprudently—bipolar formulation of what is at stake: we are asked to choose between "the individual and the state" or "The First Amendment and the Community" or the "private and the public sectors." With such dualisms before us, we are a people riven by unsavory choices between what passes as absolute power on the one side and liberty on the other; the state on one side, the individual on the other; the community, or the majority by which it is supposedly represented, on one side, and the First Amendment, standing for the rights of the individual against the community and the majority, on the other. Such stark oppositions derive from the classical liberal model of society and politics in the West, particularly in England and the United States, and are applied without reference to the real political situation. (Louis Hartz of Harvard University once quipped that the American majority was a puppy-dog tethered to a lion's leash!) On the dichotomous liberal model, liberty is protected by separating the state as the embodiment of sovereign power from the individual as the embodiment of freedom (negatively construed as the absence of all power) and then interposing between the two domains firm constitutional barriers. As James Madison makes clear, the American Constitution enumerates powers in part in order to delimit them and so itself becomes a wall separating and protecting individuals from abuse by government (the Constitution "is a Bill of Rights," Madison insisted). In the founding era, however, Jefferson won this particular argument with Madison and we have relied not on rights implicit in the Constitution but on an explicit Bill of Rights as the primary instrument of protection for individuals and their autonomy interests against the inroads that the common and collective interests of majorities, communities, and other collectivities thought to be hostile to individuals are potentially capable of.

With this model in place, it is easy enough to identify any breach in the constitutional wall that affords the state an opportunity to penetrate the private sector (which is the cultural sector) as "censorship" or "state repression." By the same token, if the private sector overflows its boundaries denying to the sovereign its regulatory and governing mission, we identify this distending of the private sphere as "anarchy"—free expression transmogrified into licentiousness and the obliteration of public norms. Liberal states offering only these alternatives constrain citizens to constantly patrol the borders between private and public, watchful for vulnerabilities, perpetually fearful that the system will degenerate into licentiousness on the one hand or into censorship on the other. Understandably, questions relating to this policing of the boundaries become the chief concern of legal and political—no less than of journalistic and popular—debates and tend to crowd out other less dualistic concerns.

The question we must ask is whether this widely employed model of liberalism rooted in the classical conception of state power in radical opposition to individual freedom really captures the full character of the sorts of social relations that serve as the real world context for debates about censorship, pornography, and freedom of expression. There is a much richer understanding of society in which liberalism's two sharply delineated opponents need not always be the chief players. To begin with, we need to recall that liberalism has itself displayed an affinity for romanticism that in the nineteenth century created a literary alliance which was associated with the rise of nationalism and of revolutionary art. (The French Revolution offered a particularly clear mirror of the alliance). In literature, liberal romanticism constructed a vision of "The Artist as Rebel," "The Artist as Dissident against the State," and "The Artist as Anarchist Hero" that endowed economic liberalism's *homo economicus* with a soul even as it further vilified the state as an "Intolerant Aggressor" against individuals and literature—a repressive and intolerant "Enforcer of Public Standards." The quarrel that originated in the nineteenth century debate between John Stuart Mill and James FitzJames Stephen over whether the state is obliged to respect private liberty or enforce moral norms and that has been rehearsed in recent times by H. L. A. Hart and Lord Devlin is the reflection in law and philosophy of the controversy among liberal romantics. If the moralists see the state as art's guide and censor, the romantics see art as the state's critic and nemesis. Thus, James Agee could insist in the 1930s, "a good artist is a deadly enemy of society."

Romanticism's spin on the liberal dichotomization of state and individual managed then, if anything, to exacerbate the polarization. The artist as anarchist becomes a permanent and implacable adversary of the political process itself; self-expression becomes inherently oppositional. And of course when society is democratic, the adversarial artist becomes not merely an enemy of the state but an enemy of the people — an anarchist or a Nietzschean *Übermensch*. Whether the individual artist is understood in terms of the romantic rebel or, to use Lionel Trilling's phrase in his study of the liberal imagination, "the solitary esthete," or even as "the narcissistic genius," her space — his space — is the artist's own: sacred, private, inviolable. A liberal society opts to protect such unencumbered conceptions of the individual artist via the Bills of Rights and other constitutional guarantees, sometimes turning the artist (all too often, with the artist's enthusiastic cooperation) into a kind of paradigmatic recluse, the liberal individual defined not just by freedom but by solitude and homelessness.

This same dichotomous perspective is found in modern liberal political philosophy. The priority of liberty is a feature of nearly all modern liberal theory from John Rawls to Robert Nozick, from social welfare liberalism to anti-statist libertarianism. To prioritize liberty is to privilege it, to cast it as an inertial resting point, any movement away from which demands justification. "Born free" and "natural freedom" are two expressions of liberty's privileged position in liberal theory. It is not the individual and individual freedom but the community and community's common objectives that demand prima facie legitimization, the community's encroachments on the individual that are to be justified.

These observations suggest that much of the character of the contemporary discussion of censorship and the First Amendment derives from a conception of players who — whether they are artists or individuals — are either self-segregating, rights-bearing individuals, or overbearing and intolerant collectivities. Liberalism's privileged "private ones," whether they are advancing private opinions or telling prophetic truths or forging novel science or creating new art, locate themselves in a space outside of the state and segregated from society's public places and thereby place themselves in ineluctable tension with the community, which always appears to them as a censorious collectivity pursuing goals whose commonality can be secured (they believe) only at the expense of their liberty — the liberty of the individual. The choices this conception of the individual affords are few; indeed, the conception itself reflects a certain contempt for the mediated and the dialectical. As a consequence, those who buy into this conception find it easier to take positions on the extremes than in the middle. They are forced into a kind of First Amendment absolutism that continues to make political choices in the domain of censorship stark and unpalatable.

Contrarily, defenders of the rights of communities wishing to posit and secure common mores are compelled by the divisive liberal rhetoric of rights to mimic Lord Devlin's harsh language invoking state enforcement of morals. Perhaps that is why American moralists like Jesse Helms, or more temperately, William Bennett, despite their conservative distaste for governmental intrusions into the private realm in the economic domain, fall so easily into the language of enforcement and social repression when they take on social issues such as birth control, Hollywood films, porn on the Internet, or heterosexual divorce and gay marriage. And, although communitarians like Amitai Etzioni have been careful to avoid letting the concern for community rights become an excuse for statism, the communitarian persuasion often lapses into repressive moralism and the enforcement of moral codes and norms on recalcitrant, supposedly self-absorbed individuals.

In a debate where rights' absolutism and communitarian repression are the only available alternatives, it is not always so easy to locate mediating positions in a hypothetical civil center. Ensuing controversy tends, as a consequence, to be divisive and constricting and (perhaps more importantly) abstracted from actual conditions and hence largely unreal. Whether the argument is conducted in the heated rhetoric of Catharine MacKinnon's *Only Words,* where speech *is* action, and where consequently words are susceptible to censorship on the same grounds that permit the state to constrain behavior; or whether it is conducted in the liberal judiciary's preemptory language that not only privileges individual speech but allows it to trump all other competing values so that individual rights always triumph over community norms, our choice seems to be either to enthrone the majority and ignore the individual's liberties or to secure absolutely the freedom of private persons by turning communal goals into synonyms for tyranny. A paltry menu of choices at best!

I start then with the premise that if we are to progress beyond such a menu we need to start by exploding the dualistic, the dichotomous, the radically two-celled version of state and individual, of power and liberty, of community and artist, that is liberalism's favorite paradox. In place of the two-celled model, I propose we employ an approach that describes social space with at least three cells or sectors where the lines between the community and the individual are blurred and their overlapping character becomes visible. This three-celled model exposes the economic marketplace not simply as a variation on the private sector or civil society but as a domain unto itself not only distinctive from civil society but with a potential for corrupting it. For what the two-celled version of the state and

individual obscures is precisely the capacity market economics has to undermine the associative ties that typify civil society. The absence of an
economic perspective, of a willingness to scrutinize the impact of the
market on art, on culture, and on self-expression in free societies represents
a telling and remarkable lapse and leaves a gargantuan hole in the debate
about self-expression and censorship. If we fail to acknowledge the hidden
and soft forms of censorship found in the marketplace, we ignore a peril to
both community and individuals, a peril nearly as invidious as, because so
much less obvious than, that of tyrannical governments.

Let me suggest, then, that instead of positing a two-celled world of states
and individuals, we assume a social world in which there are at least three
cells and thus three distinctive forms of social identity (or asocial identity). Two of the three are the familiar domains of state (politics) and
individual (private sector), but consider now between them a putative
third sector, neither governmental nor private but independent—civil society understood precisely as (to use the name of a well-known national civil
association) "the independent sector." In civil society understood as a third
sector, individuals encounter one another neither as voters or politicians
or citizens under the formal, legal arrangements of the constitution, nor
as producers or consumers or clients in the economic market; rather, they
encounter one another as neighbors, friends, and collaborators. Even when
they are strangers, they are "commoners," or, in the broadest generic sense,
citizens—not simply voters or taxpayers or jurists or opinion mongers but
as women and men who are perpetually active, taking responsibility for
their local communities, working in local block associations or participating in local charities or organizing neighborhood social movements,
say, in protest against redlining or a toxic waste site.

In this more complex picture of a three-celled social universe in which
citizens need neither be assimilated to majorities nor reduced to private
consumers, a number of important things happen to the debate about free
speech, political discourse, and cultural expression. Foremost among them
is the recognition that an overweening government, a too intrusive state,
an intemperate majority, loathsome as they are to unfettered individuality,
are far from being the only enemies of liberty or the sole potential censors
of free expression and political discourse. There are also forms of "censorship," that is to say, ways of chilling expression and effectively repressing
speech, that do not take the form of state sanctions or rely on the heavy
onus of public opinion (de Tocqueville's worry), but emanate instead from
the dynamics of a market sector that is driven by profit alone, and that is
often competitive (and thus pluralistic in the useful democratic sense) in
name only. Such bonds, if that is not too strong a term, are far less visible:
harder to discern, more difficult to talk about, and certainly less capable
of being defended against by the kinds of formal barriers raised by legal

institutions, constitutions, or bills of rights. The bonds of the market are braided cords of velvet and feel soft, even comfortable, and thus seem welcome.

When Madison reminded us that bills of rights were but "parchment barriers" against tyranny, he was thinking about the kinds of civil and moral institutions necessary to make democracy work. Thus did Jean-Jacques Rousseau, after detailing in the first two books of his *Social Contract* the mechanics of democratic decision-making in the process he called general willing, acknowledge that a purely formal approach was insufficient. And so he went on in the third and fourth books to stipulate the background conditions upon which real democracy depended for its successful functioning (austerity, a young and simple people, common mores, a civil religion, and so on). Rousseau spoke in this spirit when he talked about the dependence of democratic institutions on an underlying democratic culture. It seems evident that if bills of rights cannot in themselves even be counted upon to obviate political tyranny, then in themselves they are likely to do still less to avert the softer forms of censorship that arise out of the private market sector, where we see ourselves, first of all, as producers and consumers and only later, if at all, as neighbors, citizens or members of a political community capable of adducing common goods.

Once we have replaced a stark oppositional portrait of public and private with a three-celled perspective that encompasses state, civil society, and the private market, the sharpness of the distinction between power and liberty is softened and the boundaries separating the individual and the community are blurred. With civil society understood to be a domain separate from the market, we can for the first time take the market seriously as a domain separate from and potentially invidious to culture. New questions become possible: Is art also a commodity, and as a commodity does it condition the free speech of artists? Can the products of free expression be treated as a special kind of property, namely intellectual property? Does that mean they can be bought and sold? Writers nowadays are all too familiar with the phrase "work-for-hire," which treats the writer as a laborer, a producer of artistic commodities whose labor power can be purchased and whose labor output ("art content") become a wholly owned property of the purchaser. The writer who does work-for-hire neither owns her words not preserves any rights—economic, legal, or artistic—over them. It is not art but the artist who is bought, both the artistic talent as well as the words and images it produces.

Another telling feature of the special role the economic domain has come to play in altering how we see free expression and the First Amendment is evident in the field of advertising. Traditionally, it has been argued by historians like Walter Berns that the primary concern of the founders as they harped on the protection of free expression was with political speech—that affinity for debate, controversy, and pluralism of opinion that they regarded as the sine qua non of democracy. Yet because the liberal model identifies the individual with the private sector and the private sector with commerce, the federal courts have today not only ceased to distinguish commercial from political speech, but seem to have arrived at the conclusion that commercial speech is as worthy of or perhaps even worthier of protection than mere political speech. Sometimes it seems that those who burn the American flag in protest are less likely to get a sympathetic public hearing than those who stitch it into designer underwear. And, in an odd reversal, what passes as political discourse on television— the kind of polarizing, uncivil, anti-rational discourse we are proffered by programs like *The McLaughlin Group* and *Crossfire* that do mimic political discourse in a certain sense—seems as interested in commerce (ratings, selling soap) as in political education. Free expression in the arts on the other hand, although not necessarily contributory to political debate directly, does undergird the variety and creativity of the civic sphere and engenders the imaginative powers that are democracy's guarantors. Yet it finds far fewer defenders than does commercial speech. In a domain in which success is measured by profit, however, neither political nor cultural expression is necessarily very secure. We need not agree entirely with Walter Bern's view that the First Amendment's primary objective was to protect political speech and thereby secure democracy to understand that pornography and commercial speech were not foremost on the constitutional agenda of the founders. Nor did they seem to fear that censorship of pornography sent a democracy careening down some slippery slope that bottomed out only with the destruction of the Constitution and the eradication of all liberty. The slipperiness of slopes depends in any case on their angle of incline, on their surfaces, and on the agility of those who negotiate them—all matters of historical and social context. Goats are not known to fall down rocky mountainsides however steeply inclined, while bugs in a jar slide back down the sides into the center. It may be that in a civil society with a centrist U-shaped profile like ours, the political ground slopes upward on either side from the center as it approaches the extremes, leaving things to slide, if anywhere, back toward the center. In a Lockean consensual society, one might say, slippery slopes all lead back to a safe middle ground, and so we have little to fear from them.

The courts certainly have a prominent role to play in protecting unpopular but obviously political speech. But the problem is more complex with respect to free expression in the civic culture generally, where civil society is understood to be a shared domain of citizens, of spectators, of artists, of cultural creators, and thus a domain which, while distinct from both the government and the market sectors, is crucial to the healthy functioning of both. Civil society has its own softer governance procedures, it has its own rules, and it has forms of speech that can neither be fully secured by, nor easily prohibited by, either the state or the market, although both the state and the market can influence their flowering or decline. The Bill of Rights cannot by itself keep civic culture from decay any more than the private sector can "buy" a flourishing civil society by treating art and culture as for-profit commodities. Civic relations are not the same as commercial and contract relations, and the reciprocity of neighbors, the interactivity of women and men who participate in local governance, or who interact as artists and audience around cultural activities, look very different from the relations of buyers or sellers (or at least ought to look different).

It is in civil society, in fact, that the crucial institutions nourishing to a free society and to free expression are found. Yet the civil domain all too often plays little or no role in the debates about censorship and the First Amendment. Similarly, although it is through education—particularly civic education and arts education—that a climate can be created in which it is possible to cultivate reciprocal speech, tolerance, and a popular willingness to accept that artists may from time to time have to take risks or appear "offensive" or worse, education strategies aimed at cultivating such a climate are rarely discussed. In sum, only in civil society away from the raucous discourse of rights are we likely to be able to instill (and to benefit from) positive attitudes towards culture and to cultivate ("cultivate" as in "culture") an environment in which art is appreciated. Only under these circumstances will artists be released from uncertain dependency on the courts to protect them from what are supposed to be their audience and their supporters.

In fact, ironically, the arts may actually become more fragile when we place a wall between the artist and society and treat the two as potential adversaries. As we demand from a democratic culture an appreciation of the vital role artists play, even when they are being subversive and offensive, we have to demand from artists an appreciation of the concerns a community may have about the impact of subversive and offensive art on its communal norms. To put it another way, the rights that artists enjoy under a rights-oriented constitution to express themselves freely, although formally speaking a matter of law, depend in practice on the willingness of artists to take a certain responsibility for the communities to which they belong. Decoupling rights from responsibilities here as elsewhere ultimately weakens not only the moral appeal of obligation but the moral force of rights. Artists uninterested in arts education, a society unwilling to fund arts education in the schools—and we know that the first curricular domain to be sacrificed when schools are de-funded is arts education— mean a society unlikely to see a flourishing of the artist, let alone tolerance for his or her sometimes perverse, always provocative artifacts. That remains true whatever the laws say, and whatever stipulations may be found in constitutional protections of speech.

By the same token, an America, a Europe, a world in which civil society is diminished because it offers neither the time nor the space for public discourse, will be a world in which culture is vulnerable and the place of artists ambiguous. As civic culture declines, so the role of culture is diminished and the compass of free expression constricted.

New York City boasts a remarkable theater called Town Hall. Art galleries, theaters, and museums are all, at their best, town halls made for the public, open to the public, constitutive of what a public is. In small towns, the town hall is often itself also the community hall, the amateur theater, even the occasional gallery for a local exhibition. One of the tragedies of suburbanization in America (and over 55 percent of Americans now live in suburbs) is the vanishing of public space. There are no town halls, no granges, no public squares, no downtown churches or galleries or schools, because there are no "towns," no uptowns or downtowns, no center cities. The few public dwellings that exist like schools and municipal works buildings are spread around everywhere, adjacent (literally) to nowhere, usually abutting an interstate, just a few *Minutes from the Blue Route* in the title of Tom Donaghy's black comedy about the suburbs. In the psychic and political place where the public square could once be found are now shopping malls. Strip malls, enclosed malls, these are the new "public" spaces of suburbia, often named after our vanished public squares ("Bridgewater Commons"), except there is nothing public about them. In many states they have been declared "private" by state courts, and everywhere they are dominated by a single pervasive activity: consumerism.

How then are we to develop a political discourse, a flourishing arts culture, a respect for language and a tolerance of, even an appetite for civil disagreement, in a world in which there are no public squares? Where do citizens have a chance to confront and argue with one another? Not simply to interact vertically with elites but to interact laterally with one another? Can the idea of public speech be meaningful in the absence of the public square? The death of small towns and the death of the large city neighborhood and its replacement by soulless and townless suburbs may do more to "repress" speech and art in this country than any amount of state censorship could ever do. Nor can government funding create a thriving culture in a marketplace made barren by its single-minded devotion to consumption. Yet such soft forms of—we cannot really say "repression," so let us say constraint—are largely invisible and cannot be countered by court order. In a public world reduced to the private marketplace, it is not only politics that vanishes but the very concept of a public and thus of public goods, public will, and public interest. Culture and art are public goods: without public space and a community to inhabit it, they too disappear, transmogrified into private commodities.

When visitors come to my hometown of Piscataway, New Jersey (across the river from Rutgers University) and suggest to me, "Let's go to town," I never know where to take them. There is no town, no center, no public square. There are a couple of corporate parks, strip malls galore, heavily trafficked throughways, a Township Offices building off of a four-lane highway, but there is literally no town. There must have been one once upon a time, because Piscataway was incorporated in 1766. Head out to one of the upscale enclosed malls in the "neighborhood" (we might more accurately call it the "mallhood"), and you will find neither an amateur theater nor an art gallery nor a child-care center nor a storefront mayor's office. Not even a real restaurant; they interfere with shopping, so food in the form of shopper's fuel is offered only in a fast food court guaranteed to prevent shoppers from lingering over coffee. What you will find of course are stores, stores, stores—an efficient instrument of retail commerce in which consumption is the only activity permitted. Even the stores are likely to be boutiques and gadget palaces like Brookstone's or The Sharper Image that cater, quite precisely, to image rather than to real need (try to find a hardware store or dry cleaners at the mall). These new commercial spaces serve only one dimension of our humanity—the impulse to consume.

The consumer is obviously an identity that defines one part of our being as human animals. And consumption can be a pleasant activity an hour or two a day. But increasingly we live in a world where the only thing we can do in our "free" time is shop. Television and the Internet are also being turned into instrumentalities of the market, with "push" technologies displacing real interactivity. The new technological pushers have a lot in common with street-pushers: they both pretend to cater to needs which they are in fact busy helping to manufacture. Consumption marginalizes both the creation and appreciation of art, turning it into product and commodity. No wonder that the discussion of free speech is for the most part an issue for elites—for intellectuals, writers, and artists about whom the country at large is little concerned. It is probably not realistic to expect a people who understand culture and free expression to refer to commercial soft-core pornography or *Crossfire* scream matches to be much interested in their protection.

By the same token, one might say that the need for censorship vanishes in a society dominated by commerce because the market provides its own forms of soft censorship. Two examples: when I first came to New Brunswick in the 1970s, there were only two movie theaters in what was then a decaying central Jersey blue-collar town from which the only two viable white-collar enterprises, Rutgers University and Johnson & Johnson, were hoping to escape (though both later changed their minds). Both movie-houses showed a menu of commercial films of the kind that could be found throughout America. One might say, within Hollywood's rather con-stricting menu, people had a choice. In the mid-70s, there was a radical and discomfiting change. Both theaters started showing nothing but por-nography. Locals could no longer choose between genres and types of films. Yet no tyrannical decision had been taken by a totalitarian govern-ment, no prurient de Sadian censor had been at work winnowing out all but the filthiest works. On the contrary, the abrupt constriction of choice was a direct product of market freedom, of commercial forces that made it cheaper and more profitable for local filmhouses to distribute and show porn than traditional Hollywood fare. Had some wayward government announced, "From this moment on, you will only see pornography! Every other kind of entertainment will be banned!" there would have been a riot, a political revolution. But this was the work of the market, so people wrung their hands, shrugged their shoulders, and went silently on.

A similar tyranny is now at work around the world where, in nations that once had robust indigenous film industries, American films are now showing on 90 percent of the screens. And even in America, in all but a few cosmopolitan cities, you will see only a few dozen films—the same ones, not porn but Hollywood hoopla—everywhere. One shoe fits all. There is no question of censorship here, no Star Chamber watching from above. Yet the effects on our diversity are surely just as significant as if the state had ordained that only those large-scale Hollywood films would be shown. We speak about the self-regulation of the film industry via the ratings systems (and now V-chips), but the most serious self-regulation comes from the market's catering to centrist, majority tastes where ratings are sovereign and profits are king. The self-rating system is itself a kind of censorship since few filmmakers or distributors can afford losing their market edge by accepting, say, an NC-17 or even an R rating on films from which they hope to make a significant profit. Hence, when the courageous defenders of the First Amendment (as Milos Forman and Oliver Stone portrayed themselves) who made *The People vs. Larry Flynt* came to the question of whether to actually show onscreen the misogynist and racist porn that had made *Hustler* magazine a success, they demurred. The market can defend the First Amendment but thinks twice before actually showing the stuff the First Amendment is being celebrated for protecting! Had director Forman done so with his romanticized Larry Flynt, not only would he have turned his putative hero into the money-grubbing bigot he was and thereby have lost the audience's sympathy, but he would have received an X rating and would have failed to win general distribution and so would have been denied both profitability and fame (Academy Award consideration, for example).

When we homogenize and sanitize from below in the name of marketing strategy, we impose a form of silencing less tyrannical but perhaps even more effective than anything censoring governments do. The market controls through homogenization—trickle-up censorship via an increasingly plastic culture in America and an increasingly homogenous culture around the globe I have called "McWorld".

When I first spent time in Europe in the 1950s as a student, my experience was one of a stunning and seemingly unassimilable diversity. The cultural changes (within what was already hoping to become a single Europe) one found as one journeyed from Stockholm to Paris, from London to Rome, from Davos in Switzerland to Cracow in Poland, were staggering. Such differences in cultures, speech, politics, and identity are the very essence of what it is we mean to protect with devices like the Bill of Rights. In our diversity, after all, lies one essential dimension of our humanity. That dimension is perhaps the most crucial object of the protections we direct toward free expression and free speech. Rights help preserve diversity, pluralism, and our individual and group distinctiveness, but they cannot combat the corrosive effect of a uniformitarian commercial culture whose depredations are actually implemented in the name of freedom.

It would be an insult to those who have lived under the political despotisms once called "totalitarianism" to refer to the power commerce has to homogenize and destroy civic space as totalitarian, but I would propose that there is something inadvertently totalizing about it—which is what led Herbert Marcuse in the 1960s to speak of "one-dimensional man," and caused earlier critics to worry about "art in the age of mechanical reproduction" and about the "culture industry" (Walter Benjamin, Theodore Adorno, Max Horkheimer). There are artists who claim to feel freer under explicitly repressive political regimes than they do under free market conditions: "We were never so free as under the Occupation," wrote Sartre in paying ironic tribute to the capacity of direct repression from above to keep the spirit of resistance alive. It is the market's greatest virtue and its most infuriating vice that it offers no resistance to subversives and rebels. Like toffee, it yields and absorbs and swallows up, neutralizing without ever acknowledging its radical critics. The possibilities for a resilient human diversity are not then necessarily expanded by the marshmallow market where the lure of profit and reputation gradually, but surely, undermine the forms of creative expression and individuality despotism once tried, unsuccessfully, to vanquish overnight.

I flew directly from London to Phoenix to offer the original lecture version of this essay. It is hotter and drier in Phoenix, but parts of London today are indistinguishable from Tempe—or Berlin or Hong Kong or, for that matter, Beijing (where Kentucky Fried Chicken and McDonald's have set up shop and Disney is planning a theme park and international hotel chains are cloning their remorselessly international style). Japan has one of the world's most distinctive cultures, but without any government intervention or regulation the number one and two (by volume) restaurants in the country are McDonald's and Kentucky Fried Chicken. Defenders of global markets insist that cultural assimilation is a two-way path, and that as pop music, fast food, and the Internet ring the world and transform its once diverse cultures, it in turn transforms them. Look at reggae, they retort. Notice how in Paris, you can drink wine and read *Le Monde* in fast-food emporia. Perhaps. But, McWorld is a python, and the cultures it gobbles up are so many hares; and while a python who has consumed a hare does, it is true, acquire the rotund profile of a hare for a day or two, at the end of the week the hare is gone and the svelte python, looking very much like the snake he is, is still oiling his way around, stalking new prey.

The urban metropolis, once a site of diversity and cultural heterogeneity, is gradually succumbing to a malling that is also a mauling. As London becomes Tempe and Tempe becomes Los Angeles, all cities become parodies of themselves. Take that paradigmatic city, New York. As the communication and information conglomerates such as Disney/ABC and the Bertelsman Company move into Times Square, Manhattan is being "saved" and renovated by being robbed of its particularity. Even as its image is cloned to create a facade for a Las Vegas casino, the original is undergoing radical surgery to look more like suburban Las Vegas. Potsdammerplatz in Berlin (on what was the border between East and West) is being treated to a similar makeover, though the architects there at least began with a wasteland. In neither city has government been allowed more than a facilitating role—"helping" the market through tax breaks and an appropriately deregulatory mien. And since it is the market that is master, no one would dare speak of government tyranny or architectural censorship. But could any political tyrant ever imagine he might redesign and thus redefine a great city so painlessly, with so little resistance, no, so much cooperation from those being reconstructed in someone else's plastic image of their own vanishing true selves? With the market, self-liquidation always feels like freedom, and always ends up as freedom trivialized, as with that mid-Western baked potato chain that advertises its all-American character by mouthing the all-American mantra "We give you liberty!" and then hastily adds, "The liberty to choose your own toppings!"

How is it then that our own consumer choices can create a homogenous, repressive, uniform society? By the magic of the market—through what pass as our own free choices which, when made one by one, have collective consequences we cannot predict but for which we are held responsible.

This is not an argument about manipulated consumer freedom (although there is such an argument to be made—otherwise, the global advertising industry would presumably not be spending a quarter of a trillion dollars a year trying to change our minds). It is rather an argument about the social impotence of private choices. For *private* choices have *public* consequences that can only be dealt with via public institutions for which the market does not provide and against which market ideologues wage a silent war.

The aim of this rather ferocious critique of the market is to thicken our description of the social context that surrounds controversies about the First Amendment—to move them out of the bi-polar debate about state and individual and put them into the context of civil society ("missing" civil society). To do so is to recall that there are ways to control the human soul far more effectively than a gun pointed at the head, or manacles attached to wrists, or a cage around the body. When, at the end of *Mother Courage* we see Bertolt Brecht's weary protagonist still pulling the trader's wagon that ties her fate to war and has cost her the very lives of her children, it is her ignorance and "heroic" blindness that fasten her to the heavy cart, not someone else's bonds. She need only let go of its draft handles to be free of everything it stands for—above all the reciprocity of war and commerce. But that it is a bondage of her own "choosing"—if the discretion of ignorance can be called choice—only makes that bondage the more powerful and poignant.

The market rules because we reach out to grasp it; to be rid of it, we need only let go. But that turns out to be harder than severing chains imposed on us by others against our will. The enemies of free discourse and unencumbered artistic expression turn out to be not just narrow-minded and prurient politicians like Senator Jesse Helms or Representative Tom Coburn (who deemed Steven Spielberg's holocaust film *Schindler's List* unsuitable for television because of what he perceived as its raunchy nudity and disgusting violence), such adversaries can be countered both in our courts of law and in the court of public opinion (Coburn quickly backed down). Far more dangerous are the invisible restraints of the market—precisely because the market is "free."

I will not here rehearse the arguments I have developed in *Jihad vs. McWorld* about the ways in which the free global market is being occupied by transnational conglomerates that turn a putative zone of freedom into an actual realm of monopoly. Yet the question of who owns McWorld impinges in obvious ways on the question of whether the market is free or not. If diversity, pluralism, and the contest of ideas—if different voices and different views are the crux of what it means to be an artist, to be a democrat and to be a citizen—then surely, the growing control by fewer and fewer corporations of all media, of the means and modes of communication, and of the conduits of information and entertainment is a disaster for free expression. For both art and democracy have at their core how we communicate with one another, and those who control communication control art and democracy, offering a far greater threat to our liberties than, say, the National Endowment for the Arts' funding priorities.

Ben Bagdikian showed with clarity in his *The Media Monopoly* that since 1945, when control over America's newspapers, magazines, radio stations, ballparks, and publishing houses was spread out among hundreds and hundreds of companies in a lively competition that often pitted three or four (or more) papers against one another in a single town and featured legal prohibitions by a conscientious government against one kind of media firm from owning another, there has been a gradual contraction of ownership capped by the vertical integration mergers and acquisition frenzy of the last fifteen years that have resulted today in just a half dozen firms—transnational companies that own film studios, satellite television systems, publishing houses, theme parks, sports teams—who hold more than half of the global business in information, communication, and entertainment in their hands. The effects of this conglomeration on our capacity for diversity, free speech, and cultural expression are just beginning to be felt. Broadway can support only mega-hit musicals; the dozens of dramatic plays that once enjoyed the favor of audiences there have vanished. Publishing houses, now almost entirely subsidiary to corporations for whom books are merely another commodity, produce mainly celebrity books while the "middle novel" and the serious, small circulation mid-list nonfiction title are disappearing. They are not viable in a world where publishers struggle to earn the mega-profits expected from their non-publisher owners. An 8 to 10 percent profit margin, on which many traditional publishers survived for a century or more, is no longer acceptable. No new laws have been passed mandating mass marketing, but the unwritten economic law of blockbuster marketing ("Don't do it unless it has a chance to be a market-smashing monster-hit!") is far more efficient than the mandates of Stalinist tyrants trying to impose some ideology or other.

When we come then to debate the First Amendment, we need to shift our gaze from the formal, legal, and constitutional to the informal, social, and economic. When we do so, it becomes apparent that many of the real threats to free expression, diversity, and artistic freedom cannot be addressed by courts or the application of liberal rules demarcating the state and private spheres. The enemies of freedom who today stalk the private sector are part of the market's defining essence. If we hope to preserve the rights of artists, we will have to nourish the responsibilities of citizens. If we want a zone of free expression, we need a place for civil society. If we hope to preserve free expression, we will have to secure genuine economic competition—the kind of real entrepreneurial capitalism that prohibits monopoly, regulates trusts, and guarantees variety. That will only happen when democratic governments are again allowed to play their mediating role on behalf of citizens.

Liberty in all its forms depends on an independent sector. To be sure, independence from statist coercion is one important condition for that sector's autonomy. But independence from market forces, commercial homogenization, and consumer uniformity is equally important. And until we find a surrogate for what the First Amendment does in protecting the individual from political tyranny that will also protect the citizen and the artist from market constraints, neither free expression nor cultural creativity will be secure, and all the political and legal debates about the First Amendment and censorship that occupy us today will in a certain sense remain moot.

Part III

EDUCATION FOR DEMOCRACY: CIVIC EDUCATION, SERVICE, AND CITIZENSHIP

CHAPTER 12

Thomas Jefferson and the Education
of the Citizen

IN THE YEARS following World War II, as education became professional-ized and vocationalized, it was increasingly decoupled from the life and practice of democracy. Today, while education is widely discussed, the focus on performance, standards, global competition, and outcomes has largely eclipsed the linkage to citizenship.* Yet civic pedagogy and public schooling have always been central to those who advocate democratic forms of governance. Nowhere is this more evident than in the thought of Thomas Jefferson, where the nurturing of education often seemed more crucial than the nurturing of politics in the Jeffersonian account of demo-cratic practices. Dumas Malone has noted the relationship between politi-cal liberty and the cultivation of the spirit in Jefferson, and Merrill Peterson has argued that Jefferson's faith in freedom and self-government was at bottom a faith in education.

From the time of the Greeks, who spoke of *paideia* as the educational and cultural practices around which a just republican society rooted in the rule of the demes could alone be established, the very meaning of citizenship has been informed by reference to particular understandings of civic education and the transformation of ordinary private human be-ings into citizens. The citizen, it has been argued, is the calculating egoist *educated* to public judgment; the citizen is the corrupt merchant *induced* to virtue; the citizen is the bigoted individual *conditioned* to tolerance; the citizen is the impulsive actor *trained* to deliberateness; the citizen is the adversary *taught* to seek common ground with her opponent. The standards will vary, but all traditional political theory—liberal, republi-can, and democratic—insists that citizens are created rather than born,

* This essay was originally written as part of a Library of Congress symposium on Jefferson and Education, and in addition to this general discussion, it included several focused analyses of conference papers. After several years of delay, it appears that the collected papers (in-cluding an earlier version of this one) will be published by the Library. In the meanwhile, I have edited out specific references to these papers (to which I do refer in several notes). Nonetheless, my own expression of views here owes much to the spirit of the four authors with whom I originally interacted. The four are Douglas Wilson, Richard D. Brown, Herbert A. Johnson, and Jennings L. Waggoner, Jr., and I remain in their debt for their careful scholarship on Jefferson's educational philosophy and practices. I also benefited from the commentary of other conference participants, in particular Gordan Wood's contribution.

products not of nature but of educational artifice. As human beings we may be born free, but civil liberty is an acquisition for which we need education. It is not democratic theorists but only their inattentive detractors who have asserted that democracy is only the rule of the mob and that citizens are only self-interested individuals operating in the political arena.

For democratic theorists, education has defined not merely citizenship, but democracy itself. Where is the apostle of democracy who advocates the unbridled governance of masses? More even than the critics of democracy, the proponents have worried about the fitness of the people to govern themselves. That it is their natural right does not in itself capacitate them to do so. The right is not the ability. The normative claim of democracy is disclosed by the phrase "government by, of, and for the people," but its effective operationalization depends on government by, of, and for citizens—a people educated in the arts of liberty.

Without education, democracy may mean little more than the tyranny of opinion over wisdom. From Plato to Alexander Hamilton and Allan Bloom, critics of democracy have complained that to empower the people is to elevate ignorance to the throne. Indeed, many Federalist founders distrusted popular government (if not central government) to a point where they were willing to exercise quite extraordinary constitutional ingenuity in circumventing the popular sovereignty nominally undergirding their new republic. Representative government can be seen as their compromise between natural republican aristocracy in which the best govern a sovereign people whose sovereignty is limited to accountability, and democracy in which the subjects and the rulers are one and the same, and in which all citizens partaking regularly in the affairs of government govern themselves. The compromise of representation (sometimes call Madisonian) permitted the many to choose the few, but vested governing power in the few, thereby filtering out the passions and prejudices of the sovereign many. With its astonishing panoply of representative institutions—the college of electors, the indirect election of the president and Senate, state nominating conventions—representative government was meant to guarantee excellence without violating the spirit of popular sovereignty. Its multiple filters insulated the people from their prejudices by separating the prejudiced from the rulers, distancing the best from the rest, assuring a government of natural excellence in a setting of popular sovereignty.

Now Thomas Jefferson was no less exercised by the possibility that democracy might enthrone ignorance than were his fellow Virginians. He too sought a system of filtration by which government might be insulated from passion. His appeals to elective aristocracy have been duly noted by critics of direct democracy. But Jefferson's discriminating "filters" were to be installed within rather than between men. Rather than separate men from government, he wished to school them in government. People in power are often indiscreet, for power breeds indiscretion in the wise as well as the foolish.

> Cherish therefor the spirit of our people keep alive their attention. Do not be severe upon their errors, but reclaim them by enlightening them. If once they become inattentive to public affairs, you and I and Congress and Assemblies, judges and governors, shall all become wolves. (Letter to Edward Carrington, January 16, 1787)

The trick was, however, not to take from the people a power that was rightfully theirs (and which, in other hands, would be vulnerable to still more dangerous abuses); not to withdraw a power they might use indiscreetly, but rather to "inform their discretion."[1] Jefferson never imagined that the common birthright of liberty meant the actual equality in talent and ability of all those born free. The birthright of freedom was a study in immanence, and the actualization of liberty required much more than just getting born. While no less devoted to the idea of a natural aristocracy of talent than was any founder, he believed that popular sovereignty entailed popular government and popular government could transcend popular ignorance only by way of popular education. In this knowledge, he drafted the 1779 Virginia Bill for the More General Diffusion of Knowledge, and made the founding of a public university in Virginia the primary work of his postpresidential years. On his gravestone he memorialized not his presidency but his role as founder.

Precisely because he saw in democracy a test of discretion and judgment, he made education the keystone of the governmental arch. To filter the passions by filtering the potentially passionate out of government not only risked error—who could assure that it would not be the wealthy or the privileged (the artificial aristocracy) rather than the wise and judicious (the natural aristocracy) who found their way into service?—but it violated the fundamental logic of democracy. If men could not be trusted to govern themselves, how on earth could they be trusted to govern others? No, Jefferson concluded:

> [T]he people, especially when moderately instructed, are the only safe, because the only honest, depositories of the public rights, and should therefore be introduced into the administration of them in every function to which they are sufficient. (Letter to A. Coray, October 31, 1823)

To put it simply, Thomas Jefferson preferred education to representation as democracy's guarantor. In his case, this choice was a necessity because he did not think a democracy could survive rooted solely in indirect governance and in that version of original consent which for many members of the founding generation was sufficient to establish a liberal republican constitution. Like Rousseau, he worried that representation forced people to alienate their liberty. If one took seriously the claim that liberty was inalienable—the central claim of the social contract tradition—then a form of representative government in which liberty was alienated to representatives risked the destruction of the self-evident rights on which the constitution rested. In a Kantian language that was certainly not Jefferson's but one he might nevertheless appreciate, we might say that autonomous principles first agreed on by unanimous consent (the social contract itself as a founding covenant) quickly become heteronomous when passed on to succeeding generations. The laws of usufruct applied to precepts as well as produce: principles belong to those who use and embrace them rather than to those who merely inherit them. Thus, Jefferson insisted, constitutions were not to be looked upon with "sanctimonious reverence" but had to be reinvoked, reembraced, reinvigorated generation by generation—if necessary, by blood struggle.

In Jefferson's take on liberty, one senses a certain kinship between democracy and revolution, a linkage which Richard Mathews has placed at the center of his work. The democratic will had to reassert itself spontaneously in each generation and within each citizen. The birthright of liberty as potential came alive only in the practice of liberty. Whereas champions of the social contract reasoned that the original consent of founders coupled with the tacit consent of those who subsequently obeyed its precepts sufficed to legitimize a government as democratic, Jefferson understood democratic legitimacy to reside in a series of ongoing choices made afresh by each generation of citizens.

To understand the place of revolutionary ardor in Jefferson's perspective on democracy, we need to look at the spirit associated with political spontaneity—that sense of fresh ownership that each generation brings to a constitution or political order through its participation in the political process. Jefferson was hardly a model for Trotsky, but there was a sense in which he embraced the idea of permanent revolution. For his object was in a certain sense to make revolution commonplace, to make it a permanent feature of the political landscape rather than just leaving it as a founding mechanism for a new, more legitimate politics of stasis. Democracy's chief guarantor was not accountability but participation, not representation but local government. The cry "divide the country into wards" with which Jefferson liked to conclude letters and speeches during one phase of his career was a reminder to the young republic that devolving power into the hands of citizens was a surer way to protect against the abuse of power than to insulate the power holders from popular prejudice via representative institutions.

Following Rousseau's insight that liberty represented was liberty lost (at least with respect to the fundamentals of the sovereign will), Benjamin Rush had reminded would-be democrats that though in the American system "all power is derived from the people, they possess it only on the days of their elections."[2] Jefferson, who loved "dreams of the future more than history of the past" (letter to John Adams, August 1, 1816),[3] had a special sensitivity to the centrality (and fragility) of revolutionary zeal. He warned against looking "at constitutions with sanctimonious reverence, and deem[ing] them like the arc of the covenant, too sacred to be touched" (letter to Samuel Kercheval, July 12, 1816), and he is known famously for his insistence that "the tree of liberty must be refreshed from time to time with the blood of patriots and tyrants. It is its natural manure" (letter to Col. William Stevens Smith, November 13, 1787). These sentiments were linked both to his conviction that constitutions must change with the times,[4] and to his belief that "the earth belongs in usufruct to the living" and "that the dead have neither powers nor rights over it" (letter to James Madison, 1789). But it was finally the preservation of the revolutionary spirit itself that was at issue: a "little rebellion now and then," he had argued, was a "good thing" in and of itself.[5] In later life, he certainly distanced himself from the specifics of the French Revolution, whose spirit he had rather naively celebrated at the outset of the event, but he never ceased to believe in the need for a refreshing of principle and a reembracing of founding precepts as a condition for the survival of democracy.[6]

There is of course a paradox here, since a revolution is always a founding (and thus a foundation) as well as the kindling of a certain spirit of spontaneity hostile to foundationalism. As Hannah Arendt has observed, in America the revolutionary spirit founded a constitution at odds with that spirit—as social contracts and fixed laws are always likely to be at odds with the spirit of innovation that creates them.[7] Jefferson saw democracy itself, more particularly ward government and active participation by citizens in self-governance, as the remedy to the inevitable ossification of a democratic constitution founded on an original compact that successor generations could only approach as an ancient artifact in a spirit of abstract loyalty. Like Rousseau before him and Robert Michels after him, Jefferson worried that representative government could swallow up a people's liberties and lead to an "elective despotism," the worse for being legitimized by a social contract rooted in the very notion of direct voluntary consent being violated by representation. He preferred the internal filter of education to the external filter of representation in part because, as we have seen, he feared that in representation, the distancing of individuals from their prejudices was won only at the cost of distancing them from the responsibilities that defined and gave life to their liberties.

The call for ward government and full participation by citizens "not merely at an election one day in the year, but every day" (letter to Joseph Cabell, February 12, 1815) was to Jefferson a way of critiquing representation as well as a way of advocating participation. Ward government not only secured negative liberty by decentralizing the sovereign power of that state to the neighborhoods; it secured positive liberty by turning right into an affirmative participatory principle in which freedom was not merely preserved but also exercised—in which rights were recoupled with the responsibilities that alone could make rights more than parchment parapets (as Madison had it) from which to defend liberty. The lesson taught by Jefferson is that the celebrated principle of original consent as derived from the foundational principles of natural right (the essence of social contract reasoning) is wholly inadequate to the democratic mandate.

It is in this Jeffersonian mood that I have spent so much of my career trumpeting the benefits of strong, participatory democracy. For according to this persuasive Jeffersonian logic, it is not just foundationalism, but foundings themselves that imperil the democratic orders they establish. The tension between constitutional order and the revolutionary spirit has been the subject of two recent books that pointedly capture the contradictions between founding and democracy: Gordon Wood's *The Radicalism of the American Revolution* (winner of the 1992 Pulitzer Prize in history) and, equally suggestively and rather more provocatively still, Bruce Ackerman's *We the People*.[8] Ackerman offers an account of "dualist democracy" in which "Rights Foundationalists" face advocates of the actual exercise of popular sovereignty in a contest over the meaning of democracy and of the Revolution that made it. Ackerman sees in historical moments like the Founders' rejection of the Articles of Confederation (and the procedural principles the Articles mandated) or like Roosevelt's New Deal, revolutionary emblems of the nation's true democratic spirit. "Americans have not been 'born equal' through some miraculous act of immaculate conception," Ackerman argues. "To the extent that we have gained equality, we have won it through energetic debate, popular decision, and constitutional creativity." His conclusion is Jefferson's: "Once the American people lose this remarkable political capacity, it is only a matter of time before they lose whatever equality they possess—and much else besides."[9]

Gordon Wood also treats the American founding, understood in terms of the Revolution more than in terms of the Constitution, as far more than a rejection of the previous monarchial constitutional order. It did not simply refound a social contract on the basis of popular sovereignty and thereby create a republic, "it actually reconstituted what Americans meant by public or state power and brought about an entirely new kind of popular politics and a new kind of democratic officeholder."[10] The American founding was more than a legitimizing event: it was the beginning of a self-renewing and self-perpetuating process whose legitimacy depended less on its origins that its ongoing character and the objects after which it strived. In this sense the Declaration of Independence and subsequent founding documents defined not a point of origin but a destination; not a naturalistic starting point but an artificial ideal. Not something to be built upon but something to be brought into being and accomplished over time. James MacGregor Burns thus has it exactly right in the title of his book on "the pursuit of rights," *A People's Charter*.[11] Rights are what the American political system was designed to pursue and bring into being. They may be celebrated as constitutive of a founding moment, but their realization depends on a permanent democratic politics that secures them "for all" only through painful struggle over a long period of time.

Recent critics of Jefferson have reveled in what they deem his overarching hypocrisy. The democrat who boasts on his gravestone about his authorship of the Declaration of Independence and pronounces all men born equal is in truth not merely a slaveholder who in his latter penurious days comes to depend on slavery for his economic security, but a racist persuaded of the generic inferiority of the African race. To Connor Cruse O'Brien, Jefferson is a hypocrite and a mountebank posturing as the defender of liberty even as he profits from the American caste system.[12] Yet Jefferson's democratic politics and his devotion to a progressive political process are what save him from his institutional and period prejudices. He may have despised the Negro race, but he embraced a participatory politics that opened the way to a struggle for rights within rather than against the political system. He may have hypocritically excluded from inclusion in the vaunted rights of the Declaration and the Bill of Rights the rights of people of color (as well as Native American Indians and women, about whom he also expressed himself in extraordinarily derogatory terms), but he set those rights in a context of revolutionary expectations that allowed abolitionists in the 1850s and women in the 1890s and again civil rights marchers in the 1960s to organize under their banner and fight not for the overthrow of the system but for inclusion.[13]

Democrats and egalitarians owe him a debt less as a "founder" than as a devotee of an antifoundationalist participatory politics of the present and the future that allowed what might have become a stultifying system of stasis to become a revolutionary instrument each new generation of Americans might employ in their own struggle for enfranchisement and rights. In short, it is not so much Jefferson's principles in the Declaration but the practical politics and civic education those principles justified to which egalitarians ought to pay tribute. The critics have called his integrity into question by contrasting his principles with his practices as a slaveholder — but the whole point of the principles in question was to subject all principles to constant criticism. Jefferson is important to modern democrats because he expounds the most essential (and paradoxical) of all democratic principles: that politics always trumps principle. In the short term, this may dismay upholders of the "right" principles (such as the principles of right). But in the long run, it is the only hope for both principles and for rights. We need not engage in Jeffersonian hagiography to acknowledge this and give Jefferson his due.

Democratic foundationalism, Jefferson recognized, although it represents an authoritative establishing of the credentials of democracy, may undermine democracy. Representation can successfully distance government from popular passion, but it can also erode popular responsibility and destroy active citizenship. Michael Oakeshott once said rationalists are "essentially ineducable," by which he meant that, wedded to formal models of truth and cognition, they were closed to the evidence of their senses about the here and now, and the commonsense conversation of those around them.[14] Citizens, on the other hand, are defined by their civic educability: they are not only eminently educable, but they are constituted by that capacity, which is part of the meaning of republican civic virtue. Democracy enjoins constant, permanent motion, a gentle kind of permanent revolution, a movable feast that affords each generation room for new appetites and new tastes, and thus allows political and spiritual migration to new territory. Yet for this radical version of democracy to work, the citizens upon whom the burden of its success rests must be fit for their responsibilities. Which brings us back to the crucial role of education in Jefferson. The logic of the arguments offered here suggests that it was precisely Jefferson's commitment to autonomous, participating citizens, his distrust of representation, and his belief in the necessity of revolutionary ardor in vitalizing everyday democracy that made civic pedagogy and public education central to his political philosophy.

There are of course some critics who have suggested not only that Jefferson was a bigot and a racist, but that his attachment to natural aristocracy and his distrust of central government made him a far less fervent ally of radical democracy than enthusiasts like Richard Mathews or I allow. Gordan Wood has made this kind of argument, suggesting that Jefferson would have inevitably been caught up in the distrustful temper of the times. Yet a careful reading of the letters proves again and again that while Jefferson distrusted central government, he did not distrust either republicanism or the people. He had none of that liberal fear of the unwashed masses that typified so many of his peers. Indeed, it is precisely this faith in the populace of France (and America) that has exercised his critics. They take for granted that his enthusiasm for the French Revolution is prima facie grounds for distrust. But of course it was not just revolution in the abstract he endorsed; he also defended real rebels of the kind who had unnerved the young country in Shay's Rebellion. "I like a little rebellion now and then," he had written to L. J. Cappon, for it helps "keep alive" that valuable "spirit of resistance" on which popular government depends.

There is then no convincing way to enlist Jefferson in the battles of those modern antidemocrats whose "liberalism of fear" (bred by Europe's twentieth-century wars and holocausts) begins with a deep suspicion of popular government. Europe's teeming cities may have given their government a reason to fear the malcontent urban mob, but to apply their lessons to "the independent, the happy, and therefore orderly citizens of the United States" was to do them a grave injustice (letter to John Taylor, 1816). Jefferson refused the politics of anxiety. Well after his supposedly youthful flirtation with the French Revolution, he could still write to Samuel Kercheval (July 12, 1816): "I am not among those who fear the people." On the contrary, he tells the Marquis de Lafayette (November 4, 1823), it was "the sickly, weakly, timid man" who "fears the people" and who was thus a "Tory by nature. The healthy, strong and bold, cherishes them." Nor did Jefferson, like so many of the founders, prefer property to the people. To John Taylor (1816) he wrote to excoriate the arrangements that excluded "like Helots, from the rights of representation" that "one-half of our brethren who fight and pay taxes . . . as if society were instituted for the soil and not for the men inhabiting it."

There was to be sure a certain American naïveté in Jefferson's earliest and most ardent embrace of European revolutionaries that was to be rehearsed again in succeeding generations by Walt Whitman (his "To a Foiled European Revolutionaire") and made transparent in Melville's brilliant account in *Benito Cereno* of the innocent American ship captain who cannot fathom the corruption and evil that confront him when he boards a Spanish slave ship that has been seized by its human cargo. Jefferson misjudged and underestimated the appetites for slaughter of the French revolutionaries (though not much more than the critics of the Jacobins misjudge and overestimate the tolerance and goodwill of the established ecclesiastic and secular hierarchies against whom the revolutionaries acted). His later retreat from his encomiums was not however a retreat from his belief either in democracy or in democratic education—celebrated to the very end in the epitaph he composed for himself.

It remained clear to Jefferson to the end of his life that a theory of democracy that is rooted in active participation and continuing consent by each generation of citizens demands a civic pedagogy rooted in the obligation to educate all who would be citizens; and, since the reverse was also true, to make citizens of all who are educated—another eventual Jeffersonian-style justification for the abolition of slavery in the face of educated men like Frederick Douglass. (Douglass overheard an overseer comment, "If you teach that nigger how to read, there would be no keeping him. It would forever unfit him to be a slave." And, we need only add, outfit him to be a citizen.) The spirit of new world democracy destined the people to govern themselves, and Jefferson's radicalism insisted democracy had to mean self-government; under such circumstances, there was no alternative to educating citizens, and then enfranchising the educated.

Citizen education was then neither a concern merely contingent to Jefferson's politics nor a narrow obsession arising out of his involvement in educational curriculums at the College of William and Mary and the University of Virginia. It was the central, defining moment of his political and moral philosophy; everything else turned on it. When he peered through his telescope mounted on the hill above Richmond where he had built his blessed Monticello, down at the university whose buildings he had designed, whose curriculum he had written, and whose faculty he had helped appoint, it was not merely as its parent but as the father of democracy, who understood democracy as a process dependent on education. The juxtaposition on his epitaph of two founding documents of rights and the founding of America's first public university evinces the forceful logic by which Jefferson grounded liberty's claims in education, thereby giving to rights a living meaning and a defensible reality. Education makes citizens; citizens make bills of rights; rights make democracy. There is no democracy without citizens, no citizens without public education. The questions raised by this logic confront crucial democratic controversies of our own time no less than Jefferson's: how much democracy, and for whom? What kind of democracy—egalitarian or liberal?—and at what price to reason? Who should be educated and how, and to what end?

While Jefferson's commitment to civic education is indisputable, what was entailed by his conception of civic education may be a good deal more controversial. Basic literacy clearly plays a fundamental role in forging the crucible of civic capacity, so civic education is about a good deal more than civics. Legal education plays a special role, especially at the time of the Founding, because the training of lawyers in citizenship and of citizens in the law was clearly a prerequisite of a free society founded on laws.

Douglas Wilson offers us a portrait of Jefferson as a Ciceronian advocate of natural excellence who in contrast to many of his countrymen nonetheless believed that Everyman could be educated to an excellence sufficient to the tasks of self-government. This was not a whim but, as Wilson writes, a belief in which Jefferson persisted "over the course of a long life. . . . If anything, he became even more convinced."[15] If education was the keystone in the arch of democratic government, literacy was for Jefferson the keystone in the arch of education. Books were the chief instruments of popular education. Judicious citizenship required not just specifically civic training but a "general knowledge and sensibility among the people." Where these prevailed, Jefferson was sure, "arbitrary government and every kind of oppression have lessened and disappeared in proportion."

When in 1778 Jefferson comes to draft legislation to establish a public school system in Virginia, he urges in his Bill for the More General Diffusion of Knowledge "illumination" as the cure to tyranny. History was "the common school of mankind, equally open and useful to great and small," and bookishness was thus the paradoxical route to usefulness. Jefferson combined a faith in book learning with an abiding practicality that made book learning a road to (and road map for) real-life experience, and this rich if not wholly tension-free mixture was reflected in all his educational proposals. Libraries are for Jefferson not reclusive monasteries to which men flee when tired of society, but windows on society that facilitate judicious participation in it.

Nor do bookishness and the appeal to history suggest a conservative Jefferson on the model of Hume or Burke. While Cathy Davidson and others have challenged postrevolutionary uses of literacy by John Adams and his countrymen as a legitimation device meant to enforce popular compliance and quiescence, such a view of Jefferson makes little sense. Self-assertion and rambunctiousness in standing up to authority were precisely what Jefferson was looking for in educated citizens.

The emphasis on education that was Jefferson's obsession was shared by many other Americans in the founding era, from George Wythe to Benjamin Rush.[16] John Adams of Massachusetts was less egalitarian than Jefferson, but uses the English Whig tradition to insist on the necessity of literacy and civic education in the proper functioning of republics. In Puritan New England (Massachusetts and Connecticut) taxes had been levied to support free schools for all free boys as early as the seventeenth century, allowing John Adams to boast in 1765 that nowhere in the world could one see "so much knowledge and civility among the common people" than in Massachusetts—where Adams said "a native who cannot read and write is as rare as a comet or an earthquake."[17] Still, these prerevolutionary patterns were checkered, and following independence there were "no generally accepted, clearly understood models to imitate." As with their new constitution, revolutionary leaders would have to invent the kind of public education they thought the ideal of the informed citizenry would require. The most significant (and costly) innovation was the making of a statutory commitment to public education—for which Adam's New England public school provided one vital model.

The Virginia Bill for the More General Diffusion of Knowledge can then be understood as Jefferson's effort to mount a first line of defense against the rise of tyranny. Education alone could permit men to "know ambition under all its shapes" and prompt them to "exert their natural powers" against it. The Virginia Bill (which never passed) called for establishing grammar schools throughout the state at one-hundred-acre-lot intervals and building brick or stone—that is, permanent—schoolhouses with lodgings for selected scholars and their teachers. These schools would offer access to all on the basis of ability alone ("the best geniuses will be raked from the rubbish annually," Jefferson wrote, in that amazing Jeffersonian rhetoric that at once celebrated and demeaned equality). The state would, in other words, make scholarships available to the poor. One gratis scholar from each grammar school would be sent for three years to William and Mary at public expense (this probably sealed the fate of the bill, publicly funded education being an alien notion to eighteenth-century Americans). John Adams indicted the ignorance that democracy potentially empowered as the enemy of virtuous government, but like Jefferson was inclined to think that educating the ignorant was the appropriate remedy in a Whig republic. Adams thus managed to persuade his Massachusetts brethren to enact as legislation the suggestions of his 1778 homily calling for the public encouragement of all "useful knowledge."

The Massachusetts Constitution of 1780 thus recast traditional Puritan language as a "broad republican" call "for comprehensive public responsibility, not merely for education at all levels, but for an advanced, enlightened, knowledgeable and progressive society." Republican institutions, it made clear, "could survive only in the custody of a virtuous and informed citizenry."[18] Public religion was encouraged, and Harvard was given special responsibilities that went far beyond its original Christian and civic missions. As Jefferson had linked the Virginia Statute of Religious Freedom and the establishment of a public university, the Massachusetts Commonwealth's new constitution made "wisdom and knowledge, diffused generally among the body of the people" indispensable to "the preservation of their rights and liberties."

Jefferson's educational philosophy is entangled with his views of legal training.[19] Jefferson was himself trained in the law and his early leisurely apprenticeship of five years with George Wythe exposed him both to the blue ribbon practices of the General Court and Chancery Court in Williamsburg where Wythe practiced and to the scientific and humanistic studies to which, as an Enlightenment man, Wythe was devoted. These two poles, theoretical and practical, set the parameters for Jefferson's own attempts to merge law studies and legal education—to introduce classical studies into law training and to introduce the law into liberal education. If Jefferson erred in striking the balance, it was on the side of law as a learned occupation rather than law as a trade.[20] Having never practiced in the mundane county courts—then as now, the forward trenches of the legal infantryman—when asked for advice on legal studies, as he often was, he recommended books. That is, he proposed a course of studies that at first glance might have seemed remote from the law: languages and mathematics, and all of the sciences along with a very heavy dose of history. As in other things, Jefferson valued books over experiential practice—one reason perhaps why he was never too successful as a litigator.[21]

Jefferson had worried about the narrowness and parochialism of the legal education offered by the private law schools at Litchfield, Connecticut, and Kinderhook, New York. He had spent the last decade of his life trying to establish a professorship of law at the University of Virginia and then trying to find a candidate to occupy it, and working to integrate legal curriculums into liberal arts education. The rupture in Jefferson between the demands of professional legal training and the civic requirements of liberal education brings us back to the question of Jefferson's radicalism: Can the radical proponent of a little revolution every generation, of an autonomy and spontaneity inseparable from classical liberal learning, really be assimilated to a relatively conservative and parochial reading of the law? Is Jefferson Hume or Burke? I argued above in citing the passage from Hannah Arendt about the paradoxical character of the American founding, that law itself is from a certain radical democratic perspective an adversary of autonomy, impressing itself on the will of the people with an indelible stamp inimical to true freedom. In the heart of every zealous liberal lives an anarchist. The lawyer's job is after all to enforce convention; the citizen's is to challenge and reinvent it. Can their education be identical? Is a nation of lawyers and a nation of citizens really the same thing? Are the talking skills of lawyering and the listening skills of citizenship inculcated in the same fashion?

In most university law schools, the models of Litchfield and Kinderhook have prevailed, with technical legal training in torts, corporations, property, civil, and criminal law not merely taking precedence over philosophy, history, and social science, but driving them wholly out of the curriculum. It is not too much to say that many law schools today aim at "deprogramming" liberal arts students by surgically removing their reflective and critical faculties and replacing them with a legal (and lethal) logic whose foundations are rendered incontestable or at least invisible and, thus, unchallengable. Law board scores that can be improved substantially by LSAT courses do not suggest a way of thinking that is deeply critical. Yes, critical legal studies at Harvard, legal and political philosophy at Yale, and constitutional studies at Virginia do acknowledge the limitations of legal method, but they do not alter the fact that legal training for the vast preponderance of American lawyers consists of technical training, technical training, and more technical training in a vocational mode that makes Litchfield and Kinderhook look like Aristotle's Lyceum.

I see in Jefferson's attempts to innovate in the field of legal education an attempt to radicalize the law and remove it as an obstruction from the path of citizenship. He did not err in privileging theory over practice and classical studies over legal studies: he made a conscious choice to take law away from lawyers and return it to citizen philosophers who both knew its limits and, by making it their own, could free themselves from its hold over them. To think otherwise is to make Jefferson a far more conservative and legalistic thinker than is warranted by every other fact of his intellectual biography: his prior devotion to literacy, to civic education, to public schooling, and to the maximal public spread of knowledge.

The deep belief in education is nowhere more evident than in Jefferson's Bill for the More General Diffusion of Knowledge, where he insists that "providing for the education of the people" is "the most legitimate engine of government"—strongly reinforcing the claim that public expenditure for general education is the New World's most radical innovation. Jefferson's linkage of specific education objectives to large democratic aspirations was the key to his political thought.

Now, to be sure, there can hardly be a doubt that Jefferson both recognized and celebrated what he understood to be the natural aristocracy of talent in human beings. After all, he inaugurated what almost appears as a scientific argument for the inferiority of women, and of men and women of African ancestry. But with respect to education, the limits of Jefferson's democratic radicalism appear to me to arise out of the boundaries he posits between the body of citizens and others who are not citizens rather than the boundaries within the body of citizens—the boundaries, for example, between the natural and artificial aristocracy, or white male property holders who are learned and those who are foolish. For it is the virtue of Jefferson's radicalism that education not only makes the naturally wise more judicious but makes the naturally foolish wiser. Education may create the conditions for the progress of the whole species but its most important political use is its role in capacitating as citizens those Jefferson deemed qualified.

When we turn to the education of those who are not part of "we the people," however, Jefferson looks as dimly undemocratic as any of the New York bankers he regularly contemns. He not only excoriates blacks and assimilates Native American Indians to the new country's bountiful flora and fauna, but treats women with a paternal dismissiveness that reads as misogynist even in his own not yet modern times. His remonstrations to his daughters to be neat and learn how to please their husbands, to learn how to spell and dance (though only prior to marriage, after which "gestation and nursing leave little time to a married lady when this exercise can be either safe or innocent"), betray someone persuaded of women's second-class nature. Because Jefferson urges both sexes to be moral and to find happiness, some have deemed him (relatively speaking) a gender egalitarian. I do not. The practical education Jefferson recommends for girls that fosters only efficient home economics, and the practical education he urges on men that fosters responsible citizenship are worlds apart with respect to liberty and power, and the fact that both are practical seems inconsequential. Being "serviceable to others" (a Jefferson objective) means serving the community of equals for male citizens, but for women it means serving men—not exactly the same thing. Jefferson treated his slaves and his women with the respect a civilized gentlemen offers useful (even beloved) inferiors, but radical democracy, which is to say, liberty, clearly ended for him at the frontiers of citizenship.

Finally, if commentators like Dumas Malone and more recently Jennings L. Waggoner, Jr., give too little attention to Jefferson's unsavory treatment of Native Americans, slaves, and women, Waggoner for one seems to give too much credence to Daniel Boorstin's claim that Jefferson's educational program was vocationally directed and that Jefferson himself had set a "largely conservative task" for education.[22] The notion that Jefferson's commitment was to an education that was uncritical and conservative is gainsaid by everything he wrote and did about the role of education in cultivating a new "New World" democracy.

In any case, the issue today seems to me to be more elementary: our society has pretty much abandoned the notion that education is above all a training ground for citizenship, the place where we acquire the arts of liberty. On the contrary, we train for job competition and we train for the vocations, and occasionally we uphold ivory tower intellectualism as an end in itself, but we do not educate for citizenship, and we seem neither to try nor to care. The responsibility of the state to provide for public education is acknowledged neither by taxpayers unwilling to fund schools equitably nor by many politicians who argue for the privitization of schooling via vouchers, as if the "public" in public education was an accident of infelicitous speech. There has been a great deal of discussion about the paltry condition of American democracy today: Is it possible that the problem arises directly out of the paltry condition of education? Surely Thomas Jefferson would have thought so, as he watched us ignore his principles in the name of an obsession with *his* unsavory practices, all the better to promote unsavory practices of our own.

NOTES

1. "There is no safe depository of the ultimate powers of the society but the people themselves . . . and if we think them not enlightened enough to exercise their control with a wholesome discretion, the remedy is not to take it from them, but to inform their discretion by education." Letter to William C. Jarvis, September 28, 1820. (Unless otherwise noted, all Jefferson citations are from *The Writings of Thomas Jefferson*, ed. Paul Leicester Ford [New York: G. P. Putnam's, 1892–99]).

2. Cited by Hannah Arendt, *On Revolution* (New York: Penguin, 1963), p. 236. See Robert Michels, *Political Parties* (1959).

3. Note that this was later in his life, when some claim his revolutionary ardor had cooled!

4. "I know also that laws and institutions must go hand in hand with the

progress of the human mind. . . . We might as well require a man to wear still the coat which fitted him when a body, as civilized society to remain ever under the regimen of their barbarous ancestors." Letter to Kercheval, July 12, 1816.

5. "I hold it that a little rebellion now and then is a good thing, and as necessary in the political world as storms in the physical." Jefferson to James Madison, January 30, 1787.

6. Recent Jefferson skeptics like Joseph Ellis have argued that Jefferson was ashamed of his early enthusiasm for the revolution and had accordingly doctored early correspondence to modulate its zealotry. But they misread a temperamental preference for ongoing popular participation in the affairs of government that persisted throughout Jefferson's career as a sometime and quite contingent enthusiasm for France supposedly born of his firsthand acquaintance with the country immediately prior to the revolution. See Joseph J. Ellis, *American Sphinx: The Character of Thomas Jefferson* (New York: Alfred A. Knopf, 1997).

7. "Paradoxical as it may sound," wrote Arendt, "it was in fact under the impact of the Revolution that the Revolutionary spirit in this country began to wither away, and it was the Constitution itself, this greatest achievement of the American people, which eventually cheated them of their proudest possession." *On Revolution*, p. 242.

8. Gordon Wood, *The Radicalism of the American Revolution* (New York: Vintage, 1991); and Bruce Ackerman, *We the People: Foundations* (Cambridge: Harvard University Press, 1991).

9. Ackerman, *We the People*, p. 27.

10. Wood, *Radicalism of the American Revolution*, p. 8.

11. James MacGregor Burns and Stewart Burns, *A People's Charter: The Pursuit of Rights in America* (New York: Alfred A. Knopf, 1991).

12. Besides O'Brien and Ellis, see Leonard Levy's *Jefferson and Civil Liberties: The Darker Side* (New York: Quandrangle/New York Times Book Company, 1963); and Paul Finkelman, "Jefferson and Slavery: 'Treason against the Hopes of the World,'" (1992).

13. In his *Notes on Virginia* (1787), he treats the Native American tribes with seeming affection as a feature of the New World's flora and fauna rather than as a part of the distinctively human race.

14. Michael Oakeshott, *Rationalism in Politics* (New York: Basic Books, 1962), p. 32.

15. Douglas Wilson, in his paper for the Library of Congress Conference on Jefferson, 1994.

16. Richard D. Brown offers a comparative study of the complementary educational projects for an "informed citizenry" developed by Jefferson for Virginia and John Adams for Massachusetts in his unpublished paper for the 1994 Library of Congress Conference on Jefferson. Brown explores the birth of public education in America from "Radical Whig and Enlightenment Traditions," which were combined with "diverse strands of secular and religious ideology," and shows how publicly funded education became the instrument by which the ideal of an "informed citizenry" was realized.

17. Brown cites a 1762 North Carolina statute that "held masters accountable for the literacy of even their colored apprentices." In Virginia, justices of the peace

had "consistently held parents and masters responsible for the education of their children and servants" (ibid.).

18. Although the founders differed about the role of religion, Professor Brown concludes that "for Adams and Jefferson, indeed the entire generation of Revolutionary leaders, the success of liberty and of republican government and society rested on the crucial equation of virtue and knowledge." And while the equation was deeply rooted in civic republican and Radical Whig ideology, "it was the mobilization of colonial opposition to imperial reform that made it relevant to everyday politics and led Revolutionary leaders to invest it with more urgent importance than ever before" (ibid.).

19. In his as yet unpublished paper for the Library of Congress Conference on Jefferson (1994), Herbert A. Johnson addresses the "stable requirements for the training of would-be lawyers" as they were differently refracted through the very different lenses of clerkship in the colonial era, colleges in the period between the Revolution and the constitutional founding, private law schools from about 1790 to 1830, and emerging models of modern professional law schools thereafter. Johnson links legal training to issues of literacy, citizenship, and civic virtue that account for changing notions of appropriate legal training. To balance professional and technical training is the goal. Jefferson clearly favors a training that keeps legal education popular.

20. While "working with George Wythe," Johnson notes, he might have "lost some practical training deemed so precious by [a] clerkship-trained lawyer, [but] he gained a more generous understanding of law and its impact on society."

21. In pursuing the evolution of law studies in young America, Johnson necessarily moves beyond Jefferson's career and views, looking briefly at a number of other lawyers and law professors such as Wythe and one of Wythe's first students after he had occupied the new professorship of law and police at William and Mary in 1779, John Marshall. He pursues the trail down to associate Justice James Wilson, whose Philadelphia College law lectures offered nothing less (in Professor Robert McCloskey's words) "than the presentation of a complete political theory, grounded on theology and psychology and leading to a philosophy of American law" and which saw in the science of the law "the study of every free citizen, and of every free man." Robert G. McCloskey, ed. *The Works of James Wilson* (Cambridge: Harvard University Press, Belknap Press, 1967), 1:37. This language is repeated again and again by Jefferson and by no less than his Federalist enemies Marshall and Marshall's associate Joseph Story, who eventually took the Dane Professorship of Law at Harvard and who not long after Jefferson's death wrote in a surprisingly Jeffersonian tone: "many of our most illustrious statesmen have been lawyers; but they have been lawyers liberalized by philosophy and large intercourse with the wisdom of ancient and modern times."

22. See the paper of Jennings L. Waggoner, Jr., for the Library of Congress Conference on Jefferson, spring 1994.

CHAPTER 13

The Civic Mission of the University

THE MODERN American university is embroiled in controversy, fueled by deep uncertainty over its pedagogical purposes and its civic role in a "free" society. At times the college establishment seems to know neither what a free society is nor what the educational requisites of freedom might look like. Nonetheless, both administrators and their critics have kept busy, for like zealots (classically defined as people who redouble their efforts when they have forgotten their aims), they have covered their confusion by embellishing their hyperbole. They wring hands and rue the social crises of higher education—apathy, cynicism, careerism, prejudice, selfishness, sexism, opportunism, complacency, and substance abuse—but they hesitate when faced with hard decisions, and prefer to follow rather than challenge the national mood.

Students, reflecting the climate in which they are being educated, are, well, a mess. Minority students at Dartmouth receive anonymous hate letters from their peers, and feminists are sent notes enclosed in condoms reading, "You disgust me." Students at the University of Utah are voting members of the "Who Cares?" party in student government, embracing their promises to pay their way by "panhandling, and running strip bars, raffles, and prostitution." Youthful hijinks, perhaps: after all, a decade earlier students at Wisconsin had elected the "Pail and Shovel" party into office (its platform: stealing and wasting as much money as possible); and panty raids of one kind or another have been campus staples for a century. Yet one can only feel uneasy when these newer signs of distress are read in conjunction with the wave of racism, overt sexual discrimination, and homophobia that is sweeping America's campuses; or when they are correlated with national patterns of student political apathy (less than one-fifth of the 18-to 24-year-old population voted in the 1986 congressional election, less than one-half of the 37 percent of the general population that voted); or, more pointedly, when they are seen to induce paralysis among school administrators who have necessarily abjured the infantalizing tactics of "in loco parentis" without, however, having a clue about what might take its place.

The privatization and commercialization of schooling continues apace. At the college level, we still honor teaching in the abstract, but we mainly reward research. To be sure, the two should be congruent, and administrators are fond of saying that only great scholars—superb researchers toiling on the frontiers of their discipline—can be good teachers. But good teachers need to spend at least a few hours a week in the classroom. No matter how gifted, the educator cannot practice the teaching craft in front of a computer, in the laboratory, or at the library.

The reality is, as Jacques Barzun recently pointed out, that research and scholarship have not only become ever more narrow and specialized and thus remote from teaching, but they have taken the very culture which is their putative subject and held it hostage to their reflexive scholastic concerns. "Since William James, Russell, and Whitehead," Barzun reminds us, "philosophy, like history, has been confiscated by scholarship, and locked away from the contamination of cultural use." And, we might add, from the contamination of educational use. The new scholasticism that is academic specialization has in fact turned the study of culture into the study of the study of culture—self-conscious preoccupation with method, technique, and scholarship displacing a broad humanistic concern for culture itself. We no longer simply read books, we study what it means to read books; we do not interpret theories but develop theories of interpretation. We are awash in what W. Jackson Bate of Harvard calls "self-trivialization," pursuing an intellectual quest that takes us farther and farther from students and the world in which they are supposedly being educated to live.

TWO UNIVERSITIES

There are two positive models of the university being purveyed today to address the current crisis in education. Mirror images of each other, one calls for a refurbished ivory tower, while the other calls for an uncritical servitude to the larger society's aims and purposes (read whims and fashions). Neither is satisfactory. We may call the first the purist model and the second the vocational model. The first is favored by academic purists and antiquarian humanists and is an embellishment on the ancient Lyceum or the medieval university. In the name of the abstract pursuit of speculative knowledge, it calls for insulating the university from the wider society. Learning for learning's own sake: not for career, not for life, not for democracy, not for money; for neither power nor happiness, neither career nor quality of life, but for its own pure sake alone. To the purist, knowledge is radically divorced from time and culture, from power and interest; above all it eschews utility. It aspires to reconstruct Aristotle's Lyceum in downtown Newark—catering, however, to the residents of New Athens rather than of New Haven or Newark.

In the Lyceum, knowledge is mined from the great intellectual veins running through the canyon of the canon. What the canon teaches is that there is a knowledge that is not conditioned by culture and interest, that is not some other century's fashion or some other culture's dominant paradigm, but which—transcending time and space—has earned the status of, if not universal truth, at least universal wisdom. This claim to universality uproots the canon from the contexts that might once have created it. (That Eton in the nineteenth century had one science master, one math master, one modern languages master, and twenty-seven classics masters teaching Latin and Greek and the cultures they mediated is seen as a product of the canon, rather than a force conditioning its modern incarnation.) On the other hand, belief in the independent and objective veracity of the canon does not prevent purists from seeing all other knowledge, all deviations from the canon (such as feminist studies or comparative religion), as the subjective effects of contemporary cultural contexts that are transient, contingent, and subjective; that is to say, the product of liberal pedagogical conspiracies and political interest.

The vocational model abjures tradition no less decisively than the purist model abjures relevance. Indeed, it is wildly alive to the demands of the larger society it believes education must serve. Where the purist rejects even the victories of modernity (equality, social justice, universal education) as so many diseases, the advocate of education as vocational training accepts even the ravages of modernity as so many virtues—or at least as the necessary price of progress. The vocationalist wishes to see the university go prone before modernity's new gods. Service to the market, training for its professions, research in the name of its products are the hallmarks of the new full-service university, which wants nothing so much as to be counted as a peer among the nation's great corporations that serve prosperity and material happiness. Forging dubious alliances with research companies, All-American U. plies corporations for program funding and stalks the public sector in search of public "needs" it can profitably satisfy. In each of these cases, it asks society to show the way, and it compliantly follows.

If this requires that teaching be subsumed to research and research itself reduced to product-oriented engineering, so be it. If it means taking bribes, such as advertising, that privatize and commercialize education in ways wholly inconsistent with learning, that is the price of survival. If it requires that education take on the aspect of vocational training, and that the university become a kindergarten for the corporate society where the young are socialized, bullied, and otherwise blackmailed into usefulness, then the curriculum must be recast in the language of opportunism, careerism, professionalism, and, in a word, commerce. Where the philosopher once said all of life is a preparation for death, the educational careerist now thinks all of life is a preparation for business—or perhaps, more bluntly, that life is business.

A DIALECTIC OF LIFE AND MIND

The first of our two models is aristocratic, humanistic, and poignantly nostalgic—not merely Luddite in C. P. Snow's sense, but profoundly anti-modern: it wishes to educate the few well and perceives in the democratic ideal an insuperable obstacle to excellence.

The vocationalist knows these predilections for sequestration to be dangerous and probably impossible. For him, education and its institutional tools are for better or worse embedded in the real world. His pedagogical tasks are socialization not insulation, integration not isolation. Education must follow where society leads: support it, ape it, reinforce it, chase it, undergird it, affirm it, preserve it. Whatever society wants and needs, the university tries to supply. Indeed, society defines the university rather than the other way round. Society says what, the scholar as researcher shows how; society says Yes or No, the teacher helps the pupil pronounce the words; society says I need doctors, I will pay lawyers, students nurture medical skills and acquire legal credentials. Education as vocationalism in service to society becomes a matter of socialization rather than scrutiny, of spelling out consequences rather than probing premises, of answering society's questions rather than questioning society's answers. Where once the student was taught that the unexamined life was not worth living, he is now taught that the profitably lived life is not worth examining.

Neither purist nor vocationalist recognizes that education is a dialectic of life and mind, of body and spirit, in which the two are inextricably bound together. Neither acknowledges how awkward this makes it for a liberal arts university at once to serve and challenge society, to simultaneously "transmit" fundamental values such as autonomy and free thinking, and to create a climate where students are not conditioned by what is transmitted (transmission tends toward indoctrination), and where thinking is truly critical, independent, and subversive (which is what freedom means). For such a university must at once stand apart from society in order to give students room to breathe and grow free from a too insistent reality; and at the same time it must stand within the real world and its limiting conditions in order to prepare students to live real lives in a society that, if they do not mold it freely to their aspirations, will mold them to its conventions. To live eventually as effective, responsible, critical, and autonomous members of communities of discourse and activity, students must be both protected from a too precipitous engagement in them and acclimatized by responsible and critical participation in them.

If the young were born literate there would be no need to teach them literature; if they were born citizens, there would be no need to teach them civic responsibility. But of course educators know that the young are born neither wise, nor literate, nor responsible—nor, despite the great rhetoric to the contrary, are they born free. They are born at best with the potential for wisdom, literacy, and responsibility, with an aptitude for freedom which is, however, matched by an aptitude for security and thus for tyranny.

THE CIVIC MISSION

Thomas Jefferson regarded habituated belief as an enemy not only of freedom but of usable conviction, and argued that "every constitution and every law naturally expires at the end of 19 years." Canons, like constitutions, are also for the living, and if they do not expire every 19 years they surely grow tired and stale and heteronomous as time passes. Which is not to say they must be discarded: only that they must be reassessed, relegitimized, and thus reembraced by the current generation. A canon is no use if it is not ours, and it becomes ours only when we reinvent it—an act impossible without active examination, criticism, and subversion. That is why teachers cannot teach the canon properly without subverting it. Their task is not to transmit the canon but to permit their students to reinvent it. Paradoxically, only those "truths" founded on abstract reason which students can make their own, founded on their own reason, are likely to be preserved. Waving the *Republic* at the young will do nothing for restoring literacy or extending the truths of the old.

What I wish to urge is a far more dialectical model of education: one that refuses to prostrate itself, its back to the future, before the ancient gods of the canon, but is equally reluctant to throw itself uncritically, its back to the past, into the future as envisioned by the new gods of the marketplace. This argument suggests not that the university *has* a civic mission, but that the university *is* a civic mission, is civility itself, defined as the rules and conventions that permit a community to facilitate conversation and the kinds of discourse upon which all knowledge depends. On this model, learning is a social activity that can take place only within a discursive community bringing together reflection and experience. On this model, knowledge is an evolving communal construction whose legitimacy rests directly on the character of the social process. On this model, education is everywhere and always an ineluctably communal enterprise.

I mean to suggest much more than that democracy and education are parallel activities; or that civic training and the cultivation of knowledge and judgment possess a parallel structure. I am arguing that they are the same thing: that what distinguishes truth, inasmuch as we can have it at all, from untruth, is not conformity to society's historical traditions or the standards of independent reason or the dictates of some learned canon, but conformity to communicative processes that are genuinely democratic and that occur only in free communities.

The conditions of truth and the conditions of democracy are one and the same: as there is freedom, as the community is open and inclusive and the exchange of ideas thorough and spirited, so there is both more democracy and more learning, more freedom and more knowledge (which becomes, here, ideas conditionally agreed upon). And just as no argument will be privileged over other arguments simply because of how or from whom it originates, so no individual will be privileged over other individuals simply because of who he is (white or male or straight) and where he comes from (old money, good Protestant stock, the United States of America).

Once this is understood, we can move beyond the old instrumental arguments on behalf of democracy that rest the case for citizen training inside the university on the prudential need to shore up democracy outside the university. These arguments are powerful—neither education nor research can prosper in an unfree society, and schooling is the only way we are likely to be able to produce citizens who will uphold freedom—but they are prudential. The prudent Jefferson is known for his linkage of education and democracy: if, Jefferson writes in his *Notes on Virginia,* the people are "the ultimate guardians of their own liberty," then we had best "render them safe" via a prudent and thorough education. "The only sure reliance for the preservation of our liberty," he writes to James Madison in 1787, is to "educate and inform the whole mass of the people."

However, my argument here goes well beyond Jefferson's instrumental formula making education "the guarantor of liberty." It suggests that liberty is the guarantor of education; that we not only have to educate every person to make him free, but we have to free every person to make him educable. Educated women and men make good citizens of free communities; but without a free learning community you cannot educate women and men.

THE SENSE OF COMMUNITY

Walt Whitman, who refused to wall off democracy from life, or life from poetry, or poetry from democracy, mocks those who try to cut the fabric of democracy to the sorry measure of their own tiny imaginations (he must have had the first political scientist in mind!):

> Did you too, O friend, suppose democracy was only for elections, for politics, and for a party name? I say democracy is only of use there that it may pass on

and come to its flower and fruits in manners, in the highest forms of interaction between men, and their beliefs—in religion, literature, colleges and
schools—democracy in all public and private life.

The point where democracy and education intersect is the point we call
community. For if democracy is a mode of associated living, then it is also
true, Dewey has written, that "in the first place, the school must itself be a
community life." Dewey is framing a careful philosophical argument
rather than just a provocative metaphor. He is insisting that the "realization of the meaning of linguistic signs . . . involves a context of work
and play in association with others." He is saying that in the absence of
community there is no learning; that language itself is social, the product
as well as the premise of sociability and conversation.

We should comprehend him, for underlying the pathologies of our society and our schools—beneath the corruptions associated with alcohol and
drugs, complacency and indifference, discrimination and bigotry, and violence and fractiousness—is a sickness of community: its corruption, its
rupturing, its fragmentation, its breakdown; finally, its vanishing and its
absence. We can no more learn alone than we can live alone, and if little
learning is taking place in American schools and colleges it may be because
there is too much solitude and too little community among the learners
(and the teachers too). Schools that were once workshops of intimacy have
become as alienating as welfare hotels and as lonely as suburban malls.
They lack neither facilities nor resources, neither gifted teachers nor able
students; but they are for the most part devoid of any sense of community.
And without community, neither the almighty canon nor the almighty
dollar can do much to inspire learning or promote freedom.

Dewey's conception of education is often deemed "progressive," yet in
fact it harks back to classical and neo-classical models of *paideia* and *Bildung*. *Paideia* was the term the Greeks used to encapsulate the norms and
values of public life around which citizenship and learning were organized. To be an educated Athenian was to be a free and participating citizen. These were not two distinctive roles, two parallel forms of training;
they were a single identity revolving around common norms each individual made his own. Imagine Socrates recommending a canon to his pupils,
or telling an Athenian youth that what he learned in the Lyceum was not
meant to apply to life beyond the bleached stones where the two of them
sat in the sun conversing. The German Enlightenment term *Bildung* possessed the same unifying cultural thrust; it brought together under the
rubric of life, learning, and self-reflective experience the same ideals of
the fully developed citizen of a civil cosmopolis. The education of Emile
(Rousseau) or the education of the young Werther (Goethe) was a lifetime
task in which schooling represented only a phase. Emile did not imagine

his pupil could separate the cultivation of his civility from the reading of books; Goethe never imagined that Werther could or should wall off his life from his learning.

The trouble with the purist's canon is that it renders knowledge a product stripped of the process by which it is endowed with its quickening vitality and its moral legitimacy. The canon does not produce the cultural education the Germans called *Bildung; Bildung* produces the canon, which consequently needs to be no less flexible and mutable than the life processes that make it. The trouble with the vocationalist's servitude to society is that it fails to distinguish society or society's fixed conventions from the free society and the unique educational prerequisites that condition freedom. A free society does not produce *Bildung,* which is always critical of it; *Bildung* produces a free society, keeping it from ossifying and perishing— helping it to overcome its most difficult contradiction: the institutionalization and petrification of the spirit of freedom that animates it.

COMMON LIVING

We can address these troubles, both those of the purists and those of the vocationalists, by insisting on the centrality of community to both education and democracy, both convention and freedom. Where in the quest to preserve the canon is a concern for the communal conditions of learning upon which its revival (and thus its preservation) depend? In the rush to serve the society that beckons from beyond the schoolyard, what has happened to the schoolyard's own precious community, whose delicate ties alone permit the young to learn the art of civility and to create a common language in the face of private differences, so that they might conduct a conversation about common knowledge and shared belief?

It is not really a matter of making the liberal arts university into a community; for it already is a community, however corrupt and frangible it has become or however little it is seen as such by its privatized inhabitants (students, faculty, and administrators alike). It is a matter of recognizing the communal character of learning, and giving to community the attention and the resources it requires. Learning communities, like all free communities, function only when their members conceive of themselves as empowered to participate fully in the common activities that define the community—in this case, learning and the pursuit of knowledge in the name of common living. Learning entails communication, communication is a function of community. The equation is simple enough: no community, no communication; no communication, no learning; no learning, no education; no education, no citizens; no citizens, no freedom; no freedom—then no culture, no democracy, no schools, no civilization.

Cultures rooted in freedom do not come in fragments and pieces: you get it all, or you get nothing.

The sociopathologies that currently afflict American universities (renewed racism, substance and alcohol abuse, alienation, suicide) are then anything but contingent features of higher education, mere symptoms that can be isolated and treated one by one like so many cuts on an otherwise healthy body. They speak rather to a disease of the whole, a systemic affliction of education's integral body, which is nothing less than the community of teachers and students in which education subsists.

If we wish to treat the symptoms, I suggest we try to treat the disease: the corporal weakness of community itself. I will not try here to specify what it might mean to reform our universities and colleges, focusing on the needs of community rather than the demands of a canon or the needs of a hungry society. But when I think about how crucial teaching is to all education and thus to democracy, I am put in mind of a remarkable stanza that brings Walt Whitman's "A Song of Occupations" to its conclusion. Whitman writes:

> When the psalm sings instead of the singer,
> When the script preaches instead of the preacher,
> When a university course convinces like a slumbering woman and child
>   convince . . .
> I intend to reach them my hand and make as much of them as I do of men
>   and women.

Whitman always reminds us of the obvious; perhaps because it is the obvious that we always forget. Canons don't teach; teachers teach. Poems cannot enchant; only poets can do that. History will not preserve us from the errors of the past, but historians just may, if they are teachers.

Education is finally a matter of teachers teaching students; and where teachers teach and students learn, there we will discover community. Or, to put it the other way around, only where there is a genuine community will there be genuine teachers and students and anything resembling genuine learning.

Does the university have a civic mission? Of course, for it is a civic mission: the cultivation of free community; the creation of a democracy of words (knowledge) and a democracy of deeds (the democratic state). Perhaps it is time to stop complaining about the needs of society and worrying about the fate of the canon and despairing over the inadequacies of students, which after all only mirror our own. Perhaps the time is finally here to start thinking about what it means to say that community is the beginning and the end of education: its indispensable condition, its ultimate object. And time then, if we truly believe this, to do something about it in words and in deeds.

CHAPTER 14

Service, Citizenship, and Democracy: Civic Duty as an Entailment of Civil Right

DEFINING THE PROBLEM: THE DECLINE OF SERVICE AS A FUNCTION OF THE BANKRUPTCY OF CITIZENSHIP

We live in times when rights and obligations have been uncoupled, when the government has to compete with industry and the private sector to attract service people to the military, and when individuals regard themselves almost exclusively as private persons with responsibilities only to family and job, but with endless rights against a distant and alien state of which they view themselves, at best, as watchdogs and clients and, at worst, as adversaries and victims. The idea of service to country or obligations to the institutions by which rights and liberty are maintained has fairly vanished. "We the People" have severed our connections with "It" the state or "They" the bureaucrats and politicians who run It. If we posit a problem of governance, it is always framed in the language of leadership: why are there no great leaders anymore? Why can't we trust our representatives? What's gone wrong with our political institutions?

In the last decade a healthy American distrust of outsized or overbureaucratized government has become a zany antipathy toward all government; not even public schooling or progressive taxation are regarded as necessarily legitimate. As the reputation of government has declined, the reputation of markets—seen in their most abstract and innocuous eighteenth-century form—has skyrocketed. Apparently government can do nothing right, and markets can do nothing wrong. Governments are thus afflicted with every social malfunction from corruption to unintended consequences, but markets operate perfectly, right out of the textbook.

Yet those modern attitudes toward government are symptoms rather than causes of deeper changes—above all in the meaning and importance of the idea of citizenship in Western democracy. The long-term effect of representative institutions, which have been crucial in the preservation of accountability and a thin version of democracy in mass societies where more participatory forms of government seem untenable, has often been to undermine a vigorous participatory citizenship and to reinforce the distance between voters and their governors. We view the democratic state as one more hostile exemplar of those bureaucratic Leviathans that encroach on our private lives and jeopardize our private freedoms. Freedom is associated with the absence of government, and national service is regarded as a species of tyranny or involuntary servitude: "Them" coercing "Us" to serve "It" (the state). That service might be a condition of citizenship and citizenship the premise for the preservation of freedom is an argument that has little resonance in modern mass society where *voluntary* means market and *market* means a kind of formal equality (each dollar is worth each other dollar, each vote worth each other vote, and so forth) that is simply assumed, whatever the actual conditions (skewed, monopolistic, unbalanced) of real markets. Where the idea of citizenship has lost its vigor as a correlate of freedom, the idea of service appears as a function of coercion; where markets are regarded uncritically, coercion appears as solely governmental, and all behavior that is nongovernmental is, by definition, regarded as voluntary or free. Thus, the school dropout watching television all afternoon is perceived as acting voluntarily: "Let's see now, what should I do this afternoon? I can read Virgil in Latin; I can put on that new recording of *Parsifal*; or I can watch 'General Hospital' . . . mmm, think I'll watch 'General Hospital.'" The teenager washing up at McDonald's is likewise simply exercising his market freedom: "Should I be a bank president, a senator, a nuclear physicist, or a dishwasher at McDonald's? Gee, tough choice, guess I'll opt for being a dishwasher at McDonald's. I like those late-night shifts."

Yet although meaningful choice in the private sector bears no relationship to the ideal conditions assumed by advocates of the market, choice in the public sector has also been radically truncated by the erosion of citizenship. It is my argument here that service has lost much of its political potency precisely because citizenship has lost its currency. It is a notion so thin and wan nowadays that it means little more than voting, when it means anything at all. Democratic politics has become something we watch rather than something we do. As political spectators and clients of governments for which we otherwise feel no responsibility, it is no wonder that service should appear legitimate only as an alternative to government —a product of voluntarism or altruism or philanthropy. To serve retains its moral character, but as an imperative of the private person rather than a concomitant of citizenship; its obligations are entirely supererogatory and can never be the subject of political imperatives. The model is compassion: charity, where people give to others who are needy out of love or pity, but not out of duty. Charity flourishes as a counter to the private sector's vices: greed, narcissism, and privatism, which, from the point of view of competition and productivity, may be virtues, but, as conservative critics of libertarianism note, can undermine social mores. It functions as a safe antidote to Reaganism overdone: Donald Trump spending Thursday evenings in a soup kitchen feeding the homeless his runaway development projects have helped to create. To the extent that service has been reduced to charity and that civic obligation and civic service have lost their place in our nation's political vocabulary, it is because we long ago bankrupted our practice of citizenship.

These observations notwithstanding, there are ample signs of a burgeoning interest in service in the United States today, an interest for the most part, however, that has been segregated from the discussion of citizenship. Some of the bills pending in Congress tie service to the federal college loan program, and many others (along with most of the school and college service programs) embrace a spirit of private sector voluntarism that seems at odds with, rather than reinforcing of, the obligations of citizenship. We continue to think of service as an apt punishment for white-collar felons on the grand scale (Colonel Oliver North, for example). No wonder young Americans have a hard time understanding service as a function of citizenship when legislators insist it is retribution for crime or (same thing?) poverty. The successful resuscitation of the idea of service will not proceed far without refurbishing the theory and practice of democratic citizenship—which must be any successful service program's primary goal.

A vigorous conception of citizenship was not bankrupted by choice or design. Rather it has been an inevitable consequence of historical conditions that have combined with the characteristically liberal distrust of democracy to favor a less active understanding of the citizen than was current in the republican tradition from which modern democracy issued. The entire history of citizenship in the West, from ancient Athens to the great democratic revolutions of the eighteenth and nineteenth centuries, has been one in which, as the compass of citizenship has expanded, its significance has contracted. More and more people have gained access to a civic status that has entailed less and less, but grown evermore defensive and rights oriented. A small handful of property-owning males once exercised a prodigious everyday franchise; now universal suffrage permits every man and woman to cast a ballot once a year in what many think of as an exercise in meaninglessness. Or they conceive of themselves exclusively as rights bearers (a vital function of citizenship as dissent) without duties.

Before considering modern remedies to the defects of thin democracy or advancing feasible programs for strengthening service in an appropriate educational setting, let us briefly review this ironic tradition in which, as the compass of the franchise grew, the value of the citizenship it conveyed depreciated.

A BRIEF HISTORICAL SURVEY
OF THE GROWTH OF THE FRANCHISE
AND THE DECLINE OF CITIZENSHIP

We derive our richest conception of citizenship from classical Athens in the fifth century when, paradoxically, a slave society that excluded women, immigrants, resident foreigners, and slaves from the ranks of its citizens nonetheless afforded that one-fifth of the population that was politically active an extraordinarily powerful role in governance. The citizen was required to participate in legislative assemblies that met every ten days or so and acted as the sovereign authority of the polis, making policy on foreign and domestic issues from war and empire to tariffs and weights and measures. The citizen also served regularly on juries with five hundred, a thousand, and sometimes more members hearing cases concerning minor civil matters as well as capital crimes and treason. He could be chosen (by sortition) for roughly half the civic magistracies through which Athens was governed on a day-to-day basis and had to pay for and serve in the military campaigns he had, as a citizen of the assembly, decided to pursue.

When Aristotle wrote in *The Politics* that man was a *zoon politikon* (political animal), he meant that man was born to civic membership in a polity. Unlike the gods and the beasts, who were capable of solitude, men were naturally sociable and found their identity in their membership in a community. Extrapolitical pursuits — both familial (regulated by women) and economic (undergirded by slave labor) — were secondary, utilitarian activities aimed at providing for procreation and sustenance, but little better than what all animals were required to do for survival and something less than constitutive of what it meant to be human.

Pericles was doing more than boasting when in Thucydides' account of the Funeral Oration he exulted: "We do not say that a man who takes no interest in politics is a man who minds his own business; we say that he has no business here at all." Even Socrates, no friend to Athenian democracy, refused to choose exile over death and reflected (in the *Crito*) on how much he owed to Athens's laws under which (he acknowledged) he was educated, provided for, and allowed to live. To a Greek, then, ostracism *was* a fate worse than death. To be outside the city, beyond the polis, was to forgo living as a human being; to be an individual was, quite literally, to be an *idiot*. When King Oedipus sought a punishment for himself as horrific as his crimes, he chose not death but exile from Thebes.

Citizenship to the Greeks was as knowledge is to philosophers: a cherished object of veneration. It entailed, to coin a term, a veritable *philopoliteia,* a love of the political so strong that it outweighed most other concerns. This powerful sense of politics has been replicated only occasionally—often in small, homogenous civic polities such as the Italian republics of the late Renaissance and the Swiss confederation of the fifteenth and sixteenth centuries—but has largely vanished in the modern world, where politics is the last refuge of scoundrels and things private are by far more venerable than things public (the old *res publica*). Nostalgic yearners for the old *philopoliteia* like Hannah Arendt or the disciples of Leo Strauss suggest that the demarcation line between antiquity and modernity is also a demarcation between virtue and corruption, justice and commerce, public goods and private greed. But the ancient ideals of civic virtue and civic participation are gone along with the belief that citizenship expresses the highest in human character, the most precious possession a man has to lose, a citizenship that—even as it facilitates common living—defines individual being.

Citizenship had already lost some of its moral luster by the time of the Romans, who learned a lesson from the example of the Athenians. The Athenians had tried futilely to extend an empire while jealously guarding the narrow boundaries of their citizenship and had ended up losing both empire and democracy. Roman citizenship grew along with imperial ambition. Beginning with their legendary conquest over the neighboring Sabines, the Romans gave to the vanquished survivors of their slaughters the gift of Roman citizenship. As their empire grew, the conquered became Romans. By the second century A.D., when Rome's territory began to match its imperial imagination, peoples in distant Gaul and Alemannia, whose language and customs were utterly alien to Rome's and who knew Romans only as efficient, irresistible warriors, nonetheless carried the name *cives* and shared minimal legal rights with those who had vanquished them. In time, all of Europe and much of the Mediterranean became Roman; the idea of Roman citizenship, however, had lost the immediacy and vitality of its Athenian cousin. Active participation had been replaced by minimal legal rights, with many more men enjoying far fewer powers. But Rome persisted where Athens had gone under, and the modern concept of citizenship as a form of thin legal personhood rather than a rich and textured human identity took root. Rights flourished, participation eroded.

After the Renaissance, and the rediscovery of Aristotle, antiquity enjoyed a renewed fashion, and early modern political theorists from Machiavelli to James Harrington again took up classical conceptions of citizenship and civic virtue and developed a tradition of republican thought that influenced polities in the burgeoning nation-states of Europe. Nationalism inspired a new understanding of the citizen-subject with obligations to the crown that included military service, and the rise of national armies—how Machiavelli admired them!—reinforced the idea of a civic polity. But the focus was shifting. The economic market, previously a locus for secondary private activity, came to be seen as the crucial arena of human productivity and, thus, of potential human virtue. As the classical weighting of the public and political over the private and economic was inverted, *liberty* ceased to mean only license and *individual* ceased to mean only anarchist or idiot. Where once commerce had been associated with the insufficiency of individuals and virtue had been understood as a wholly public commodity, by the eighteenth century commerce had come to denote a system whereby virtue might acquire a private meaning (if only by such indirect devices as the invisible hand—today's supply-side economics). Freedom became increasingly associated not only with dissent against illegitimate authority but with private agency even against a legitimate state. Thus did the state—above all the democratic state—come gradually to be perceived as liberty's primary nemesis.

The writings of Machiavelli and Montesquieu on the continent, as well as those of Harrington and his fellow republicans in England, struggled to restore vigorous citizenship and civic virtue to the political center. But the privileging of economic activity as the basis for social growth, and the concommitant stress on individual activity and private choice, both shaped and placed limits on the republican revival. The founding of new republics, above all the United States, brought to the surface the deep controversy over whether public virtue or private economic activity was to be the basis for a productive and stable society. Calvinist doctrine tried to bridge the two conceptions, as John Patrick Diggins has shown in his remarkable book *The Lost Soul of American Politics,* but even where civic virtue held its own in theory, commerce seemed to prevail in practice. For the virtuous republic modeled on antiquity relied above all on the cultivation of citizenship and demanded civic education, civic participation, and sufficient civic activism to guarantee a responsible electorate. In contrast, the new commercial republic called for a limited state whose primary function was to protect the market and for individuals whose primary motives were economic—the good citizen as productive capitalist or efficient worker—and who held the state and the democratic majority in suspicion, if not outright contempt. Religion, Tocqueville and others hoped, might continue to tether people to the civic polity and ground responsibility; but the secularism it was meant to prop up was religion's chief adversary, and public space had been stripped bare long before Richard John Neuhaus wrote his *Naked Public Square.*

Ironically, the coming of capitalism gave a push to the franchise even as it presumed a limited and privatized conception of what the franchise entailed. The final victory of capitalism over feudalism in England arrived with the nearly simultaneous abolition of the Corn Laws (and thus trade barriers) and the radical extension of the franchise in the first half of the nineteenth century. Markets, which stood for a theoretical equality that workers hoped to turn into political practice, offered a challenge to organizers, spurred the syndicalist and socialist movements, and motivated labor. Motivated labor in turn demanded the vote. In challenging feudalism in the name of capitalism, Adam Smith, David Ricardo, and Thomas Malthus assailed economic parasitism and privilege in a manner that invited an assault on political privilege and property and class limits on the franchise. If real property could not bar capital from electoral representation, why should capital bar productive (though propertyless) labor from representation? The outline of Marx was already visible to a careful reader of Ricardo and Malthus.

Democracy was thus born in the modern world with capitalism as its midwife—a capitalism that, however, was simultaneously transforming the classical values that constituted its core. More and more people shared in a power that meant less and less. Property owners without noble titles, then capitalists without real property, and in time workers with neither capital nor property won the rights of the citizen, only to discover that those rights were reactive and cautionary rather than empowering and participatory—giving citizens protection against the state but little control over it. Hoping to win the right to self-government, men (and in time women) found themselves relegated to the passive role of watchdogs, guardians of rights that no longer seemed to entail obligations, private persons whose liberty was defined exclusively by the absence of state power.

The advocates of strong democratic participation acknowledged that self-government by a community was feasible only under limited conditions: a homogenous population sharing a common history, a common religion, and common values; an uncomplicated economic frame characterized by modesty, relative austerity, and rough equality; and a limited territory ensuring both commonality and equality. Such conditions, theorists like Rousseau warned, were fast disappearing in Europe and seemed incompatible with almost everything associated with modernization.

Certainly the French Revolution seemed to provide ample evidence that the attempt to introduce radical democracy in the setting of an urban, industrializing mass metropolis was likely to result in tyrannical collectivism as well as equality and in terror as well as liberty. Indeed, to the extent partisans of individualism, property, liberty, and the modern market felt threatened by the populist tradition, they argued not merely that democracy was atavistic, but that it was undesirable. Today many Americans—still students and disciples of that powerful tradition of liberalism running from William Godwin, Alexis de Tocqueville, and Benjamin Constant to Walter Lippmann, Robert Nozick, and Milton Friedman that places the fear of majoritarianism first among its many anxieties—retain a distrust of participatory democracy, equating it with mob rule or the tyranny of opinion. This fear may seem out of all proportion to the actual danger, above all in a republic as thoroughly hemmed in by constitutional constraints as ours. Louis Hartz observed with more frustration than wit that the majority in America has forever been a puppy dog tethered to a lion's leash. Neo-Hamiltonian critics still insist that the public mind must be filtered and refined through the cortex of its betters: Give the franchise to all, but don't let them do much with it. Protect them from government with a sturdy barrier of rights, but protect government from them with a representative system that guarantees they will not themselves be legislators. In short, let them vote for the governors, but do not let them govern.

The hostility to citizenship and the contempt for *res publica* have taken a toll even on the limited notion of citizenship permitted by limited government and by the dominion of market forces over political forces. Only half the eligible electorate participates in presidential elections (and the numbers fall off quickly in lesser elections), plummeting to 15 percent or less in local primaries—where, however, millions of dollars are spent by eager candidates. (Leonard Lauder, a candidate in a 1980s New York mayoralty primary, spent $13 million *losing* the Republican nomination!) The public airwaves are licensed to private corporations who sell them back to the public during elections at fees so exorbitant that a free electoral process can hardly be said to survive. Young Americans vote less often than old, Americans of color less than white, poor Americans less than the well-off. Whether nonvoting is, as Frances Fox Piven argues, a political act of resistance or simply a sign of the morbidity of electoral politics, democracy even in its thin version seems to be in some trouble.

Yet despite the growth of elephantine and unaccountable corporate bureaucracies, liberal and libertarian critics continue to single out the democratic state as liberty's most dangerous foe. No wonder then that the renewed call for national service uses the rhetoric of voluntarism, charity, and good works rather than the rhetoric of citizenship and responsibility. These bring us full circle to the problem with which we began: the civic vacuum in which the issue of national service is discussed today, even by its advocates.

SERVICE UNDER THIN DEMOCRACY: A PROPOSAL FOR MANDATORY CITIZEN EDUCATION AND COMMUNITY SERVICE

For all the welcome interest in the idea of service today in the United States, little can be expected from it unless it inspires a renewed interest in civic education and citizenship. Simply to enlist volunteers to serve others less fortunate or those at risk (we are *all* at risk) or to conscript young people to do some form of national service in the name of improving their moral character or forcing them to repay the debt they owe their country (the language of market contracts applied to politics and the public good) will do little to reconstruct citizenship or shore up democracy. Rather it sells short the growing desire to do service, for that desire carries within it a longing for community, a need to honor what the sociologist Robert Bellah (following Tocqueville) identifies as the "habits of the heart" nurtured by membership in communal associations. This need must be met by healthy democratic forms of community in a democracy or it will breed unhealthy and antidemocratic forms: gangs, secret societies, conspiratorial political groups, hierarchical clubs, and exclusive communities. Participatory democratic communities permit an identification with others that is compatible with individual liberty.

Service to the nation is not a gift of altruists but the duty of free men and women whose freedom is wholly dependent on and can survive only through the assumption of political responsibilities. The confounding of service with altruism (charity) and volunteerism is radically ahistorical and thus particularly troublesome, for the history of the United States suggests a nation devoted to civic education for citizenship. The traditional American wellspring of service was not the nineteenth-century poorhouse or its corollaries like noblesse oblige, but the older idea of the responsible citizen as a primary objective of liberal education. In this tradition service is something we owe ourselves or that part of ourselves that is embedded in the civic community. It assumes that our rights and liberties do not come for free, that unless we assume the responsibilities of citizens we will not be able to preserve them.

For these reasons citizenship and service have historically been the first concern of the public (and private) educational system. American colleges and universities were founded in the seventeenth and eighteenth centuries on the idea of service: service to church (many began as training seminars for the ministry), service to the local community, and service to the emerging nation. Because so many wealthy parents sent their children to school in England, American schools emphasized training the young to become what the famous farmer Crèvecoeur called in 1782 "this new man, the American." This was true among the schools founded before the Revolution (Harvard, William and Mary, Yale, and Princeton, to take the four oldest) and of Queens College in New Brunswick (Rutgers University in its first incarnation), chartered in 1766 to "promote learning for the benefit of the community."

By the nineteenth century, Benjamin Rush's call for the nation's colleges to become "nurseries of wise and good men" who might ensure a wise and good country had become the motto of dozens of new church-related schools and land grant colleges. The Gilded Age took its toll on this spirit, however, and by the beginning of the twentieth century Woodrow Wilson was worrying that "as a nation we are becoming civically illiterate. Unless we find better ways to educate ourselves as citizens, we run the risk of drifting unwittingly into a new kind of Dark Age—a time when small cadres of specialists will control knowledge and thus control the decision making process." Wilson urged—against the specializing spirit of the new German-influenced research universities like Johns Hopkins—that the "air of affairs" be admitted into the classrooms of America and that "the spirit of service" be permitted once again to "give college a place in the public annals of the nation."

The call for a liberal education relevant to democracy gets renewed in each generation: during World War II the fate of the war in Europe and the Pacific was seen as hinging in part on the capacity of America's schools and colleges to produce civic-minded, patriotic young Americans who understood the meaning of democracy and who (Paul Fussell notwithstanding) knew the difference between what they were fighting for and what their enemies were fighting for. In the 1960s, concern for democracy and the civic education of the young led many colleges to experimentation in the name of relevance. Few reached so far or waxed as hyperbolic as Rutgers' Livingston College, which issued the following inaugural bulletin toward the end of the 1960s:

> There will be freedom at Livingston College! For Livingston will have no ivory towers. It cannot; our cities are decaying, many of our fellow men are starving, social injustice and racism litter the earth. . . . We feel a strong conviction that the gap between the campus and the urban community must be narrowed.

Although many colleges' aspirations were more modest, they were led, if only by their students, to question the relationship of the ivory tower to the democratic nation, and a number tried to develop programs of some value to the country's democratic agenda.

In the 1980s the spirit that put civic questions to the complacent professionalism and research orientation of the modern university is again alive. In their 1981 study *Higher Learning in the Nation's Service*, Ernest Boyer and Fred Hechinger asked that "a new generation of Americans . . . be educated for life in an increasingly complex world . . . through civic education [that] prepares students of all ages to participate more effectively in our social institutions."

Over the past few years interest in civic education and community service has fairly exploded. At the beginning of the decade the Kettering Foundation issued "The Transition of Youth to Adulthood," a report calling for national youth service of at least a year for all young Americans. Meanwhile the Committe for the Study of National Service at the Potomac Institute issued a report, "Youth and the Needs of the Nation," asking for closer coordination between and a unified national policy for programs like Peace Corps, Volunteers in Service to America, the Young Adults' Conservation Corps, and the Job Corps. Charles Moskos both surveys and embraces the decade of effort in his *Call to Civic Service*, a book that has promoted the cause of service on Capitol Hill, where members of Congress have introduced nearly a dozen bills in search of a workable program of national service. These legislative efforts, along with President Bush's national Points of Light Foundation, reflect a salutary interest in service. But they do not fully connect service to citizenship and to civic education, and many draw a misleading and (to democracy) dangerous picture of service as the rich helping the poor (charity) or the poor paying a debt to their country (service for college funding) — [an oversight largely remedied by President Clinton's Corporation for National Service, founded years after this essay was written.]

The Rutgers Program

In the spring of 1988, the late President Edward Bloustein of Rutgers University gave a commencement address in which he called for a mandatory program of citizen education and community service as a graduate requirement for all students at the State University of New Jersey. In the academic year 1988–89, I chaired the Committee on Education for Civic Leadership charged with exploring the president's ideas and developing a program through which they could be realized.

Nine governing principles are the foundation of the practical program:

1. That to teach the art of citizenship and responsibility is to practice it: so that teaching in this domain must be about acting and doing as well as about listening and learning, but must also afford an opportunity for reflecting on and discussing what is being done. In practical terms, this means that *community service can only be an instrument of education when it is connected to an academic learning experience in a classroom setting*. But the corollary is also true, that *civic education can only be effective when it encompasses experiential learning of the kind offered by community service or other similar forms of group activity*.

2. That the crucial democratic relationship between rights and responsibilities, which have too often been divorced in our society, can only be made visible in a setting of experiential learning where academic discussion is linked to practical activity. In other words, *learning about the relationship between civic responsibility and civic rights means exercising the rights and duties of membership in an actual community, whether that community is a classroom, a group project, or community service team or the university/college community at large*.

3. That antisocial, discriminatory, and other forms of selfish and abusive

or addictive behavior are often a symptom of the breakdown of civic community—both local and societal. This suggests that *to remedy many of the problems of alienation and disaffection of the young requires the reconstruction of the civic community,* something that a program of civic education based on experiential learning and community service may therefore be better able to accomplish than problem-by-problem piecemeal solutions pursued in isolation from underlying causes.

4. That respect for the full diversity and plurality of American life is possible only when students have an opportunity to interact outside of the classroom in ways that are, however, the subject of scrutiny and open discussion in the classroom. *An experiential learning process that includes both classroom learning and group work outside the classroom has the greatest likelihood of impacting on student ignorance, intolerance, and prejudice.*

5. That membership in a community entails *responsibilities and duties which are likely to be felt as binding only to the degree individuals feel empowered* in the community. As a consequence, *empowerment ought to be a significant dimension of education for civic responsibility*—particularly in the planning process to establish civic education and community service programs.

6. That civic education as experiential learning and community service must not discriminate among economic or other classes of Americans. If equal respect and equal rights are two keys to citizenship in a democracy, then *a civic education program must assure that no one is forced to participate merely because she or he is economically disadvantaged, and no one is exempted from service merely because he or she is economically privileged.*

7. That civic education should be communal as well as community based. If citizen education and experiential learning of the kind offered by community service are to be a lesson in community, *the ideal learning unit is not the individual but the small team, where people work together and learn together, experiencing what it means to become a small community together.* Civic education programs thus should be built around teams (of say five or ten or twenty) rather than around individuals.

8. That the point of any community service element of civic education must be to teach citizenship, not charity. If education is aimed at creating citizens, then it will be important to let the young see that *service is not just about altruism or charity, or a matter of those who are well-off helping those who are not. It is serving the public interest, which is the same thing as serving enlightened self-interest.* Young people serve themselves as members of the community by serving a public good that is also their own. The responsible citizen finally serves liberty.

9. That civic education needs to be regarded as an integral part of liberal education and thus should both be mandatory and should receive academic credit. Because citizenship is an acquired art, and *because those least likely to be spirited citizens or volunteers in their local or national community are most in* *need of civic training, an adequate program of citizen training with an opportunity for service needs to be mandatory. There are certain things a democracy simply must teach,* employing its full authority to do so: *citizenship is first among them.*

On the basis of these principles we developed a program that representatives of the student body and the Board of Governors have endorsed and duly constituted faculty bodies are currently reviewing. It calls for

A mandatory civic education course organized around (though not limited to) a classroom course with an academic syllabus, but also including a strong and innovative experiential learning focus utilizing group projects. A primary vehicle for these projects will be community service, as one of a number of experiential learning options; while the course will be mandatory, students will be free to choose community service or nonservice projects as their experiential learning group project. The required course will be buttressed by a program of incentives encouraging students to continue to participate in community service throughout their academic careers at Rutgers.

Course content will be broad and varied, but should guarantee some coverage of vital civic issues and questions, including the following:

1. The nature of the social or civic bond; social contract, legitimacy, authority, freedom, constitutionalism—the key concepts of political community.

2. The meaning of citizenship—representation versus participation, passive versus active forms of civic life; citizenship and service.

3. The university community—its structure and governance; the role of students, faculty, and adminstrators; questions of empowerment.

4. The place of ethnicity, religion, race, class, gender, and sexual orientation in a community: does equality mean abolishing differences? Or learning to respect and celebrate diversity and inclusiveness? How does a community deal with differences of the kind represented by the disequalizing effects of power and wealth?

5. The nature of service: differences between charity and social responsibility; between rights and needs or desires. What is the relationship between community service and citizenship? Can service be mandatory? Does a state have the right to mandate the training of citizens or does this violate freedom?

6. The nature of leadership in a democracy: are there special features to democratic leadership? Do strong leaders create weak followers? What is the relationship between leadership and equality?

7. Cooperation and competition: models of community interaction: how do private and public interests relate in a community?

8. The character of civic communities—educational, local, regional,

and national. What is the difference between society and the state? Is America a community? Is Rutgers a community? Do its several campuses (Camden, Newark, New Brunswick) constitute a community? What is the relationship between them and the communities in which they are located? What are the real issues of these communities—sexual harrassment, suicide, date rape, homophobia, racism, and distrust of authority?

A supervisory board will oversee the entire program, including its design and development, its standards and its operation. This Board will be composed of students, faculty, community representatives, and administrators who will act as the sole authority for the civic education program and who will also supervise the planning and implementation process in the transitional period. The Board will work with an *academic oversight committee,* a senior faculty committee responsible for academic design and for ongoing supervision over and review of course materials. This committee will work closely with community representatives and School of Social Work experts to assure quality control over community service and other group projects. Course sections will be taught by a combination of volunteers from faculty, graduate students, and more advanced students who have graduated from the program and wish to make seminar leadership part of their continuing service.

Variations on the basic model will be encouraged within the basic course design, with ample room for significant variations. Individual colleges, schools, and departments will be encouraged to develop their own versions of the course to suit the particular needs of their students and the civic issues particular to their disciplines or areas. The Senior Academic Committee and the Supervisory Board will assure standards by examining and approving proposed variations on the basic course. Thus, the Engineering School might wish to develop a program around the responsibilities of scientists, the Mason Gross School for the Performing Arts might wish to pioneer community service options focusing on students performing in and bringing arts education to schools and senior centers in the community, or Douglass College might want to capitalize on its long-standing commitment to encourage women to become active leaders by developing its own appropriate course variation.

Experiential learning is crucial to the program; for the key difference between the program offered here and traditional civic education approaches is the focus on learning outside the classroom, integrated into the classroom. Students will utilize group projects in community service and in other extraseminar group activities as the basis for reading and reflecting on course material. Experiential learning permits students to apply classroom learning to the real world, and to subject real world experience to classroom examination. To plan adequately for an experiential learning focus and to assure that projects are pedagogically sound and responsible to the communities they may engage, particular attention will be given to its design in the planning phase.

The team approach is a special feature of the Rutgers proposal. All experiential learning projects will be group projects where individuals learn in concert with others, where they experience community in part by practicing community during the learning process. We urge special attention be given to the role of groups or teams in the design of both the classroom format and the experiential learning component of the basic course.

Community service is only one among the several options for experiential learning, but it will clearly be the choice of a majority of students, and is in fact the centerpiece of the Rutgers program. For we believe that community service, when related to citizenship and social responsibility in a disciplined pedagogical setting, is the most powerful form of experiential learning. As such, it is central to our conception of the civic education process.

An incentive program for continuing service is built into the Rutgers project, because our objective is to install in students a spirit of citizenship that is enduring. It is thus vital that the program, though it is centered on the freshman year course, not be limited to that initial experience, and that there be opportunities for ongoing service and participation throughout the four years of college.

Oversight and review are regarded as ongoing responsibilities of the program. In order to assure flexibility, adaptability to changing conditions, ongoing excellence, and the test of standards, every element in the program will be subjected to regular review and revision by the faculty and the student body, as represented on the Supervisory Board, the Academic Oversight Committee, and the administration. This process of review will be mandated and scheduled on a regular basis, so that it will not come to depend on the vagaries of goodwill.

[Today (1997), this program encompasses not a single mandatory course but over three dozen service-learning courses enrolling over one thousand students.]

CONCLUSION

The Rutgers program depicted here is only one possible model. But some form of civic education seems necessary. For democracy to be capable of withstanding the challenges of a complex, often undemocratic, interdependent world, creating new generations of citizens is not a discretionary activity. Freedom is a hothouse plant that flourishes only when it it carefully tended. It is also, as Rousseau reminded us, a food easy to eat but hard to digest, and it has remained undigested more often than it has been assimilated into a democratic body politic. Without active citizens who see in service not the altruism of charity but the necessity of taking responsibility for the authority on which liberty depends, no democracy can function properly or, in the long run, even survive. National service is not merely a good idea; it is an indispensable prerequisite of citizenship and thus a condition for democracy's preservation. The Rutgers program offers a model that integrates liberal education, experiential learning, community service, and citizen education. Using the nation's schools and colleges as laboratories of citizenship and service offers an attractive way to develop civic service for all Americans without establishing some elephantine and costly civilian surrogate for the Pentagon and provides a means by which we can restore the civic mission of our educational institutions.

CHAPTER 15

Cultural Conservatism and Democratic Education: Lessons from the Sixties

STUDENTS cannot finish revolutions, but they have often started them, lending to rebellion their youth, their education, their optimism, their inexperience, and their foolhardiness. Because the future looms large before them and the past is but a small space immediately behind them, they have little to lose. They live in a world of artful imagination, free from the onus of reality. "Die Gedanken sind frei!"—our thoughts are free!—they have always gloated in their poetry and their songs.

From the free speech movement at Berkeley to the Columbia occupation, from the Free University movement to the Kent State killings, the revolution that was the sixties was above all a student revolution. The counterculture was a student culture, the war against the war in Vietnam, a student war, the home turf of the rebels, student turf—schools, colleges, universities. The leading organization was run by students devoted to a democratic society (they thought). Democracy may have been, as a pamphlet from the era put it, "in the streets," but the streets were filled with students.

Students start revolutions, but are rarely successful revolutionaries; advanced solely by students, there were revolutions in civil rights, in the war on poverty, in the struggle to turn Vietnam into a respectable issue for the middle class—but there was little power in flowers and no enduring political legacy for a movement that was unable to rally potential allies in the unions, the racial minorities, and the other constituencies that might have been capable of winning serious victories at the polls.

Yet there has been one legacy that has lasted, precisely where one would most expect it (after all, this was a student revolution): in education. The agenda for the educational debates of the eighties was fixed in the sixties. *The Closing of the American Mind* capitalizes on the contemporary mood of reaction; but it is first of all a book about what happened twenty years ago at Cornell, where Allan Bloom, then a young professor of political philosophy, looked on in horror as the real world of race, guns, and power intruded on his intellectual sanctuary. And when William Bennett shakes his fist at Stanford's faculty for trashing their great books curriculum (well, actually they only knocked a few "classics" off the list to make room for representative women, nonwhites, and non-Western writers, but let's not quibble) there is little doubt that for him the trouble really started when students first raised the cry of "relevance" in the sixties. As conservatives have noticed, the revolutionaries of that era have not really vanished; they have become teachers. The generation that challenged the professoriate twenty years ago is today itself the professoriate, or an influential part of it. The long hairs have gone gray but the ideals that inflamed these now balding pates continue to infuse sociology lectures on mutualism and political science seminars exploring Green politics or revisioned feminist liberation.

Of course the majority of the would-be rebels have gone into law or business where they have been sufficiently constrained by the responsibilities of money and power to set aside their inconvenient ideals. No such constraints affect those who live and work on that periphery where in our society serious education takes place. Impotent to affect power and irrelevant to the "action" in market America, teachers have had little reason to cultivate conservatism or for that matter that form of responsibility that for Americans means quiescence. Irresponsibility has always been a duty of the good teacher: that was (*pace* Bloom) Socrates' most radical, most truly subversive lesson. For schools to teach only what life teaches — limits — disembowels the future.

Yet it was not always so; to an earlier generation, the schools and universities of America seemed as set against the future as today they seem, to some, set against the past. Anyone not sure of this need only pay a little attention to those who have made themselves guardians of all that the sixties threatened to undo. These stalwarts of the past are incensed not by the ageing Resisters who fled to Canada to avoid conscription or did virtuous time at Danbury to avoid being shipped out; nor by the crazies of the Weather Underground, most of whom have blown themselves up or gone to better things on Wall Street; or the zealots of the Symbionese Liberation Army who are dead, in jail, or usefully unemployed. They seethe, rather, at associate professors in Iowa who teach students how to deconstruct texts (the point for conservatives would seem to be to embalm them); or at political scientists in Tulsa who take Gramsci as seriously as Hobbes and who spice up American government courses with James Baldwin novels. What they fear most is not the specter of international communism but the specter of pedagogical progressivism: the nontraditional major, affirmative action, women's studies, cultural pluralism, form over substance, too many electives, too few requirements, a studied tolerance for civilizations other than our own.

The modern university is then a major national scandal and, as such, the sixties' greatest success. Our salient "crises" (crises are recurring problems faced by men without memory) are all correctly attributed to that era's pedagogic reforms—for the conservatives, the youthful excesses of kids out of control. The erosion of standards, the collapse of classical education, the eclipse of the great books, the watering down of substantive curriculum with "political" agendas, the substitution of form for content, the flourishing of mediocrity, the relativizing of values, creeping nihilism, and MTV are so many products of a revolution its makers thought had failed. Professor Bloom and Mr. Bennett agree that what the student reformers in the sixties sowed in innovation and reform the eighties are reaping in illiteracy and ignorance.

While other debates have acquired new contexts or a fresh rhetoric, education debates continue to revolve around issues raised in the sixties; and they in turn were a radical restatement of perenniel questions posed earlier by Dewey or Nietzsche—or perhaps even Socrates. The Roosevelt coalition and Keynesian economics are dead for liberals and conservatives alike, the cold war is passé, and even anticommunism is no longer a satisfactory substitute for foreign policy. But in education the issues are unchanged.

For education has always been about a single crucial issue: the relationship between ideals and reality, between the aspirations of the spirit and the nature of civil society. From the time of the Greeks, the educator's role was to mediate the world of the mind and the world of experience, to accommodate the ideal to reality and fix the relationship of morality to power. All of the sixties' debates about illegitimate power, the role of the university, secret research, social science positivism, the character of authority, the position of teachers, the responsibility of students were finally about the question of the place of ideals in the real world—whether the university was to be reality's way of socializing the innocent into power (useful corruption, so to speak); or a way for conscience to tether power to ideals and hence a tool by which the real world could be measured, challenged, even transformed.

In the sixties, the question gained new cogency: was the university to be an essentially *critical* institution or an essentially *socializing* institution? A vehicle of change or a vehicle of confirmation? Was its role to create civic activity or civic passivity? Was the educated citizen to be a critical thinker or a well socialized yea-sayer? Would power be reinforced or discomfited by the educators? The issue was the place of education in a democratic society, and the one thing clear to students was that the university's leading positions—value neutrality, impartiality, the separation of facts and values, positivism—were spurious, impossible in a world where knowledge was always about (among other things) power, and where truth always reflected (among other things) somebody's interests. This was Habermas's lesson in his influential *Knowledge and Interests*. To isolate cognition from influence was to disguise its relationship to society. The educational establishment that came under attack from this left had tried to conceal its establishment biases under a cloak of neutrality—the claim to an ivory-tower objectivity that heard and saw and spoke no evil; nor, for that matter, any good, since value-neutrality proscribed both opprobrium and approbation.

Social scientists led the way in arguing that the university's mission was impartial and scientific, and that students who insisted on "revealing" its political commitments were only trying to inculcate it with their own. If such models as systems theory, cross-polity survey research, and behaviorism produced a picture of government and of human behavior that seemed to legitimize the American status quo and delegitimize political change, that was but an accident, a piece of scientific serendipity. When Gabriel Almond and Sidney Verba published their influential *Civic Culture* at the beginning of the sixties, American democracy, measured against a set of "neutral" and "objective" cross-polity standards, simply turned out to be descriptively superior to the democracy of the other nations in the study— not as the result of the national origins or political preferences of the authors, but purely as a consequence of scientific investigation.

But of course as students quickly perceived, it was in truth a particular American reality (fifties stasis) that made plausible the social science paradigms of that era, by making stability, equilibrium, and passivity seem like immutable features of social reality. This became clear in the late sixties when social scientists were rocked by forms of civil protest, social unrest, and urban breakdown in their own backyard for which their models left them totally unprepared.

In a recent Presidential address to the American Political Science Association, Professor Samuel Huntington of Harvard University boasted that political science as a discipline has always been on the side of democracy. But in the 1960s and 1970s Huntington, along with so many of his colleagues, was insisting that political science could take no position on democracy (though political scientists might subjectively appreciate it); and moreover that, from the perspective of equilibrium theory, what was called democracy worked best when the public was quiescent. Active participation, political mobilization, and social movements all worked to paralyze the political system through a process of what Huntington called democratic overload. Conventional democratic theory was little more than antidemocratic theory masquerading as science.

What university critics and student rebels were insisting on in the sixties then was that the "objectivity" of the university and the "impartiality" of the social sciences were sham. The university was committed, but covertly committed, and to establishment rather than reformist values and ends. What they had discovered is what political theorists on the right as well as on the left had been arguing since the fifties: that neither the university nor the human sciences could possibly be value neutral, and that the pretense that they were would always be hypocrisy of a particularly dangerous kind, since it legitimized the powerful while concealing its own connections to power. The university was value-laden and so were its vaunted social disciplines. But its values and commitments were identical with those of the larger society and were largely invisible—the values of the powerful rather than the values of the critics; the commitments of the conservators of American dogma rather than the aspirations of the rebels of the American imagination.

The rule the reformers extrapolated from their experience was simple and enduring: there is no value neutrality, no impartial ivory tower; there are only express commitments and covert commitments. The radical values of critics cannot be disguised as "scientific" or value-neutral because they show up in sharp relief to the general background of established values. But the values of those in power vanish into the background that has produced them and permit supporters to claim neutrality on their behalf because against this background they are invisible—black cows grazing in a black forest in the middle of the night.

Against this reading of the sixties, what is to be made of the charges being leveled today by cultural conservatives such as Bennett or Bloom against the educational legacy of the sixties? Ironically, when they rail against relativism and nihilism, they seem implicitly to embrace the sixties' critique of scientism and "objectivity." Bennett and Bloom are committed to moral commitment with a fervor that is more redolent of Yippies than Yuppies. But where in the sixties a centrist, quasi-liberal establishment was insisting on value neutrality in its argument on behalf of positivistic social science, liberal tolerance, and pluralism, today the establishment is in the hands of the very conservatives who are that era's critics. From the inside, however, the critics have had to relocate their enemies on the outside: the left with which they once shared the critique of value neutrality in the university is now part of the university and must be charged with stumbling past relativism into the abyss of nihilism.

Yet the contemporary university is anything but value neutral. To the degree it is in the hands of adults who are children of the sixties, it is actively promoting substantive values—although, to be sure, they are not the values preferred by the right. Allan Bloom acknowledges as much, for while he assails value relativism in theory, it is the political and cultural practices of the educators and those they teach (as well as the values they mirror) that elicit his greatest fury. What is scandalous to him is not that the teachers believe nothing but that they believe something—something progressive, something radical, something disdainful of tradition. To the extent they are children of the sixties, they believe in equality, in disarmament, in tolerance, and in social justice, gender justice, racial justice, and a variety of other contemporary justices for which Bloom and company apparently have little use.

But schooling is only a single moment in the socializing environment that confronts the young. It would be foolish to think that the professoriate alone controls how they think and feel, or that radicalism is in any way their dominant political orientation. Most of the substantive values reflected in their attitudes mirror the popular culture in which they live and the economic cultures in which they make their careers. These cultures are powerfully value-laden and powerfully corrupting. There is a terrible hypocrisy in a society that accuses educators of corrupting the young with too many radical ideas and too indulgent a posture toward cultural pluralism, but remains silent in the face of the damage wrought by its own delicious forms of waywardness. "Do as I say," says the conservative, "not as the society I defend does." But the kids, being clever enough to know the difference between what is real and what is pretense, will always do as society does rather than as it says. They will invariably prepare themselves for a career with Finley, Kumble rather than with Milton, Virgil.

When they are not the committed democrats many professors who are veterans of the sixties would like them to be, the young are the committed privateers society wants them to become. They may as Bloom fears be agnostic as between Jesus and Buddha, but they are not agnostic as between Jesus/Buddha and hard cash. Without values? No, the students are chock full of them: they value competition, they value success, they value celebrity, they value power, and they value plain old greed. These are not expressions of a dumb neutrality or some post-Nietzschean moral torpor; and they certainly do not reflect the untoward biases of left-wing teachers. The right complains (in the title of the best-selling book by Diane Ravitch and Chester Finn, Jr.), about what our seventeen-year-olds know and don't know—about Plato, about Caesar, and about the Constitution of the United States. But in truth seventeen-year-olds know what they have to know to get ahead in America, and this has little to do with Plato, Caesar, and the Constitution of the United States. Can we really expect students to heed their teachers' calls for higher learning, when their school administrators are busy forging commercial alliances with corporations and governments for research and funding? The young have without doubt relativized religion and turned their backs on the Western tradition's defining principles, but this is the doing of modernity and all it entails rather than of yuppy puppy puerility or intellectual juvenile delinquency. The Harvard Business School has just added a mandatory course on ethics, but does anyone really believe that this scholastic exercise will offset the practical lessons graduates will find themselves being taught by Pentagon procurement officers, Wall Street arbitragers, or corporate take-over specialists?

Their problem is not ignorance; the young know the difference between the bonds of community and tax-free community bonds, between library stacks and blue-chip stocks, between writing a poem and writing a résumé. That they prefer the second to the first may be appalling, but it betokens value corruption not valuelessness, and signals the priority of socialization over schooling. We are not talking about nihilists, who spurn dollars and ideas, power and value, devils as well as angels. We are talking about value-loaded materialists and ardent careerists who have learned all too well what America (not its universities) has taught them.

The sixties critique still applies, then, in the decade of the eighties, and if the cultural right were less hypocritical it might discover it shares with critics on the left a common dismay at the contempt in which learning—understood as a critical education in values—is held by almost everyone except the long suffering teachers whom it has made the butt of its over-heated criticism.

Yet the pedagogical disagreements between right and left are not to be papered over by dwelling on their common enmity to hypocritical value neutrality. The conservative critics of sixties style progressive education do have a more probing and troubling line of criticism that can be traced back to William Buckley, Jr.'s observation that atheism was the key to the relationship of God and man at Yale and other too liberal elite universities. What the sixties did, this argument suggests, is to promote a model of education that catalyzed social disintegration. The left may have been as sharply critical of relativism and value neutrality in the sixties as the right is now. But its program of relevance, its assault on the sanctity of academia, its devotion to cultural pluralism, its subordination of scholarship to a political struggle for justice, and its conviction that the "better" and "best" of the world of excellence had no place in the leveling egalitarianism of the world of democracy, combined to undermine not just true learning but the already fraying moral bonds holding society together. It undermined attachments to nation (patriotism), divinity (religion), family (marriage), and children (motherhood), at the same time that it threw into doubt the great Western values on which these institutions rested. By creating a mood of interior skepticism and tolerance towards alien cultures and values, it left the generation which was to inherit the universities afloat on a sea of boundless subjectivity. Trying to exhibit the hypocrisy of establishment norms that passed for "objective," it destroyed all rational attempts to sustain something more than mere opinion or interest. It made knowledge the wholesale creature of power. Made over into a curriculum, this leftist critique destroyed the moral civic mission of the universities and deprived students of safe moorings. Inviting the young to take seriously the culture of poverty, the culture of women, the culture of the third world, it led them to ignore, neglect, even to derogate their own.

These criticisms go to the heart of educational and cultural conservatism. Their real target is not simply value relativism or materialist philistinism—for far from being sins of the left, these are themselves targets of leftist criticism; the true villain is modernity itself. After all, conservatives define themselves by their distrust of "progress," their discomfort with "liberation," their suspiciousness in the face of an "egalitarianism" that in the first instance appears to them as a leveling mediocrity and an incapacity to discern standards of excellence. Their quarrel is with what the secular, post-Enlightenment world has done to the traditional bonds which once held societies together. Like Alasdair MacIntyre, they mourn the loss of ancient virtues, and the pathologies that have accompanied both liberation and its therapeutic catalysts. Like him too, however, they seem not to notice that the virtues they rue were destroyed by historical forces that ran their course long before Tom Hayden or Abbie Hoffmann came crashing onto the American scene. The defect of conservative thought lies not so much in the criticisms of bourgeois modernity it has shared with the left at least since Nietzsche, but in its unwillingness to acknowledge the reality of the world it condemns.

The unraveling of societies that have lost the cohesive power of religion is a story at least as old as the French Revolution, as old as Rousseau and Tocqueville—both of whom urged the remedy of a "civil religion" on cultures in which natural religion and the bonds of traditional consensus had vanished. Our schools today can aspire to provide artificial civic and cultural bonds but they cannot revivify natural ones. Tocqueville knew that. He feared the loss of cohesion emancipation brought in its train, but he understood it to be inevitable, understood that creeping moral anarchy could not be avoided in a society organized around freedom. He worried that the emerging egalitarianism of America's vibrant local democracy could nourish envy, comformity, and a fatal leveling, but he also realized that equality was the currency by which the Americans had purchased their freedom and was understandably of great value to them. Modern conservatives share Tocqueville's fears but have neither his dialectical hopefulness (grasping the rose that springs from within the cross), nor his realism, that permitted him to recognize the ineluctability of the modern age—even in its more noxious manifestations. Bloom, Bennett, and company are moved by anxiety, sometimes—it almost seems—by terror, and rush forward to reclaim a vanished past. They urge curricula modeled on a golden age (an age that never actually existed, since the eighteenth and nineteenth century's "great books" were not necessarily ours), and they scapegoat teachers for having *created* the brave new world teachers are trying to help students learn to live in and to challenge.

The conservative's antipathy to democracy is in fact rather peculiar, for democracy is how women and men emancipated from the consoling certainties of authority (religious, political, and metaphysical) try to govern themselves in a world without definitive values. It is as much a political response to the terrors of modernity, as modernity's monstrous creation. Bloom, MacIntyre, and the others can only call for an impossible restoration of the world we have lost. The prudent democrat, on the other hand, teaches how we might survive the passing of values in a world that provides neither escape routes back into the authoritarian past nor ladders leading up into the aeries of the philosophers' republic. The democrat may even promise more: to transform survival into a virtue, by forging an art of politics capable of holding together and giving meaning to beings emancipated from the roots that once imprisoned their spirits even as it grounded their values.

The condition of modernity is above all America's condition: that is both our brave boast and our tragic fate, and it is what gives democracy its powerful American resonance. Educators are faced with teaching possible futures in a nation that too often pretends it has no past. Discontinuity is at once America's pathology and its virtue. It frees immigrants from the onus of a past from which they have fled even as it denies their children a history they need. Education for us must then always be civic education, education for and about living together in the absence of a common history or blood nationhood and in the face of pluralism's defining uncertainties. An America settled by rival religions and competing nationalities was in no position to cultivate cultural monism—however sustaining such a monism might have been to patriotism, national cohesion, and shared values. America allowed itself to be defined by the absence of common definitions: this is what the conservatives have never really understood or accepted. In a certain sense, their battle is a battle against America and the civic values produced by its melting pot politics. Women and blacks are only the most recent contenders for recognition in a culture that is constituted by plurality. When conservatives oppose curriculum reforms introducing race or gender into Western "culture" they signal their resistance to this plurality. But the pluralism they challenge is not an ideological weapon of the cultural left, it is a fact, perhaps *the* fact, of our cultural identity.

A thoughtful teacher under assault from cultural conservatives for teaching women's studies or third world literature might then be forgiven for concluding that behind the concern to protect Western Culture from modernity's ravages is a certain sense of cultural anxiety, posing as cultural monism, cultural superiority, even cultural imperialism. Dominant cultural paradigms have always sought the legitimacy of Truth or History or Tradition to protect themselves against fresh voices, even when those voices came from *within* the paradigm. Cultural conservatives have in fact succeeded in making their world-view a dominant paradigm of the eighties, allowing themselves to forget that dominance from within the paradigm. In making their world-view dominant, cultural conservatives have also allowed themselves to forget that not so long ago they were outsiders denouncing the "hypocrisy" of liberals and positivists who claimed the new science of liberal society as the leading paradigm of their culture.

As the conservatives knew then, the lesson of other cultures or of voiceless subcultures within a dominant culture need not be a lesson in relativism. The knee-jerk nativist reaction to Margaret Mead's style of anthropology (if we acknowledge that *they* practice polygamy, *our* devotion to monogamy will be undermined!) is silly. That there is more than one form of Truth does not necessarily entail the demise of all truth. That prudence is contextual and that practice takes different forms in different societies does not make prudence unvirtuous or practice immoral. In the significant artifacts, the "great books," the religious principles, of a great many societies are to be found the common threads of a common spirit. Universalism—to the degree it is possible in a pluralized world—must be a matter of parallel, complementary or mutually non-exclusive principles rather than of identical values and customs. To read the Mahabarhata is not to desecrate the Bible. The case for reading Virginia Woolf does not turn on the case for not reading Shakespeare. The war of good and evil, the struggle between the earthly and the transcendental, the tension between individual and community, the contest of liberty and power, the striving for eternity and universality pitted against the reality of mortality and particularity, the unending battles of men and women, of parents and children, of public and private, are all features of a common global condition; just as the eroding of authoritative values by scientific "progress" and the secularization of societies under conditions of industrialization and prosperity appear to be features of a common global fate. To deny the reality of this fate is to substitute power for judgment and to try to conceal our own forms of particularity (Western or white or male or propertied) behind a mask of universalism. *We* are what is universal, we say; *our* particularisms becomes Truth, all other particularism are merely particular.

But the idea of the universal, if it is to survive modernity's many skepticisms, will have to be an encompassing rather than a restricting idea, taking in and making sense of contradictions and differences. Student rebels, educational reformers and all those other children of Dewey who helped produce the educational revolution of the sixties got a good many things wrong, but they got a few things right as well. They saw that to expose the power biases of conventional science and "neutral" scholarship was less to undermine the pursuit of genuine truth than to clear hypocrisy from truth's way. And they appreciated that by including studies of and by women, blacks, and other dispossessed groups within Western society, they were not narrowing but enlarging the notion of Western culture.

That culture is in trouble—left, right, and center acknowledge as much.

We may weep along with Bloom, Bennett, and MacIntyre at how queasy we feel living in a world after virtue, at how difficult it is to discern the good in a world no longer shadowed by the authority of an eternal God or guided by a metaphysician's account of the eternal verities. Indeed, even modernity's fans may shudder a little at a world where modernity's great teacher—science—has been de-mythologized and forced to seek out a sociological legitimacy no longer automatically vouchsafed it by empiricism or rationalism. Nonetheless, it is this world for which educators must prepare the young—a world of doubts and puzzles, a world of too much materialism and too few great books, of more than enough selfishness and not enough civic education, a world where culture must mean the globe or mean nothing at all (though this could well result in it meaning nothing at all). But clinging to values that have lost their resonance, blaming outsiders for the loss of what the culture has failed to preserve from within, assailing the teachers for failing to teach the young what the old clearly do not want them to learn, is more than just hypocritical, it is dangerous.

From all those endless teach-ins, from the campus riots and student rebellions, from the campaigns against secret research and the anti-ROTC demonstrations, from the foolish innovations and the curricular novelties, from the free speech movement and the free university ideal, have come some saving truths. Equality is not the enemy of freedom; power must not be the determinant of culture; pluralism is not a recipe for nihilism; the opening of the schools to all need not spell the closing of the American mind; to acknowledge the plurality of culture is not to deny the universality of cultural aspirations; the rise of liberal education is not the same thing as the fall of Western culture, and finally, all education is and ought to be radical—a reminder of the past, a challenge to the present and a prod to the future. It will be worth something to set aside sufficient space in the pedagogy of the nineties to accommodate these hard-earned lessons of the sixties. For they are small but precious truths capable of securing an American future in a world that, however much the cultural conservatives curse it, is not going to be exclusively American, or white, or male.

CHAPTER 16

America Skips School:
Why We Talk So Much about Education
and Do So Little

ON SEPTEMBER 8, 1993, the day most of the nation's children were scheduled to return to school, the Department of Education Statistics issued a report, commissioned by Congress, on adult literacy and numeracy in the United States. The results? More than 90 million adult Americans lacked simple literacy. Fewer than 20 percent of those surveyed could compare two metaphors in a poem; not 4 percent could calculate the cost of carpeting at a given price for a room of a given size, using a calculator. As the DOE report was being issued, as if to echo its findings, two of the nation's largest school systems had delayed their openings: in New York, to remove asbestos from aging buildings; in Chicago, because of a battle over the budget.

Inspired by the report and the delays, pundits once again began chanting the familiar litany of the education crisis. We've heard it all many times before: 130,000 children bring guns along with their pencils and books to school each morning; juvenile arrests for murder increased by 85 percent from 1987 to 1991; more than 3,000 youngsters will drop out today and every day for the rest of the school year, until about 600,000 are lost by June—in many urban schools, perhaps half the enrollment. A lot of the dropouts will end up in prison, which is a surer bet for young black males than college: one in four will pass through the correctional system, and at least two out of three of those will be dropouts.

In quiet counterpoint to those staggering facts is another set of statistics: teachers make less than accountants, architects, doctors, lawyers, engineers, judges, health professionals, auditors, and surveyors. They can earn higher salaries teaching in Berlin, Tokyo, Ottawa, or Amsterdam than in New York or Chicago. American children are in school only about 180 days a year, as against 240 days or more for children in Europe or Japan. The richest school districts (school financing is local, not federal) spend twice as much per student as poorer ones do. The poorer ones seem almost beyond help: children with venereal disease or AIDS (2.5 million adolescents annually contract a sexually transmitted disease), gangs in the schoolyard, drugs in the class-room, children doing babies instead of homework, playground firefights featuring Uzis and Glocks.

Clearly, the social contract that obliges adults to pay taxes so that children can be educated is in imminent danger of collapse. Yet for all the astonishing statistics, more astonishing still is that no one seems to be listening. The education crisis is kind of like violence on television: the worse it gets the more inert we become, and the more of it we require to rekindle our attention. We've had a "crisis" every dozen years or so at least since the launch of *Sputnik,* in 1957, when American schools were accused of falling behind the world standard in science education. Just ten years ago, the National Commission on Excellence in Education warned that America's pedagogical inattention was putting America "at risk." What the commission called "a rising tide of mediocrity" was imperiling "our very future as a Nation and a people." What was happening to education was an "act of war."

Since then, countless reports have been issued decrying the condition of our educational system, the DOE report being only the most recent. They have come from every side, Republican as well as Democrat, from the private sector as well as the public. Yet for all the talk, little happens. At times, the schools look more like they are being dismantled than rebuilt. How can this be? If Americans over a broad political spectrum regard education as vital, why has nothing been done?

I have spent thirty years as a scholar examining the nature of democracy, and even more as a citizen optimistically celebrating its possibilities, but today I am increasingly persuaded that the reason for the country's inaction is that Americans do not really care about education—the country has grown comfortable with the game of "let's pretend we care."

As America's educational system crumbles, the pundits, instead of looking for solutions, search busily for scapegoats. Some assail the teachers— those "Profscam" pedagogues trained in the licentious Sixties who, as aging hippies, are supposedly still subverting the schools—for producing a dire illiteracy. Others turn on the kids themselves, so that at the same moment as we are transferring our responsibilities to the shoulders of the next generation, we are blaming them for our own generation's most conspicuous failures. Allan Bloom was typical of the many recent critics who have condemned the young as vapid, lazy, selfish, complacent, self-seeking, materialistic, small-minded, apathetic, greedy, and, of course, illiterate. E. D. Hirsch in his *Cultural Literacy* and Diane Ravitch and Chester E. Finn Jr. in their *What Do Our Seventeen-Year-Olds Know?* have lambasted the schools, the teachers, and the children for betraying the adult generation from which they were to inherit, the critics seemed confident, a precious cultural legacy.

How this captious literature reeks of hypocrisy! How sanctimonious all the hand-wringing over still another "education crisis" seems. Are we ourselves really so literate? Are our kids stupid or smart for ignoring what we preach and copying what we practice? The young, with their keen noses for hypocrisy, are in fact adept readers — but not of books. They are society-smart rather than school-smart, and what they read so acutely are the social signals emanating from the world in which they will have to make a living. Their teachers in that world, the nation's true pedagogues, are television, advertising, movies, politics, and the celebrity domains they define. We prattle about deficient schools and the gullible youngsters they turn out, so vulnerable to the siren song of drugs, but think nothing of letting the advertisers into the classroom to fashion what an *Advertising Age* essay calls "brand and product loyalties through classroom-centered, peer-powered lifestyle patterning."

Our kids spend 900 hours a year in school (the ones who go to school) and from 1,200 to 1,800 hours a year in front of the television set. From which are they likely to learn more? Critics such as Hirsch and Ravitch want to find out what our seventeen-year-olds know, but it's really pretty simple: they know exactly what our forty-seven-year-olds know and teach them by example — on television, in the boardroom, around Washington, on Madison Avenue, in Hollywood. The very first lesson smart kids learn is that it is much more important to heed what society teaches implicitly by its deeds and reward structures than what school teaches explicitly in its lesson plans and civic sermons. Here is a test for adults that may help reveal what the kids see when they look at our world.

Real-World Cultural Literacy

1. According to television, having fun in America means
   a) going blond
   b) drinking Pepsi
   c) playing Nintendo
   d) wearing Air Jordans
   e) reading Mark Twain

2. A good way to prepare for a high-income career and to acquire status in our society is to
   a) win a slam-dunk contest
   b) take over a company and sell off its assets
   c) start a successful rock band
   d) earn a professional degree
   e) become a kindergarten teacher

3. Book publishers are financially rewarded today for publishing

   a) mega-cookbooks
   b) mega–cat books
   c) megabooks by Michael Crichton
   d) megabooks by John Grisham
   e) mini-books by Voltaire

4. A major California bank that advertised "no previous credit history required" in inviting Berkeley students to apply for Visa cards nonetheless turned down one group of applicants because

   a) their parents had poor credit histories
   b) they had never held jobs
   c) they had outstanding student loans
   d) they were "humanities majors"

5. Colleges and universities are financially rewarded today for

   a) supporting bowl-quality football teams
   b) forging research relationships with large corporations
   c) sustaining professional programs in law and business
   d) stroking wealthy alumni
   e) fostering outstanding philosophy departments

6. Familiarity with *Henry IV, Part II* is likely to be of vital importance in

   a) planning a corporate takeover
   b) evaluating budget cuts in the Department of Education
   c) initiating a medical-malpractice lawsuit
   d) writing an impressive job résumé
   e) taking a test on what our seventeen-year-olds know

7. To help the young learn that "history is a living thing," Scholastic, Inc., a publisher of school magazines and paperbacks, recently distributed to 40,000 junior and senior high-school classrooms

   a) a complimentary video of the award-winning series *The Civil War*
   b) free copies of Plato's *Dialogues*
   c) an abridgment of Alexis de Tocqueville's *Democracy in America*
   d) a wall-size Periodic Table of the Elements
   e) gratis copies of Billy Joel's hit single "We Didn't Start the Fire" (which recounts history via a vaguely chronological list of warbled celebrity names)

My sample of forty-seven-year-olds scored very well on the test. Not surprisingly, so did their seventeen-year-old children. (For each question, either the last entry is correct or all responses are correct *except* the last one.) The results of the test reveal again the deep hypocrisy that runs through our lamentations about education. The illiteracy of the young turns out to be our own reflected back to us with embarrassing force. We honor ambition, we reward greed, we celebrate materialism, we worship acquisitiveness, we cherish success, and we commercialize the classroom—and then we bark at the young about the gentle arts of the spirit. We recommend history to the kids but rarely consult it ourselves. We make a fuss about ethics but are satisfied to see it taught as an "add-on," as in "ethics in medicine" or "ethics in business"—as if Sunday morning in church could compensate for uninterrupted sinning from Monday to Saturday.

The children are onto this game. They know that if we really valued schooling, we'd pay teachers what we pay stockbrokers; if we valued books, we'd spend a little something on the libraries so that adults could read, too; if we valued citizenship, we'd give national service and civic education more than pilot status; if we valued children, we wouldn't let them be abused, manipulated, impoverished, and killed in their beds by gang-war crossfire and stray bullets. Schools can and should lead, but when they confront a society that in every instance tells a story exactly opposite to the one they are supposed to be teaching, their job becomes impossible. When the society undoes each workday what the school tries to do each school day, schooling can't make much of a difference.

Inner-city children are not the only ones who are learning the wrong lessons. TV sends the same messages to everyone, and the success of Donald Trump, Pete Rose, Henry Kravis, or George Steinbrenner makes them potent role models, whatever their values. Teen dropouts are not blind; teen drug sellers are not deaf; teen college students who avoid the humanities in favor of pre-business or pre-law are not stupid. Being apt pupils of reality, they learn their lessons well. If they see a man with a rubber arm and an empty head who can throw a ball at 95 miles per hour pulling down millions of dollars a year while a dedicated primary-school teacher is getting crumbs, they will avoid careers in teaching even if they can't make the major leagues. If they observe their government spending up to $35,000 a year to keep a young black behind bars but a fraction of that to keep him in school, they will write off school (and probably write off blacks as well).

Our children's illiteracy is merely our own, which they assume with commendable prowess. They know what we have taught them all too well: there is nothing in Homer or Virginia Woolf, in Shakespeare or Toni Morrison, that will advantage them in climbing to the top of the American heap. Academic credentials may still count, but schooling in and of itself is for losers. Bookworms. Nerds. Inner-city rappers and fraternity-house wise guys are in full agreement about that. The point is to start pulling down the big bucks. Some kids just go into business earlier than others. Dropping out is the national pastime, if by dropping out we mean giving up the precious things of the mind and the spirit in which America shows so little interest and for which it offers so little payback. While the professors argue about whether to teach the ancient history of a putatively white Athens or the ancient history of a putatively black Egypt, the kids are watching televised political campaigns driven by mindless image-mongering and inflammatory polemics that ignore history altogether. Why, then, are we so surprised when our students dismiss the debate over the origins of civilization, whether Eurocentric or Afrocentric, and concentrate on cash-and-carry careers? Isn't the choice a tribute not to their ignorance but to their adaptive intelligence? Although we can hardly be proud of ourselves for what we are teaching them, we should at least be proud of them for how well they've learned our lessons.

Not all Americans have stopped caring about the schools, however. In the final irony of the educational endgame, cynical entrepreneurs like Chris Whittle are insinuating television into the classroom itself, bribing impoverished school boards by offering free TV sets on which they can show advertising for children—sold to sponsors at premium rates. Whittle, the mergers and acquisitions mogul of education, is trying to get rich off the poverty of public schools and the fears of parents. Can he really believe advertising in the schools enhances education? Or is he helping to corrupt public schools in ways that will make parents even more anxious to use vouchers for private schools—which might one day be run by Whittle's latest entrepreneurial venture, the Edison Project.

According to Lifetime Learning Systems, an educational-software company, "kids spend 40 percent of each day . . . where traditional advertising can't reach them." Not to worry, says Lifetime Learning in an *Advertising Age* promo: "Now, you can enter the classroom through custom-made learning materials created with your specific marketing objectives in mind. Communicate with young spenders directly and, through them, their teachers and families as well." If we redefine young learners as "young spenders," are the young really to be blamed for acting like mindless consumers? Can they become young spenders and still become young critical thinkers, let alone informed citizens? If we are willing to give TV cartoons the government's imprimatur as "educational television" (as we did a few years ago, until the FCC changed its mind), can we blame kids for educating themselves on television trash?

Everyone can agree that we should educate our children to be something more than young spenders molded by "lifestyle patterning." But what should the goals of the classroom be? In recent years it has been fashionable to define the educational crisis in terms of global competition and minimal competence, as if schools were no more than vocational institutions. Although it has talked sensibly about education, the Clinton Administration has leaned toward this approach, under the tutelage of Secretary of Labor Robert Reich.

The classroom, however, should not be merely a trade school. The fundamental task of education in a democracy is what Tocqueville once called the apprenticeship of liberty: learning to be free. I wonder whether Americans still believe liberty has to be learned and that its skills are worth learning. Or have they been deluded by two centuries of rhetoric into thinking that freedom is "natural" and can be taken for granted?

The claim that all men are born free, upon which America was founded, is at best a promising fiction. In real life, as every parent knows, children are born fragile, born needy, born ignorant, born unformed, born weak, born foolish, born dependent—born in chains. We acquire our freedom over time, if at all. Embedded in families, clans, communities, and nations, we must learn to be free. We may be natural consumers and born narcissists, but citizens have to be made. Liberal-arts education actually means education in the arts of liberty; the "servile arts" were the trades learned by unfree men in the Middle Ages, the vocational education of their day. Perhaps this is why Thomas Jefferson preferred to memorialize his founding of the University of Virginia on his tombstone rather than his two terms as president; it is certainly why he viewed his Bill for the More General Diffusion of Knowledge in Virginia as a centerpiece of his career (although it failed passage as legislation—times were perhaps not so different). John Adams, too, boasted regularly about Massachusetts's high literacy rates and publicly funded education.

Jefferson and Adams both understood that the Bill of Rights offered little protection in a nation without informed citizens. Once educated, however, a people was safe from even the subtlest tyrannies. Jefferson's democratic proclivities rested on his conviction that education could turn a people into a safe refuge—indeed "the only safe depository" for the ultimate powers of society. "Cherish therefore the spirit of our people," he wrote to Edward Carrington in 1787, "and keep alive their attention. Do not be severe upon their errors, but reclaim them by enlightening them. If once they become inattentive to public affairs, you and I and Congress and Assemblies, judges and governors, shall all become wolves."

The logic of democracy begins with public education, proceeds to informed citizenship, and comes to fruition in the securing of rights and liberties. We have been nominally democratic for so long that we presume it is our natural condition rather than the product of persistent effort and tenacious responsibility. We have decoupled rights from civic responsibilities and severed citizenship from education on the false assumption that citizens just happen. We have forgotten that the "public" in public schools means not just paid for by the public but procreative of the very idea of a public. Public schools are how a public—a citizenry—is forged and how young, selfish individuals turn into conscientious, community-minded citizens.

Among the several literacies that have attracted the anxious attention of commentators, civic literacy has been the least visible. Yet this is the fundamental literacy by which we live in a civil society. It encompasses the competence to participate in democratic communities, the ability to think critically and act with deliberation in a pluralistic world, and the empathy to identify sufficiently with others to live with them despite conflicts of interest and differences in character. At the most elementary level, what our children suffer from most, whether they're hurling racial epithets from fraternity porches or shooting one another down in schoolyards, is the absence of civility. Security guards and metal detectors are poor surrogates for civility, and they make our schools look increasingly like prisons (though they may be less safe than prisons). Jefferson thought schools would produce free men: we prove him right by putting dropouts in jail.

Civility is a work of the imagination, for it is through the imagination that we render others sufficiently like ourselves for them to become subjects of tolerance and respect, if not always affection. Democracy is anything but a "natural" form of association. It is an extraordinary and rare contrivance of cultivated imagination. Give the uneducated the right to participate in making collective decisions, and what results is not democracy but, at best, mob rule: the government of private prejudice once known as the tyranny of opinion. For Jefferson, the difference between the democratic temperance he admired in agrarian America and the rule of the rabble he condemned when viewing the social unrest of Europe's teeming cities was quite simply education. Madison had hoped to "filter" out popular passion through the device of representation. Jefferson saw in education a filter that could be installed within each individual, giving to each the capacity to rule prudently. Education creates a ruling aristocracy constrained by temperance and wisdom; when that education is public and universal, it is an aristocracy to which all can belong. At its best, the American dream of a free and equal society governed by judicious citizens has been this dream of an aristocracy of everyone.

To dream this dream of freedom is easy, but to secure it is difficult as well as expensive. Notwithstanding their lamentations, Americans do not appear ready to pay the price. There is no magic bullet for education. But I no longer can accept that the problem lies in the lack of consensus about remedies—in a dearth of solutions. There is no shortage of debate over how to repair our educational infrastructure. National standards or more local control? Vouchers or better public schools? More parental involvement or more teacher autonomy? A greater federal presence (only 5 or 6 percent of the nation's education budget is federally funded) or fairer local school taxes? More multicultural diversity or more emphasis on what Americans share in common? These are honest disputes. But I am convinced that the problem is simpler and more fundamental. Twenty years ago, writer and activist Frances Moore Lappé captured the essence of the world food crisis when she argued that starvation was caused not by a scarcity of food but by a global scarcity in democracy. The education crisis has the same genealogy. It stems from a dearth of democracy: an absence of democratic will and a consequent refusal to take our children, our schools, and our future seriously.

Most educators, even while they quarrel among themselves, will agree that a genuine commitment to any one of a number of different solutions could help enormously. Most agree that although money can't by itself solve problems, without money few problems can be solved. Money also can't win wars or put men in space, but it is the crucial facilitator. It is also how America has traditionally announced, We are serious about this!

If we were serious, we would raise teachers' salaries to levels that would attract the best young professionals in our society: starting lawyers get from $70,000 to $80,000—why don't starting kindergarten teachers get the same? Is their role in vouchsafing our future less significant? And although there is evidence suggesting that an increase in general educational expenditures doesn't translate automatically into better schools, there is also evidence that an increase aimed specifically at instructional services does. Can we really take in earnest the chattering devotion to excellence of a country so wedded in practice to mediocrity, a nation so ready to relegate teachers—conservators of our common future—to the professional backwaters?

If we were serious, we would upgrade physical facilities so that every school met the minimum standards of our better suburban institutions. Good buildings do not equal good education, but can any education at all take place in leaky, broken-down habitats of the kind described by Jonathan Kozol in his *Savage Inequalities*? If money is not a critical factor, why are our most successful suburban school districts funded at nearly twice the level of our inner-city schools? Being even at the starting line cannot guarantee that the runners will win or even finish the race, but not being even pretty much assures failure. We would rectify the balance not by penalizing wealthier communities but by bringing poorer communities up to standard, perhaps by finding sources of funding for our schools other than property taxes.

If we were serious, we'd extend the school year by a month or two so that learning could take place throughout the year. We'd reduce class size (which means more teachers) and nurture more cooperative learning so that kids could become actively responsible for their own education and that of their classmates. Perhaps most important, we'd raise standards and make teachers and students responsible for them. There are two ways to breed success: to lower standards so that everybody "passes" in a way that loses all meaning in the real world; and to raise standards and then meet them, so that school success translates into success beyond the classroom. From Confucian China to Imperial England, great nations have built their success in the world upon an education of excellence. The challenge in a democracy is to find a way to maintain excellence while extending educational opportunity to everyone.

Finally, if we were serious, parents, teachers, and students would be the real players while administrators, politicians, and experts would be secondary, at best advisers whose chief skill ought to be knowing when and how to facilitate the work of teachers and then get out of the way. If the Democrats can clean up federal government bureaucracy (the Gore plan), perhaps we can do the same for educational bureaucracy. In New York up to half of the city's teachers occupy jobs outside the classroom. No other enterprise is run that way: Half the soldiers at company headquarters? Half the cops at stationhouse desks? Half the working force in the assistant manager's office? Once the teachers are back in the classroom, they will need to be given more autonomy, more professional responsibility for the success or failure of their students. And parents will have to be drawn in not just because they have rights or because they are politically potent but because they have responsibilities and their children are unlikely to learn without parental engagement. How to define the parental role in the classroom would become serious business for educators.

Some Americans will say this is unrealistic. Times are tough, money's short, and the public is fed up with almost all of its public institutions: the schools are just one more frustrating disappointment. With all the goodwill in the world, it is still hard to know how schools can cure the ills that stem from the failure of so many other institutions. Saying we want education to come first won't put it first.

America, however, has historically been able to accomplish what it sets its mind to. When we wish it and will it, what we wish and will has happened. Our successes are willed; our failures seem to happen when will is absent. There are, of course, those who benefit from the bankruptcy of public education and the failure of democracy. But their blame is no greater than our own: in a world where doing nothing has such dire consequences, complacency has become a greater sin than malevolence.

In wartime, whenever we have known why we were fighting and believed in the cause, we have prevailed. Because we believe in profits, we are consummate salespersons and efficacious entrepreneurs. Because we love sports, ours are the dream teams. Why can't a Chicago junior high school be as good as the Chicago Bulls? Because we cherish individuality and mobility, we have created a magnificent (if costly) car culture and the world's largest automotive consumer market. Even as our lower schools are among the worst in the Western world, our graduate institutions are among the very best—because professional training in medicine, law, and technology is vital to our ambitions and because corporate America backs up state and federal priorities in this crucial domain. Look at the things we do well and observe how very well we do them: those are the things that as a nation we have willed.

Then observe what we do badly and ask yourself, Is it because the challenge is too great? Or is it because, finally, we aren't really serious? Would we will an end to the carnage and do whatever it took—more cops, state militias, federal marshals, the Marines?—if the dying children were white and middle class? Or is it a disdain for the young—white, brown, and black—that inures us to the pain? Why are we so sensitive to the retirees whose future (however foreshortened) we are quick to guarantee—don't worry, no reduced cost-of-living allowances, no taxes on social security except for the well-off—and so callous to the young? Have you noticed how health care is on every politician's agenda and education on no one's?

To me, the conclusion is inescapable: we are not serious. We have given up on the public schools because we have given up on the kids; and we have given up on the kids because we have given up on the future—perhaps because it looks too multicolored or too dim or too hard. "Liberty," said Jean-Jacques Rousseau, "is a food easy to eat but hard to digest." America is suffering from a bad case of indigestion. Finally, in giving up on the future, we have given up on democracy. Certainly there will be no liberty, no equality, no social justice without democracy, and there will be no democracy without citizens and the schools that forge civic identity and democratic responsibility. If I am wrong (I'd like to be), my error will be easy to discern, for before the year is out we will put education first on the nation's agenda. We will put it ahead of the deficit, for if the future is finished before it starts, the deficit doesn't matter. Ahead of defense, for without democracy, what liberties will be left to defend? Ahead of all the other public issues and public goods, for without public education there can be no public and hence no truly public issues or public goods to advance. When the polemics are spent and we are through hyperventilating about the crisis in education, there is only one question worth asking: are we serious? If we are, we can begin by honoring that old folk homily and put our money where for much too long our common American mouth has been. Our kids, for once, might even have reason to be grateful.

Education for Democracy

IT IS EASY enough to explain the continuing assault on America's children that passes as education policy nowadays: kids are politically invisible—without significant power—and their public schools are no longer regarded as "ours" because they are predominantly nonwhite, peopled by the "invisible children" of the Invisible Man. Even so, putting the moral issues aside, it is hard to comprehend how a tough-minded realist nation can be so shortsighted. The alternatives to focusing on schools are so much more costly—and grim.

Texas skimps on education but passes a billion-dollar prison bond issue. California, which in 1980 spent roughly four dollars for education for every dollar it spent on jails, today matches every education dollar with a prison dollar. Yet nearly 85 percent of the prison population is constituted by school dropouts, and it costs three or four times as much to keep the young in prison as it does to keep them in school. It has almost become a cliché to note that one out of three young African American men is either under indictment, in jail, or on parole and that more such young men are serving time in jail than are in college. What is noticed less frequently is that 80 to 85 percent of the prison population is made up of school dropouts.

Although a fifth to a quarter of all children under six and more than half of minority children live in poverty, everything from school lunch to after-school programs is being slashed at the federal and state levels. Legislators take aim at government budgets, saying they want to spare the next generation the burden of an elephantine deficit, and then shoot down the very programs on which that next generation depends for its education and growth. There is nothing sadder than a country that turns its back on its children, for in doing so it turns away from its own future. How can a nation that has universities and graduate schools that are the envy of the educated world have public primary schools so wretched and inefficient?

If schools are the neglected forges of our future, they are also the abandoned workshops of our democracy. In attacking not just education, but *public* education, critics are attacking the very foundation of our democratic civic culture. Public schools are not merely schools *for* the public, but schools of publicness: institutions where we learn what it means to *be* a public and start down the road toward common national and civic identity.

Forges of our citizenship, they are the bedrock of our democracy. Yet we seem as a nation to want to disown them. As walls go down elsewhere, they are being raised here by a politics of fear and resentment that fences off cities from suburbs, blacks from whites, poor from rich, and public from private—where, however, public means impoverished, dangerous, squalid, and crime-prone and private means privileged, safe, wealthy, and secure. But like the walls that were once built into the *Titanic*'s superstructure to create a series of watertight compartments that would make that great ocean liner "unsinkable," the social walls we are erecting today will not save our ship of state. The "*Titanic* mentality" that drives us to compartmentalize our society cannot succeed. We stay afloat only if we recongize we are aboard a single ship.

Vilifying public school teachers and adminstrators and cutting public school budgets even as we subsidize private educational opportunity puts us in double jeopardy: for as we put our children at risk, we undermine our common future; at the same moment, in constraining the conditions of liberty for some, we undermine the future of democracy for all. I want here to deal with both sides of the argument: first to suggest that the debate about money is a diversion that exposes our children and our schools to disaster; and second to argue that the fiscal debate completely neglects the vital civic mission of public education.

Let me start with the argument about funding: it has become fashionable to deny that there is any correlation between monies expended and educational results. Comparisons are drawn to parochial schools, charter schools, and private schools where fewer bucks produce a bigger pedagogical bang. "You can't just throw money at the schools and think you can buy better education," say politicians who have been throwing money at national defense, space programs, farm and corporate subsidies, and programs for the elderly for nearly half a century. Three errors mar their argument and the data on which the argument is based:

1. In many municipalities, schools have become the sole surviving *public* institutions and consequently have been burdened with responsibilities far beyond traditional schooling. Schools are now medical clinics, counseling centers, vocational training institutes, police/security outposts, drug rehabilitation clinics, special education centers, and city shelters. They have to act both as sanctuaries from anarchic inner cities and special social service centers to address all the problems inner cities breed. Compare just the budget portion going to conventional classroom education in public schools to the money spent in private schools, and public schools look rather more efficient. But we are asking them to be all-purpose social service centers in an era where social service budgets are being slashed, and under such oppressive circumstances they can only seem in-

efficient as compared with sleek, single-mission, no-problem-student private schools.

When Kansas City "blew" more than a billion dollars without showing demonstrable improvements in children's test scores, critics scoffed that they had once again proved money solves nothing. But Kansas City spent a third of its court windfall on physical improvements (repairing a roof keeps kids dry; it doesn't in itself improve their reading scores!); another third went to court-mandated busing and transportation costs (busing gets kids to a decent school; it does not teach them math—indeed, it makes for a longer and more arduous school day); additional funds went to structural and administrative changes. Less than a quarter of the much vaunted billion plus went toward schooling in the narrow sense. And it is far too soon to tell whether this much smaller sum devoted to education can pay off (see no. 3 below).

2. Among the costs of public schools that are most burdensome are those that go for special education, discipline, and special services to children who would simply be expelled from (or never admitted into) private and parochial schools or would be turned over to the appropriate social service agencies (which themselves are no longer funded in many cities). It is the glory and the burden of public schools that they cater to *all* of our children, whether delinquent or obedient, drug damaged or clean, brilliant or handicapped, privileged or scarred. That is what makes them *public* schools. Elective schemes rooted in vouchers and private screening (parent choice and school selection) assure that only the easily educable and well motivated and parent supported are in the classroom. A "good school" generally turns out to be a school where "good" students (made so by previous circumstances, history, and education) attend. Choate and Harvard begin with the very best students: of course they are among the very best schools. Send Choate's pupils to P.S. 31 and watch it become the best public school in America except—Catch 22—it will no longer be a public school!

3. Our public schools are our point institutions in dealing with our nation's oldest and most intractable problem: racism. As Benjamin DeMott argues in his incisive book *The Trouble with Friendship,* race in America takes the form of a "caste-like stratification," whose damage can take not months or years but generations to undo. DeMott estimates that only after three generations of relative success is a family previously caught up in the caste of race likely to emerge into something resembling normal, middle-class existence. Minority test scores in a recent experiment were shown to be deeply skewed by what we might call "caste" awareness of "competition" with whites—dropping by 10 or 15 percent when test takers were told it was a "test." In informal, nontest circumstances, scores were

far better. Self-fulfilling prophecy? Living up to expectations for a certain caste? DeMott believes so.

With America divided more completely than ever into Gunnar Myrdal's, the Kerner Commission's, and Andrew Hacker's "two nations"—unequal and hostile—and with public schools more and more acting as the public institutions of last resort for the nation of African Americans (and for nonwhite immigrants), can anyone really expect that dollars spent on schools will pay off in the same fashion or with the same speed that dollars in privileged private schools do?

We might add to these three sets of issues one more general caveat. Why is "efficiency" so crucial an issue in the public education domain? Will anyone claim that defense dollars are all efficiently expended? Star Wars monies? Space race bucks? Agricultural subsidies? Even in this era of belt tightening and ideological budget slashing, Congress has seen fit to raise the defense budget and to put Star Wars back on the nation's agenda on the theory that enough is never enough when it comes to an issue as vital as national security. Will dollars alone buy the most efficient army? An impervious missile defense? Of course not. It takes ingenuity and leadership and smart ideas too. But without dollars, you can't even get started. And in any case, the silent subtext reads, what's a little waste when we're talking about national security?

Which is another way to make the point that if you want to see what a nation really values, read the subtext: find out what it is willing to "waste" dollars on. Star Wars? Tobacco subsidies? Nuclear submarines? There is no limit to waste and inefficiency here. But for schools? Overspend $3.75, and the cost accountants are at the door screaming bloody murder. Norman Mailer tells the story of an interview with a welfare mother back in the sixties when he was running for mayor of New York, just at the moment when the Great Society was beginning to receive criticism for the "wastefulness" of its inner-city antipoverty programs. The interview concluded almost before Mailer could get it under way when the woman on welfare shouted: "Where is *our* piece of the waste? We want our waste too!"

Presume the worst about waste in the schools: why is it that education is monitored for every cent budgeted while defense and market subsidies and benefits for the elderly along with a host of other "priority" programs escape even a cursory glance by the fiscal obsessives and ideological accountants? Why are benefits for the elderly "entitlements" while educational spending on the young is "discretionary"? Can it be that the children just aren't "entitled," aren't worth either spending money on or wasting money on? Can it perhaps be that when it comes to kids, "spending" is in fact itself regarded as a form of "wasting," because kids belong to a "discretionary" and "disposable" generation?

I do not, however, want to leave the argument as one concerned exclusively with issues of spending equality and fiscal efficiency. In fighting to maintain the quality of three Rs education and the kinds of vocational training that keep our workers competitive in an economy increasingly dominated by global markets and what Robert Reich has called "symbolic analyst professionals," we need to recall that education also has a central *civic* mission. Our schools are public not just in that they must educate everyone, but in that they must turn a host of "everyones" into something like a single national One: the civic entity that we call a "public." In teaching the public, they teach what "public" means and make possible common ground, public goods, and a sense of the public weal. Public schooling and the public weal are intimately bound.

When Thomas Jefferson came to consider what he would like to have inscribed on his tombstone, he omitted all mention of his two-term presidency, his acquisition of the Louisiana Territories, his founding of the Democratic Party, and his other great political achievements. Instead he memorialized only three (to him) crucial features of his biography: his authorship of the Declaration of Independence, his composition of the Virginia Statute of Religious Freedom, and his founding of the University of Virginia. Without public education for all citizens, Jefferson did not see how there could be a public and a democratic politics at all. For without citizens there could be no republic, and without education there would be no citizens. In pairing the Declaration and the Virginia Statute of rights with the founding of the University of Virginia, Jefferson's epitaph disclosed the hidden logic that linked rights to responsibilities, American independence, and democratic self-sufficiency with an educated citizenry. Bills of rights are, said Madison, parchment parapets from which no defense of liberty can be sustained. If there was to be a common American people capable of pursuing a common American good in the name of their natural rights, there had to be common schools. Although he boasted in the Declaration of Independence that men were "born free," Jefferson knew well enough that liberty is acquired, and that citizens are educated to a responsibility that comes to no man or woman "naturally." Without citizens, democracy is a hollow shell. Without public schools and universities, there can be no citizens.

This is a strain of thought that persisted from America's colonial days (when John Adams of Massachusetts boasted that the commonwealth's schools tutored every young man in citizenship with a ubiquity that put "literate" England to shame) down through the nineteenth century. Tocqueville spoke movingly of the need in democracies for "an apprenticeship of liberty," what he deemed "the most arduous of all apprenticeships." The Common School Movement informed our nineteenth-century educational practices with a sense of civic mission that left no school or college untouched. Not just the land grant colleges, but nearly every higher educational institution founded in the eighteenth and nineteenth centuries—religious as well as secular, private no less public—counted among its leading founding principles a dedication to training competent and responsible citizens. Rights were understood to be tied to responsibilities, the freedom to live well and prosper was seen as a product of civic obligations discharged with vigor, and the security of the private sector was thought to depend on the robustness of the public sector.

Sometime toward the end of the last century, with the professionalization of higher education that came to American shores with the German research university model after which Johns Hopkins was patterned, schools began to move away from their civic responsibilities. By the end of World War II, higher education had begun to professionalize and vocationalize and specialize in a manner that occluded its civic and democratic mission. Rights and responsibilities were decoupled and citizenship relegated to the occasional boring "civics" lecture—usually a harangue monumentalizing a mythical founding and a set of stereotypical heroes from George Washington to Abraham Lincoln with whom (at least as they were presented) the increasingly nonwhite population of public schools could have little sense of common cause. So far had rights wandered from responsibility that young people who explicitly professed that they cherished the system of trial by jury nonetheless argued that no one should be "required" to do jury service. And the citizens army of conscripts gave way to the "volunteer army" made up at least in part of those, black and white, for whom society offered few other opportunities.

If our nation is to repossess its civic soul, it needs to recapture the central civic responsibilities of public schools—indeed of schooling in general, K–12 and university, public and private. This means that if American schools are to be defined by the search for literacy, then civic literacy must take its place alongside science, math, English, and cultural literacy. It means that if education is to support school-to-work initiatives that adapt pedagogy to the needs of the workplace, it must also support school-to-citizen initiatives that adapt pedagogy to the needs of the public square—the civic marketplace of civil society. Lawyers and doctors are no more likely to make good citizens than dropouts if their training is limited to the narrow and self-interested world defined by vocational preparation and professional instruction. Youngsters preparing to turn their schooling to the purposes of economic competition with Japan and Germany must also be able to turn their schooling to the purposes of civic cooperation with their fellow Americans in making democracy work.

To rejoin education and liberal citizenship requires only that we take "liberal" education seriously. Liberal arts education and civic education share a curriculum of critical reflection and autonomous thought. That is how the "liberal arts" emerged in the modern era in contrast to the feudal "servile arts." The latter was job training for the unfree and indentured and subordinated learning to an apprenticeship in the vocations; the former devoted itself to free thought and what Tocqueville would many centuries later deem "the apprenticeship of liberty." In feudal times, the liberal arts were intended to serve that small minority lucky enough to be born "freemen." If schooling is to be guided once again by its democratic mission, it needs not only to be supported financially, but reendowed with a sense of civic passion. This means:

- That public schools be understood as public not simply because they serve the public, but because they establish us as a "public." Too much market ideology has left our private/public worlds all topsy-turvy. We have made Madonna's private parts public at the very moment we are demanding, via vouchers, that our last genuinely public institutions be made private. We need incentives to draw parents back into public schools, not vouchers to lure them out. We need to fix, not abandon those inner-city schools that work least well.

- That the "public" in public schools be understood as signifying plurality and diversity. America is not a private club defined by one group's historical hegemony. Consequently, multicultural education is not discretionary; it defines demographic and pedagogical necessity. If we want youngsters from Los Angeles whose families speak more than 160 languages to be "Americans," we must first acknowledge their diversity and honor their distinctiveness. English will thrive as the first language of America only when those for whom it is a second language feel safe enough in their own language and culture to venture into and participate in the dominant culture. For what we share in common is not some singular ethnic or religious or racial unity but precisely our respect for our differences: that is the secret to our strength as a nation, and is the key to democratic education.

- That schools need to be as democratic as the civic ideals they wish to teach, consistent with the authority of sound pedagogy. This suggests cooperative learning where the facile help the less facile to the benefit of both, rather than either tracking (where the quick advance at the expense of the slow) or large, undermanned detracked classes (where the slow advance at the expense of the quick). The goal is not to level down but to secure an aristocracy of everyone in which excellence is the common denominator. This suggests systems of secondary and higher education that leave room for a role for students in governance and administration. To be sure, students are a transient constituency and there are issues of hiring, curriculum, and peer review where their role should necessarily remain extremely limited. But there are also other domains where their participation, minimally on a consultative basis, is not only feasible but beneficial to the children and to their educational institutions. Simultaneously, such participation models the kind of democratic culture we presumably wish to teach.

- That learning, above all civic learning, needs to be experiential as well as purely cognitive. Serving others is not just a form of do-goodism or feel-goodism; it is a road to social responsibility and citizenship. When linked closely to classroom learning ("education-based community service"), it offers an ideal setting for bridging the gap between the classroom and the street, between the theory of democracy and its much more obstreperous practice. Our schools and colleges are not social agencies but teaching and learning communities: service is an instrument of civic pedagogy. It is a response to William James's quest for a "moral equivalent of war": in serving community, the young forge commonality; in acknowledging difference, they bridge division; in assuming individual responsibility, they nurture social citizenship.

- That to serve democratic education, service learning must be a responsibility of everyone, not just a requirement for the criminal or the needy. Teaching the young that white-collar felons or blue-collar loan seekers owe their country civic service while the well-off and wealthy do not is a poor way to inculcate the ideals of civic equality. Service is a universal entailment of what it means to live in and enjoy the rights of a free society. Loans for those who need them ought to be offered as a reciprocal right of good citizens, a consequence rather than a prerequisite of citizenship. This is the justification for the vital link the Corporation for National and Community Service has established between education vouchers and community service.

These revisions of the mission of education, aside from their possible impact on democracy, potentially have a crucial political payoff: they make schools more relevant to the needs of society generally and more pertinent to the concerns of citizens without school-age children. They thus offer burdened taxpayers reasons why they should support the flow of tax dollars to education. Polls show again and again that citizens object not so much to paying taxes but to the perceived lack of impact of the taxes they pay. They seek not so much lower tax rates but higher payoffs—better results. That our schools are committed not just to educating our children but preparing them to take responsibility for preserving and extending our democracy may make them look like a better bargain.

The rights and freedoms of all Americans depend on the survival of democracy. There is only one road to democracy: education. And in a democracy where freedom comes first—educators and politicians alike take notice—the first priority of education must be the apprenticeship of liberty. Tie every school reform to this principle, and not only education by democracy itself will flourish and perhaps even pay for themselves. Let schools sink further into poverty and privatization and we will not only put our children at risk but are likely to imperil the very foundation of their liberties and our own.

Part IV

DEMOCRACY AND TECHNOLOGY:
ENDLESS FRONTIER
OR END OF DEMOCRACY?

CHAPTER 18

The Second American Revolution

DEMOCRACY was conceived in an unwired world, one without telephones, computers, or television. When Alexis de Tocqueville visited America in the 1830s, he marveled at its "spirit of liberty," which, he concluded, arose directly out of vigorous civic activity, municipal self-government, and face-to-face interaction. Then, as now, democracy meant government by consent, and consent depended upon consensus and thus upon effective communication. In a society innocent of electronics, communications meant reading local newspapers, forming voluntary associations, developing public schools, and exploiting the American propensity for endless talk.

Democracy survives, but Tocqueville's simpler world of self-governing townships has vanished. The community of citizens governing themselves face-to-face has given way to the mass society, and live talk has been replaced by telecommunications. Once a nation of talkers, we have turned into a nation of watchers—once doers, we have become viewers—and the effect on our democracy has been profound. The average American watches television between six and seven hours a day; he votes just once a year, if that. Indeed, only one of every two Americans votes in presidential elections.

Although every schoolchild knows that television is the national pastime and politics is only one feature of its coverage, not even university professors have thought very much about the medium's long-term impact on democracy. Yet we have already passed through one major age of telecommunications technology, and we now stand on the threshold of a second. This may be our last opportunity to turn the technology of the new age into a servant of an old political idea: democracy. Democracy has a difficult time surviving under the best of circumstances.

The first age of television—from its pre-war inception through the 1970s—was characterized by the scarcity of airwaves available for television transmission. This so-called spectrum scarcity gave us a system in which three mammoth national networks monopolized public communication, the government regulated in the name of the public interest, and viewers came to perceive themselves as passive spectators willing to leave programming decisions to network executives and their corporate sponsors.

The effects of this first age of television on America's political culture were mixed. But in one clear sense, network television's homogenized programming benefited democracy: by offering the country the semblance of a national culture and national political norms, it provided a consensus indispensable to national unity. Occasionally this was a direct result of network attitudes—as in the fifties with integration, the sixties with Vietnam, or the seventies with Watergate. But more often, the television consensus was informal and indirect. National debates such as the Kennedy-Nixon exchanges; national media personalities such as Ed Sullivan, Johnny Carson, and Walter Cronkite; and such national rituals as the Kennedy funeral, the moon walk, and the mourning for Martin Luther King—all these bestowed upon the country a legacy of national symbols and myths that cut across our diverse regions, sects, interest groups, parties, races, ethnic communities, and political constituencies.

THE SAFETY OF THE CENTER

In a nation as fragmented and pluralistic as ours, where from the very beginning—in the *Federalist Papers*—the "specter of faction" loomed as the greatest peril, television has offered a common vision. If there is an American melting pot, it is fired nowadays primarily by electronic means. How else than in front of the communal fires of television could Americans have mourned together their fallen leaders? If "Roots" had not been screened in prime time on eight consecutive evenings, would the meaning of being black in America have touched so many nonblack Americans? It was a celebration not only of being black but of being American. Network television, both at its best and its worst—"Roots" as much as "Family Feud"—has helped us to subscribe to common values and to identify with a single national community. It is difficult to imagine the Kennedy Generation, the sixties, Watergate, the Woodstock Generation, or even the Moral Majority in the absence of national television. Who we are in common is what we see in common.

One aspect of this television consensus has been corrosive both to democracy and liberty, however. The dominion of a few media giants over scarce public airwaves has centralized control over information and entertainment. Democracy thrives on dissent, deviance, political heterogeneity, and individuality; network television catalyzes uniformity and homogeneity. Move a program too far off center as measured by the mass audience, and plummeting Nielsen ratings will chase sponsors away. Whether the media's middling vision is seen as the victory of bad taste (as the intellectuals claim), or of an eastern liberal elite (as Spiro Agnew used to insist), or of crass secular materialism (as the Moral Majority asserts), or of the corporate establishment (as the Left believes), there can be little doubt that it is a safe and complacent vision that offers little hospitality to alternative perspectives. A common vision may also be a homogenized, plasticized, and intolerant vision, one that distorts America's defining pluralism by imposing uniform stereotypes on a heterogeneous people.

To the extent the networks succeed in making Americans think in common, they may destroy in us the capacity to think independently. The great American television consensus of the last thirty years dismissed the aspirations of both religion and socialism (thus the hostility fundamentalists and leftists show the media today). In place of genuine American archetypes, it gave us watery stereotypes: Archie Bunker, your friendly neighborhood racist, who wouldn't do any man real harm; Sanford and son, who proved that black folks, aside from being a bit more hip, are just like everyone else; Mary Tyler Moore, who could gently mock the patriarchal world without ever truly challenging it. There were tough-but-generous cops, misguided revolutionaries, reformed junkies, urbane preachers, and decent bigots—but few vicious detectives or legitimate terrorists or victorious punks or intolerant Christians or despicable hypocrites. From the safety of the center, differences were reduced to matters of style, while the difficult choices and grim polarities of real moral and political life were ignored. The first age of television gave us unity but exacted the price of uniformity.

INNOVATIVE TECHNOLOGIES

Disturbing as these dilemmas are, they may now belong to history. For we stand, prepared or not, on the threshold of a second television age. This new age, with its own innovative technologies, promises to revolutionize our habits as viewers, as consumers, and ultimately, as citizens.

Although cable television itself relies on a technology as old as communication by wire, the convergence of a group of new technologies has made possible an entirely new system of telecommunications, one that offers us two-way and multiple-channel cable television, satellite distribution, video discs, video cameras and recorders, and access to remote computers and data banks. These technologies could bring into our homes a vastly expanded range of news and entertainment programming, diverse information services, public-access programming, security systems, and television referenda. Twenty-eight percent of American homes now receive some kind of cable service; that number will double by the end of the decade. Already in some places people use interactive television to relax, look, talk, vote, play, shop, inform themselves, express opinions, secure their homes, and go to school. State-of-the-art systems—like Warner's QUBE—will be installed in all the major cities now being franchised. The prospect of a "wired society" is real.

What will be the likely effects of this new era of telecommunications on American democracy? How will it compare to the first, now seemingly primitive era? What sort of questions ought to be put to the new industry by the federal government, the municipal franchisers, and the public at large?

At present, the government seems disposed to put the new technologies into the hands of an unencumbered private sector [this happened with the Telecommunications Act of 1996]. The Federal Communications Commission (FCC) has consistently argued that cable's multiple channels make spectrum scarcity—and the regulations that issue from it—obsolete. The Supreme Court in 1979 ruled that the FCC is not justified in requiring cable companies to provide public access. And Congress seems inclined to let "market forces" shape the development of modern telecommunications. Consequently, America is crossing the threshold of the new television age without reflection or planning; few seem aware, or concerned, that the new technologies may profoundly affect the nature of our public life and thus the character of our democracy. Yet present tendencies suggest the emergence of one of three distinct scenarios, each with far-reaching political consequences. We might call these scenarios "The New Tower of Babel," "The Corporate Big Brother," and "The Electronic Town Meeting."

THE NEW TOWER OF BABEL

From the perspective of the viewer, at least, the new technologies would appear to decentralize television. In a cable system with fifty or a hundred channels, the responsibility for selecting services and programming shifts from the supplier to the consumer. The passive spectator of homogenized network fare is replaced by the active viewer, who creates his own information and entertainment programming by choosing among the hundreds of local and national program services, prerecorded discs and tapes, and the various services two-way cable makes available.

But a political price is paid for this new activism among viewers and the apparent decentralization of television: where television once united the nation, it will now fragment it. Those it once brought together it will now keep apart. In place of broadcasting comes the new ideal of "narrowcasting," in which each special audience is systematically typed, located, and supplied with its own special programming. Each group, each class, each race, and each religious sect can have its own programs, and even its own mini-network, specially tailored to its distinct characteristics, views, and needs. The critical communication between groups that is essential to the forging of a national culture and public vision will vanish; in its place will come a new form of communication within groups, where people need talk only to themselves and their clones.

This fragmentation is already well under way. Among the proliferating new program services available today are a Hispanic network, several Christian fundamentalist networks, a black network, and a number of highbrow culture networks. The U.S. Chamber of Commerce recently announced plans for the American Business Network, a private satellite television system. "BizNet" will enable the business community to organize and to communicate more effectively—with itself.

In the New Tower of Babel, all this programming diversity and special-interest narrowcasting replaces communication with group narcissism. The tube now becomes a mirror showing us only ourselves, relentlessly screening out any images that do not suit our own special prejudices and group norms. Fundamentalists no longer have to confront Carl Sagan in the course of a day's television viewing. No longer do special-interest groups have to filter their particular concerns through a national medium and adjust their message to a pluralistic nation. Faction—the scourge of democracy feared by its critics from James Madison to Walter Lippmann— is given the support of technology; compromise, mutualism, and empathy—indispensable to effective democratic consensus—are robbed of their national medium. Every parochial voice gets a hearing (though only before the already converted), and the *public* is left with no voice. No global village, but a Tower of Babel: a hundred chattering mouths bereft of common language.

THE CORPORATE BIG BROTHER

The Tower of Babel may be a suitable metaphor for the heterogeneity and pluralism of the new media as they appear to the consumer, but to examine modern telecommunications at the supplier end is to wonder whether "Big Brother" may prove to be the more apt metaphor for television's second age.

As abundant in number as these new channels and program services seem, they are rapidly falling under conglomerate control. The potential for leviathan profits from the new industries is drawing the attention of the communications giants. A few entrepreneurial upstarts—such as Ted Turner—may remain on the scene for a while, but they almost certainly will be absorbed or conquered [Time-Warner now owns Turner's CNN]. Diversity at one end of the cable may mask monopoly at the other.

If this picture of a few corporate elites playing the role of Big Brother under the camouflage of pluralistic special-interest programming seems exaggerated, it should be recalled that cable is a capital-intensive industry.

The extraordinary cost of wiring America for cable or leasing transponder space on satellites suggests that only the most powerful corporations are in a position to sustain long-term interests in the cable industry.

Westinghouse, AT&T, Warner Communications, Time, Inc., CBS, RCA, ABC: if all the new media are controlled by these few corporate interests, we cannot expect genuine political diversity. Even if Big Brother is not watching us, we may find ourselves watching Big Brother. And it does seem likely that if we are watching Big Brother, he will eventually begin to keep an eye on us. The very features of the new technology that make it versatile and exciting also make it frighteningly vulnerable to abuse. Warner Amex's QUBE system scans subscribers' homes every six seconds, recording what subscribers watch, their answers to poll questions, the temperature in their houses (for those who have signed up for energy management systems), and even (for subscribers who buy home security services) their comings and goings. Cable systems offering transaction services such as banking and shopping will accumulate detailed computer files on all subscribers. At present, there are no safeguards to prevent the abuse of such records, other than the goodwill of cable operators. Both this and the Tower of Babel scenario, for all their differences, are equally inimical to democracy. Babel and Big Brother alike subvert citizenship by denying the significance of viewers as public persons with national identities and public obligations.

The Tower of Babel subordinates commonality and public vision to personal choice, private preference, and individual interests. It transforms the most potent medium of public communication the world has known into an instrument of exclusively private concerns. Ironically, it privatizes us even as it imperils our privacy. It takes us seriously as consumers, spectators, clients, and buyers and sellers, but it ignores us as citizens. It services lust, religious zealotry, special interests, and individual needs efficiently and pluralistically; it helps us relax or play games, exercise or buy goods, pray or learn French; but it does not help us communicate or seek social justice or formulate common decisions.

Corporate Big Brothers are no less privatistic in their methods: they control by manipulating private wants and master by guiding private tastes. Their world, like Babel, is inhabited by atomized and alienated individuals seeking personal gratification in a society in which only individual wants and corporate profits count.

THE ELECTRONIC TOWN MEETING

Ten years ago, when he was an FCC commissioner, Nicholas Johnson said, "As never before, Americans need to talk to each other. We hunger to be in touch, to reaffirm our commitment to each other, to our humanity, to the continuity of hope and meaning in our lives. . . . The ultimate promise of cable is the rebuilding of a sense of community." The new television technology has at least the potential of becoming a remarkable new instrument of public communication and collective deliberation. From the ancient world to the American founding, the great enemy of democracy has been scale: the repressive effect of mass society on the communication and participation necessary to self-government. Television in its second age can be to the problem of scale what drugs were to disease: a miracle remedy. People can be brought together across time and place and be permitted to confront one another in a continuing process of mutual exploration, deliberation, debate, and decision making.

What I have in mind has nothing to do with the instant polls and uninformed votes that have characterized the QUBE system's dalliance with politics. Voting without prior debate, polling without full-scale presentation of positions and facts, expressions of preference without a sense of the public context of choice, all do more to undermine democracy than to reinforce it.

But the true promise of interactive systems, public-access channels, and computer information banks is that they can enhance knowledge as they enlarge participation. They can equalize by informing the poor as well as the rich and, by providing access to the powerless as well as the powerful, they can help to realize the ideal of an active and informed citizenry.

In some places the democratic capabilities of the new telecommunications technology have already been proven. In Reading, Pennsylvania, an experimental project sponsored by the National Science Foundation in 1976 (and developed by New York University) used the local cable system to establish an interactive communications network for the city's senior citizens. The elderly in Reading were able to create programming for themselves and to hold their elected officials more accountable through a series of public meetings held on interactive cable television. Though this particular experiment has ended, cable's role in Reading's political system has not: today all budget and community development hearings are conducted by two-way cable. Citizens can participate on-camera by visiting neighborhood centers equipped with television equipment, or they can ask questions from home by telephone. As a result, political participation increased dramatically. Reading's experience demonstrates the new technology's potential to create a more informed and active citizenry.

Perhaps great promise lies with interactive systems like QUBE, which can link up thousands of citizens in an electronic town meeting where information and opinions can be exchanged, expert counsel called upon, and informal votes taken. In Columbus, Warner Amex hasn't seen fit to exploit this capability except as a toy. In amateur talent shows, citizens there can use their two-way cable "vote" to yank acts they don't like. Still, the potential exists.

The promise of the second age of television for democracy remains largely unexplored. Among the thousands of cable companies now serving more than twenty million homes, only a handful offer local political-access channels or services, and none has made service to public citizenship their principal product. Yet if in this conservative era of deregulation it is too much to hope for a national telecommunications service devoted to democratic and public uses of the new technology, it is surely not too much to call for a public debate on the future of American telecommunications. A number of years ago, former CBS News President Fred Friendly suggested America needed an "electronic bill of rights" to protect it from its pervasive new technology. Even more than a bill of rights, today we need an "electronic constitution"—a positive plan for the public use of a precious national resource on behalf of our nation's faltering democracy.

CHAPTER 19

Pangloss, Pandora, or Jefferson?
Three Scenarios for the Future of
Technology and Democracy

MODERNITY may be defined politically by the institutions of democracy, and socially and culturally by the civilization of technology. The relationship between democracy and technology remains ambiguous, however. Proponents of classical participatory democracy such as Rousseau have generally understood the progress of science to be corrosive to the intimacy and equality of political relations. Proponents of the liberal open society such as Sir Karl Popper and Bertrand Russell, however, have posited a close connection between the spirit of science and the success of liberal democratic institutions.

About the future role of democracy in society we cannot be certain. Because it is a fragile form of social organization, its prospects are clouded. But we do know, however we organize our political world, that we shall live in a society dominated by technology. Indeed, the theme of technology and society has become sufficiently popular to make it a favorite both with academics and after dinner speakers. An issue of the *International Political Science Review* (3, 1986) was devoted to "politics and the new communications"; the Kennedy School at Harvard University sponsored a major study (with a book) called "The New Media and Democratic Values"; and Prince Charles used his keynote address at the 350th anniversary of Harvard University to caution against the domination of society by technology, issuing a call to his listeners to restore "moral control over the things they make."

Notwithstanding it being in vogue, the relationship between technology and democracy is a matter of genuine urgency for modern men and women. Will technology nourish or undermine democratic institutions? Is technological growth likely to support or corrupt freedom? Are we finally to be mastered by the tools with which we aspire to master the world? The scientistic wisdom suggests that science and technology, by opening up society and creating a market of ideas, foster more open politics; the Soviet experience with copying machines and computers is cited as an example. Yet technology coexisted with tyrannical government in Nazi Germany, and was made to expedite the liquidation of the Jews in a fashion that suggests its utility in rendering dictatorship more efficient. And the inversion of control that attends technocratic forms of society is well enough known to cause comment by the Prince of Wales, as we have already noted.

Moreover, such generalizations as we can hazard about the connections between technology and society must remain provisional in the face of the extraordinary rate of change typical of the evolution of modern science and technology. As Arthur Schlesinger, Jr., has noticed (in his *The Cycles of American History*, [1986]), if we assume roughly 800 lifetimes separate us from the beginning of human life, there has been more change in the last two lifetimes than in the 798 that preceded them. Henry Adams had already observed at the beginning of this century that between the years 1800 and 1900, "measured by any standard known to science—by horsepower, calories, volts, mass in any shape—the tension and vibration and volume and so-called progression of society were fully a thousand times greater." Whilst for thousands of generations life for a cohort of grandchildren roughly resembled life for their grandparents, in our century there is enough change in a decade to confuse people in the fifteen years it takes to grow up.

The world's population took 10,000 years to reach a billion, around 1800. The second billion had arrived by 1900, the third by 1940, the fourth by 1960. Movable type appeared only four centuries ago, the steam engine in the eighteenth century, the telegraph in the nineteenth, and wireless at the beginning of the twentieth. The internal combustion engine, rocketry, and the typewriter came of age between the two World Wars, and television, microchips, and lasers are still more recent. The first computer built after the war filled a large room and performed less complex calculations for its ardent cybernetic attendants than a handheld instrument performs for students today.

The overall impact of these stunning developments over the last half millennium has been to shrink both time and space. Aristotle once observed that the ideal size for a democratic polity could be measured by the amount of land a man could traverse in a day—assuring that all citizens could attend a popular assembly. By this standard, Marshall McLuhan's global village is a reality that is confirmed anew each day by advances in satellite and laser optic communication and computer information systems. Technology shrinks the world, foreshortening space and conquering time. News that once took months or years to cross an ocean now flashes around the globe in seconds, and no people are more remote from the political present than the distance from a transistor radio or a short wave telephone. Orbiting satellites leave "footprints" that encompass the globe, overstepping national boundaries and treating national sovereignty like some charming vestige of a decrepit stone wall. Even the Vatican has embraced the innovations: indulgences are now granted via television to pious viewers hundreds of miles away.

We stand today on the threshold of a new generation of technology as potentially important to society as the printing press or the internal combustion engine. This technology is defined by computer chips, video equipment, electromagnetic tape, lasers, fiber optics, satellites, low-frequency transmission and, more significantly, by the revolution in information and communications made possible by *combining* these several low-price, high-speed, high-volume innovations. The possibilities for the mastery of time and space, and of knowledge and its transmission, offered by this complex, integrated technology seem almost limitless.

Can democracy, a form of government born in the ancient world and designed to bring small numbers of individuals with consensual interests together into a self-governing community where they might govern themselves directly, survive the conditions of modern mass society? Does technology help replicate the ancient conditions? Or does it underscore the distinctiveness of the modern condition? In 1752, Jean-Jacques Rousseau argued that the development of the arts and sciences had had a corrupting effect on politics and morals; has modern technology corrupted or improved our polity?

We know how profoundly simple innovations have affected social and political history in the past. Electric fences brought to an end two millennia of common grazing in Switzerland and altered the communal character of Swiss liberty; gunpowder revolutionized and ultimately democratized warfare, which was freed from the special skills of a warrior caste; the printing press destroyed both ecclesiastic and worldly priesthoods based on privileged knowledge and so, in undermining hierarchy, created the conditions for the Protestant Reformation and the rise of the democratic State; and, as George Ball said a decade ago in supporting the opening of a Fiat plant in the USSR, "the automobile is an ideology on four wheels."

Yet this is not to say that technology is wholly determining, that it overrides the plans, ideas, and institutions of man and writes its own history independent of human intentions. Where technology takes our political and social institutions will depend, in part, on where we take technology. Science and its products remain *tools,* and although the parable of the tools that come to enslave the tool-makers is an ancient one, it is not necessarily the only description of the modern technological dilemma. Rather, we must see technological determinism as one among a number of possible scenarios that depend at least in part on the choices we make about technology's use. If it enslaves us we will have chosen to act (or not act) in a fashion that permits our enslavement. I certainly do not share the neo-Luddite posture which makes the success of our free institutions depend on the suppression of technology. For better or worse, technology is with us; our fate will depend on how we use or abuse it. As with fire, gunpowder, and now atomic energy, all modern technology consists of discoveries that cannot be undiscovered, gifts of the gods that cannot be returned or exchanged. There is no way back to innocence for Prometheus; we are destined to learn to live with the booty of his visionary theft—or to die with it.

There are, in fact, at least three prospects for the future of technology and democracy—three scenarios of their relationship—that are within the realm of technological possibility. I will call them, rather fancifully, the Pangloss scenario, which is rooted in complacency and is simply a projection of current attitudes and trends; the Pandora scenario, which looks at the worst possible case in terms of the inherent dangers of technological determinism; and the Jeffersonian scenario, which seeks out the affirmative uses of the new technology in the nurturing of modern democratic life. In terms of the psychological moods they evoke, the three may be described as the posture of complacency, the posture of caution, and the posture of hope. We can aspire to hope and we should cultivate caution, but it is, of course, complacency that is most likely to attend and determine our actual future.

THE PANGLOSS SCENARIO

Anyone who reads good-time pop-futurology knows the penchant of the future mongers for Panglossian parody. Their view of the future is always relentlessly upbeat and ahistorical, mindlessly naive about power and corruption as conditioners of all human politics. They assume that the technological present and the future it will naturally produce are wholly benevolent and without costs. Without either having consciously to plan to utilize technology to improve our lives, or having to worry about the insidious consequences of such usage, we can rely on market forces to realize the perfect technological society. The invisible hand governs this scenario, carrying with it the presumption that market incentives such as profitability and consumer interest will take technology in socially useful directions without planning of any kind.

Now it is certainly true that market forces push the new technologies in directions that serve corporate efficiency, media communications, and consumer entertainment, but it is not clear that they do anything for electoral efficiency, civic communication, or political education. The untoward fate of Warner-Amex's "Qube" system—an innovation in interactive television that permits viewers to communicate with the screen via a five-position module—offers a vivid illustration. Warner-Amex introduced the device into its Columbus, Ohio, cable system, but on a purely commercial basis. Its primary use was for quick question-answer polls, for so-called gong entertainment shows which permitted viewers to "gong" acts they did not like off the air; and for video shopping, banking, and home surveillance. Although Warner-Amex originally planned to introduce Qube into all of the major cities they were cabling in the 1980s, lack of consumer interest has led them to cancel the project. The possibilities of the interactive use of Qube for electronic town meetings, voter education, and elections have never been considered, and apparently will not be. On the other hand, banks in the USA are actively merchandising home banking, relying on personal computer/telephone hookups. Private uses of the new technologies multiply, public uses scarcely exist. Thus, although several Western nations have developed videotex services aimed at public information and the public weal, the USA continues to develop them exclusively for commercial (primarily corporate) purposes. Video teleconferences are regular features of corporate communications, but are only rarely resorted to in the civic realm (for example, the Los Angeles Televote conducted in 1982). The privatization of the satellite business and its attendant modes of world communication have also thrust this important sector of the new technology into private hands. Recent failures in NASA's space program point in the same direction, have also promoted private-sector development, and what was once a public research venture is rapidly becoming the shuttle payload business.

Despite the absence of explicit political applications, the technologies themselves have had a certain market impact on political culture and economic and social structure. With the multiplication of communication spectra and the lowering of costs of hardware over the last two decades, traditional views of the airwaves as limited and therefore subject to private or (in the European case) public monopoly have been challenged. Spectrum scarcity meant government ownership in Europe and heavy government regulation in the USA. Spectrum abundance supposedly lessens the dangers of private monopoly and thus the need for public monopoly. A 1979 Supreme Court decision in the USA ruled that spectrum abundance had antiquated certain aspects of traditional Federal Communications regulations (the *Federal Communications Act* of 1934) rooted in the First Amendment—equal time, for example, or the "Fairness Doctrine," which has recently been abandoned. A new doctrine to protect freedom of information in the cable/satellite/laser age has yet to be developed. Combine the possibilities of over 200 discrete cable spectra, low-frequency and satellite broadcasting, and laser and fibre-optic technologies, and the hold of government broadcast corporations and private sector communication giants like NBC on the airwaves is patently loosened.

For a while in the USA it appeared as though new cable networks like Ted Turner's and superstations that utilized satellite broadcast capabilities would offer a major challenge to the monopoly-like networks, and create a genuinely competitive market. Increasingly, the problem faced by democracies seemed no longer to be Big Brother (Orwell imagined two-way television surveillance in *Nineteen Eighty-Four*) but a host of complacent little cousins—a plethora of broadcasting sources that would inundate the public in programming and divide the population into a series of discrete markets, each one the particular target of new "narrowcasting" strategies. In a 1982 essay (chapter 18 above), I warned against the fragmenting effect this might have on the integral American nation which heretofore had been protected from regional parochialisms by the national hearthside of network television. At the same time, I suggested that the new technological diversity might, for the first time, allow information and communication sovereignty to pass from the hands of the producers with monopolies over limited spectra to consumers who, because they now had literally hundreds of choices, could assume genuine responsibilities for what they saw and listened to. Indeed, the new plenitude appeared to challenge national sovereignty too, for anyone with a satellite dish was now able to tune into broadcasts from around the world. Armed with a VCR, a cable hookup, a satellite dish, and a television set, consumers could construct a world of entertainment and information geared to their own tastes, their own schedules, and their own needs. To this degree, the new technologies, by favoring decentralization, the multiplication of choice, and consumer sovereignty, did inadvertently benefit democratic political culture.

But in the last few years, other less benevolent market forces have conspired to work against these developments. The theoretical availability of multiple spectra has not been matched by real program or information diversification, or by any real increase in the power of the consumer over programming. This is due in part to the uncompetitive character of the real markets in hardware, software, and programming, and a surge of corporate takeovers that has shrunk this market still more. A limited number of programming and software giants have emerged from the sorting out process as monopolistic purveyors of information, news, and entertainment. Despite the fact that outlets for their product have multiplied, there has been little real substantive diversification. Thus, despite the presence of hundreds of television channels, cable stations have remained content to mimic the networks, or run movies, or develop "narrowcast" programming aimed at special audiences (religious, Spanish-speaking, sports, etc.) in search of certain profits. Although consumers are freed from traditional time constraints by video recorders and can watch live, record programs to watch at a time of their choice, or rent or buy video cassettes or laser discs, the actual content available is pretty much identical with what was available on the networks ten years ago. Moreover, the development of programming remains in the hands of the same few production companies that have always controlled films and entertainment. Indeed, such independence as the networks possessed is being eroded by their corporate takeover. Capital City Communications recently acquired ABC, General Electric purchased NBC, and CBS is a target of a number of hostile takeover sharks. Programming in the UK does not show a great deal more diversity; although sometimes a little more daring and upscale (which are often the same thing), innovative programming of the kind offered by Channel Four is not radically different from BBC1 and BBC2 programming and, increasingly, not so different from standard fare in the USA or Canada.

Elsewhere in the world, television companies (mostly national) take their cue from the English-speaking networks in the USA and the UK. Reruns of old suspense and comedy programs lead the schedule on most such networks (including those in countries with radical ideologies). Contradictions abound—*The Cosby Show* (about an average American black family) remains the most watched program in South Africa; *Dallas* (about the sexual and business escapades of the rich and meretricious in Texas) is popular in the Third World; accented mini-series from the BBC and Thames Television continue to draw a rapt American viewing audience that cannot get enough of the Royal Family it abandoned two hundred years ago; and violent, racist films like *Rambo* are regularly shown in Asia (where Rambo's Asian enemies are made to seem Arab in the overdub) and, on easily available black market cassettes, in the USSR. No wonder Thomas L. McPhail entitled his book on international broadcasting *Electronic Colonialism* (1981).

In fact, for all of its technological potential for diversification, the domination of these new technologies by the market (or by the corporate monopolies that the market conceals) assures that to a growing degree, the profit-making entertainment industry in the Anglo–American world will control what is seen, felt, and thought around the globe. It is hardly surprising that nations elsewhere are demanding a new information order. Though this demand is often construed in the West (to a degree correctly) as resulting from the tyrannical impulse to control information, it must also be viewed as a desperate reaction to the market tyranny already being exercised over world communication by Anglo–American programming and software monopolies.

None of this denies the potential of the new technology for efficient planning and information enhancement. Teleconferencing, videotex, and the interactive possibilities of this technology are being systematically exploited in the commercial world by corporations bent on enhancing efficiency through enhancing information and communication. But this has meant that a technology whose cheapness and universality promises a new communicative egalitarianism is, in fact, replicating in the domain of information the inequality that otherwise characterizes market relations in the West. Increasingly a gap can be descried between information-rich and information-poor segments of Western nations—the former, technologically literate and able to utilize the new technologies to gain mastery over their commercial and political environments; the latter, technologically illiterate and thrown more and more to the periphery of a society where power and status are dependent on information and communication.

I do not mean to suggest here a conscious attempt at control or at the sustaining of non-egalitarianism on the part of those who are major players in the "free" market—although the evidence presented here would not be inconsistent with such an interpretation. I do mean to say that even at its most innocent, the market is likely to have an impact on free and developing societies in ways unforeseen by the happy futurologists; that, at best, the market will do nothing for uses of the new technology that do not have obvious commercial or entertainment or corporate payoffs, and, at worst, will enhance uses that undermine equality and freedom.

THE PANDORA SCENARIO

Pangloss is a peril to every society, but the greater danger to democracy comes from Pandora's scenario, which envisions what might happen if a government consciously set out to utilize the new technologies for purposes of standardization, control, or repression. Clearly the new technology, which facilitates centralization of control over information and communication, enables government to retain files and "keep tabs" on all computer and telephonic communications, and makes new kinds of surveillance possible, can be a powerful weapon in the hands of a controlling political or economic elite. Brute tyrants must control by brute force, which requires constant physical control over subjects; subtle tyrants possess their subjects' hearts and minds through the control of education, information, and communication and, thereby, turn subjects into allies in the enterprise of servitude. The new technologies enhance this subtle form of control and give government instruments of indirect surveillance and control unlike any known to traditional dictators.

Nor need abuses be planned by elites conspiring to repress. The citizens of Sweden recently learned that a number of young men had been the unknowing subjects of a twenty year longitudinal surveillance that, in the name of a social scientific project, "keep tabs" on their economic, social, personal, and sexual lives—without their knowledge (let alone permission). Credit and insurance organizations in the USA and Europe are assembling mammoth information files on clients, files that are for the most part held and used at the company's own discretion without any government regulation. The Qube system, described above, offered a surveillance mode that transmitted electronic reports to a central office on the comings and goings of all residents; what and when they watched television, when lights went on and off, and so forth. Warner-Amex corporate officers "promised discretion"—a guarantee somewhat less ironclad than the Bill of Rights. Computer banking, increasingly common throughout Europe and the USA, leaves a permanent trail of files on financial transactions that permit those with access to learn the details of an individual's financial life.

Clearly the costs to privacy of the efficient operation of this new technology can be very high; neither can the individual be secured by traditional print media protections. The Fairness Doctrine, as developed by the *Federal Communications Act* of 1934, was not adapted to the new technology and has thus been laid aside. A number of commentators, including John Wicklein, Ithiel de Sola Pool, and David Burnham (erstwhile communications specialist for the *New York Times*), have decried the dangers to privacy and the individual posed by technological innovations. Fred Friendly, onetime head of CBS news, has called for an "electronic bill of rights."

Moreover, despite the diversification of communications and information channels made possible by the new technologies, control and ownership of the corporations that manufacture hardware and software and create news, information, and entertainment programming remain in the hands of a few supercorporations that exercise an effective monopoly or, as in France (and despite the recent accrediting of a private television network), of a government monopoly. Capital Cities/ABC, Gulf Western/ Warner Communications, General Electric, RCA/NBC, AT&T, Time, Inc., and IBM are conglomerates that now control hardware, software, programming, and financing. Between them they control a preponderance of what is made and produced in the communications/information field. These media giants make nonsense of the theoretical diversification of the technology. While minor players like Apple Computer or Ted Turner Broadcasting can still get into the game, the large corporations generally let them take the risks and then buy out or imitate the successes, or are taken over by them. The individual entrepreneur may still make a profit on his risk-taking, but the public is deprived of genuine competition or a real market choice.

The entertainment business provides a powerful lesson. As the television industry takes over the film industry and the film industry takes over Broadway and the West End, the English-speaking theater ceases to exist as a cultural artifact and becomes another small cog in the great profitmaking entertainment machine of the major media corporations. Shown on the hundreds of cable networks nowadays are mostly network reruns, third-rate movies never released to the theater chains, and sporting events. Innovation is commercially unviable and little supported. The "cultural" channels have mostly gone under for lack of funding, the public access channels are underutilized and unwatched (cable franchisers are often asked to put aside a channel for public access by the licensing municipality, but are never required to put aside funds to train people in the use of television, or to make available directorial and production support for groups wishing to avail themselves of public air time). Thus, no one watches. That's the market, say the cable companies (as if they would offer amateur underfunded programming of that kind to their paying viewers). The UK's Channel 4 is ingeniously financed and has developed some new programming, but it also specializes in upscale American prime-time programming (*Hill Street Blues, St. Elsewhere,* and *Cheers,* for example).

If then we measure power by the potential for monopoly and control over information and communication, it is evident that the new technology is a dangerous facilitator of tyranny. Even in the absence of conscious government abuse, this potential can constrict our freedom, encroach on our privacy, and damage our political equality. There is no tyranny more dangerous than an invisible and benign tyranny, one in which subjects are complicit in their victimization, and in which enslavement is a product of circumstance rather than intention. Technology need not inevitably corrupt democracy, but its potential for benign enslavement cannot be ignored.

THE JEFFERSONIAN SCENARIO

Despite the potential of the market for inequality and of the technology it supports for abuse, the new technologies, in themselves, can also offer powerful assistance to the life of democracy. A free society is free only to the degree that its citizens are informed and that communication among them is open and informed. Although among the three scenarios sketched here, the Jeffersonian is the least probable and, given current trends, unlikely to become more probable, it remains both technologically feasible and politically attractive. As Nicholas Johnson, former chairman of the Federal Communications Commission (FCC) noted some time ago, "the ultimate promise of the new technology is the rebuilding of community." In this sense, a guarded optimism is possible about technology and democracy, but only if citizen groups and governments take action in adapting the new technology to their needs.

At the outset, I noted that democracy is a form of government that depends on information and communication. It is obvious then that new technologies of information and communication can be nurturing to democracy. They can challenge passivity, they can enhance information equality, they can overcome sectarianism and prejudice, and they can facilitate participation in deliberative political processes.

Traditional media emphasised active programming and passive spectatorship. The new technology's interactive capability permits viewers to become active both as choosers of what they watch and respondents to programming (via interactive television, information network hookups, and public access cable channels). The old picture of passive television viewers glued to their sets for seven docile hours of complacent viewing can now be challenged by active users of a complex computer/telephone/ video set-up, who utilize the system to enhance their public and private lives.

The educational potential of computer information networks and interactive television is very great and, when appropriately subsidized, allows equal access to information by all citizens. Computer terminals equipped with user-friendly programs and manned by user-friendly technicians, if housed at public libraries, town halls, and other public places, could place the enormous banks of information available through computer networks at the disposal of the general public. Governments could offer their own networks providing information on employment, housing, zoning regulation, small business laws, and other matters of public concern. Private networks might be persuaded to offer service to public terminals at cost as a *pro bonum* return on the profits their use of public airwaves and wire make possible.

The possibilities of using the interactive capabilities of recent television technology for civic education has been underexplored. Networks run instant telephone polls on controversial debates ("are you for or against a nuclear freeze?") after half an hour of opinionated sparring by warring "experts," but have not tried to structure several programs over time aimed at actually informing opinion and giving issues full deliberation. Yet the technology is there to do so. The few times that it has been used, it has achieved unusual successes. The experiment with a civic network that began as a senior citizen and shut-in network in Reading, Pennsylvania; the "televote" experiments in New Zealand, Hawaii, and Los Angeles; and the League of Women Voters' three State teleconferences in New York–New Jersey–Connecticut are but three examples (discussed in *Strong Democracy,* as well as in chapter 18 above) of the technology's civic possibilities.

A third use of the new technology has been implicit in electronic communications from the start of the radio and television era: the overcoming of regional parochialism, local prejudice, and national chauvinism. Technology has made the metaphor of the global village an electronic reality. Satellite "footprints" know no borders and individuals or communities with a satellite dish (and perhaps a descrambler) can tune in on the world. This makes closed societies difficult to maintain, and information blackouts a contradiction in terms.

In order to be something more than the government of mass prejudice, democracy must escape the tyranny of opinion. Television often merely reinforces opinion and prejudice, but its global character and capacity for interactive communication also enable it to overcome them and sustain rational discourse and citizen education. It can, to be sure, permit instant plebiscites of the most dangerous kind where unthinking prejudices are numerically recorded to establish the momentary shape of mass prejudice on an issue (these plebiscitary dangers have been noted by various liberal critics of the new technology who, however, seem Luddite in their prejudice against alternative uses). But is also permits ongoing communication and deliberation among individuals and (via electronic town meetings) communities that can inform and improve democracy.

Imagine a situation in which the State of California wishes to offer a referendum to its citizens on a law banning Sunday retail commerce. Normally, the private sector would go to work on voters, plying them with expensive advertisements portraying the loss to the economy of Sunday closings, and church and the retail industry would indulge in a war of publicists. Voters, having passively received this bounty of misinformation, would eventually be constrained to vote their prejudices (religion versus convenience) and the matter would be "democratically" resolved. Yet with the assistance of the new technologies a very different scenario can be imagined. Every township and municipality in California might, for example, call a town meeting to discuss an issue initially. The State might fund a neutral documentary maker to produce a one hour special on the issue, which might be shown on television prior to a debate by proponents of each side. A second set of town meetings would follow this, including a video hookup (teleconference) of urban and rural meetings to let different parts of the State understand how the issue was being discussed elsewhere. This could be followed by a final debate on television coupled with an interactive hookup permitting home viewers to pose questions to the "experts." Such a multiple-phase process involving information, adversarial debate, and direct engagement by citizens within their local communities, and among the communities and the experts would offer genuine civic education. More public-regarding ways of looking at problems could emerge, and the final decision on the referendum would be both informed and more public-minded. The cumulative effect on the political competence of the electorate of a series of such procedures, replicated on different issues over several years, would be immense.

The institutional tools necessary to realize this kind of a scenario are not beyond our reach. A "Civic Communications Co-operative" in the

USA would permit an independent public corporation to oversee civic uses of the new media, and perhaps establish a model program channel. Local municipalities responsible for franchising cable operators could insist on institutional networks, public access channels with personnel and technical support, and public information terminals as a condition of the franchise (most municipalities focus on the number and entertainment quality of program channels and rarely raise issues of civic education and information).

It is then the will and not the way that is missing at present. Certainly Thomas Jefferson would not be disappointed to learn that technology has made possible a quality and degree of communication among citizens and between citizens and bureaucrats, experts, and their information banks he could not have dreamed of. It was always Jefferson's belief that the inadequacies of democracy were best remedied by more democracy: that civic incompetence was not a reason to disempower citizens, but empowerment a remedy to redress incompetence.

POSTSCRIPT IN THE FORM OF A CAVEAT

In considering the Jeffersonian scenario we do not want to fall into Pangloss's error and persuade ourselves that technology, properly used, can solve all the problems of democracy. Next to Pangloss, Pandora and Jefferson lurks Icarus, to remind us of the ultimate limits of all human technology—the modern extension of human hubris. The intractability of nature is ameliorated but not overcome by our technical mastery of the world. Our own human foibles infect our technology (as the tragedy of *Challenger* again proved), and it will never be less imperfect than the men and women who create and utilize it. If our fallibility entails the fallibility of our technology, no prudent citizen or statesman will look exclusively to technology for the solution to modern dilemmas. Democracy can be reinforced by technology and it can be corrupted by technology, but democracy's survival depends on human not machine inspiration. The posture we need in considering the relationship of politics and technology is thus one of wariness and caution—a thorough knowledge of history, a thorough awareness of what can go wrong with schemes that seem so right, a thorough and prudent modesty, rooted in a recognition of our own essential limits as transient beings in a world we control only by permitting ourselves to be controlled by it.

CHAPTER 20

The New Telecommunications Technology:
Endless Frontier
or the End of Democracy?

THE NEW telecommunications technologies are everywhere celebrated: celebrated as the key to the new global economy—this was Bill Gates's theme at the 1997 World Economic Forum in Davos, for example; celebrated as the secret of America's new global economic recovery—President Clinton and Speaker Gingrich agree on this much; and celebrated as the beginning of a "new era in American Politics" and of a new stage in the evolution of global democracy.[1] While the first and second claims may be true, the third, linking the new technologies directly to democracy, is far more controversial: palpably dangerous if not entirely false.

To be sure, innovations in communications and information technology do offer new technical opportunities for strong democrats and civic republicans to strengthen civic education and enhance direct deliberative communication among citizens. Only Luddites would dismiss the possibilities of the digital revolution as wholly nefarious. I was myself an early advocate of exploiting the democratic potential of the new technologies, and there are many responsible democrats who today are exploring in theory and practice this potential.[2] Caution has, however, been outrun by techno-Panglossians and cyber-enthusiasts who seem to think that with new technologies of communication we can overcome every defect of communication our political system has experienced.

Historically, technology has always had a special if deeply ambivalent relationship to democracy. Jean-Jacques Rousseau believed that the progress of the arts and sciences had a corrupting effect on morals;[3] Frankfurt School critics under the sway of Heidegger, from Adorno and Horkheimer to Marcuse and Habermas, have warned that the Enlightenment's faith in progress has had costs that are the more severe for their invisibility.[4] The truth seems to be not so much that technology is averse to civic ideals than that it has run away from politics and morals, evolving so rapidly that its impact on democracy as well as its vulnerability to undemocratic forces have gone largely unremarked.

TECHNOLOGY: MIRROR OF DEMOCRACY OR MIRROR OF THE MARKET?

The problem goes deep—to the very core of what democracy means. Democracy depends on deliberation, prudence, slow-footed interaction, and time-consuming (thus "inefficient") forms of multilateral conversation and social interaction that by postmodern standards may seem cumbersome, time-consuming, demanding, sometimes interminable, and always certifiably unentertaining. Computer terminals, on the other hand, make process terminable, for electronic and digital technology's imperative is speed. Computers are fast as light, literally. Democracy is slow as prudent judgment, which is very slow indeed, demanding silences as well as communicative exchange and requiring upon occasion that days or months pass by before further thought or action can be demanded. A less than human unflappability rather than a superhuman artificial intelligence is the real advantage machines hold over men, as the chess victory of IBM's Deep Blue over Kasparov proved. Unlike our computers, we humans crash frequently. We often need to cool off, ponder, rethink, and absorb the consequence of previous decisions before we can make prudent new judgments. With human intelligence, "parallel computing" entails sociability and deliberative interaction and slows rather than hastens ratiocination and decision.

Digital reasoning is binary, privileging a simple choice between on and off, A and B, yes and no. It "likes" oppositions and dualism. Political reasoning is complex and nuanced, dialectical rather than digitally oppositional. It aims at escaping the rational choice games that computer-modeled decisional processes prefer. To the question "A or B?" the citizen may reply "both!" or "neither!" or "those are not the right choices," or even "I don't care!" Imagine a computer that shrugs off a question by muttering "*Je m'en fou!*" Our tools are in a certain sense out of synch with democracy, out of control. In an epoch of antiregulatory passion and pervasive antipathy to government, as the new technologies pass into the hands of corporations organized to secure maximum profits and little else, they are likely to become ever more so. Henry David Thoreau (in his anarchist incarnation) worried about how easily we can become the tools of our tools.

Perhaps it is even worse: we may be becoming the tools of the tools of our tools—guided not by the technology itself but by how it is being utilized as a consequence of market forces. It has been decades since Fred Friendly suggested Americans might need an "electronic bill of rights" to keep pace with changes in information technology that the American Founders could not possibly have foreseen. Their Bill of Rights was designed for a world of print in which fast communication meant the pony express or a sea voyage. The Progress and Freedom Foundation has promulgated a Magna Carta for the Information Age (1994), but there has been no serious mainline attempt to update the Federal Communications Act of 1934, devised for the then "modern" world of radio and quite properly concerned to "encourage the larger and more effective use of radio in the public interest." Indeed, the recently passed Telecommunications Bill of 1996 seeks mainly to move government out of the way, turning over the question of how the new technologies will impact our civic lives and our democratic society entirely to the whims of money and markets. The only other advance has been the Communications Decency Act (of dubious constitutionality in any case), which is on the table not in the name of civic enhancement but of civic censorship of internet pornography.

While Europe has traditionally retained greater public control over its information and broadcasting utilities, it is currently under extraordinary pressure (in the name of global competition) to privatize. At the 1997 World Economic Forum in Davos, Bill Gates hectored the French for their cyber-backwardness, and met privately with representatives of the Indian government to push them toward telecommunications privatization (and perhaps a contract with Microsoft). The Munich Declaration of 1997 promulgated at the Academy for the Third Millennium's Conference on the Internet and Politics calls boldly for greater governmental and popular control and use of the new technologies for civic purposes, but it leans into the hard wind of privatization.[5] Indeed, the information superhighway is being built so fast that whatever residual regulatory powers survive the current deregulatory mania, guaranteeing privacy and controlling monopoly are likely to be left far behind. President Clinton has been reduced to high-minded jawboning in trying to persuade the private sector to control entertainment mayhem and link up public schools and libraries to the internet.[6]

How long will the vaunted "wild west frontier" of the internet hold out against the colonizing forces of commerce and corporatism? Point to point communication systems like the telephone and the internet are, it has been repeatedly argued, lateral systems and hence more inherently democratic than vertical systems like broadcast radio and television. This is perfectly true, and it offers democrats the very real promise of technologically enhanced forms of civic interaction. But those who own conduits and software platforms, those who write programs and are systems gatekeepers still wield extraordinary power. We may wish there were no gatekeepers (although I would argue that there are forms of control and intervention like editing, facilitation, and education that are necessary to democratic utilization of the net and that are legitimate forms of gatekeeping). In any case, the alternative to the visibly regulatory state is not the free market but the invisibly regulatory market, whose choices and boundaries are powerfully delimiting, but as part of the "invisible hand" of the market are largely unseen and unacknowledged. Can any regulatory body hope in the name of the public good to bring a civic dimension to a five-hundred-channel cable system, where the spectrum scarcity that once justified federal regulation has (in theory at least) vanished? or curtail the inexpensive duplication (pirating) of cassettes, compact disks, and computer programs in which the Chinese have excelled? or influence telephone companies that now have the right to compete in cable television markets? or to track and regulate global satellite companies whose stations recognize no borders and can be picked up anywhere by a dinner-plate-sized dish? Such systems are, ironically, more susceptible to corporate than to government control and are likely to serve private rather than public interests.

What these somber reflections suggest is that technology is often less a determinant than a mirror of the larger society. Who owns it, how it is used and by whom, and to which ends: these are the critical questions whose answers will shape technology's actual role in the coming century. To be sure, technology bends a little this way, a little that, and it has intimations and entailments that obviously can modify human institutions and behavior. But ultimately it reflects the world in which it finds itself. Gunpowder helped democratize a Protestant, urbanizing Europe ripe for democratizing, but in feudal China it secured the hold of grasping elites; movable type facilitated the democratization of literacy but also made possible mass propaganda and the extended thought control that marked the innovative tyranny known as totalitarianism. Interactive two-way television and keypad voting invite participation even as they expedite surveillance and marginalize thoughtfulness and complexity. But why should we finally expect our technologies to look much different than the society and the economics of the world that produces and puts them to use?

Whatever entailments technology may have in the abstract, it still will reflect concretely the premises and objectives of the society deploying it. This is precisely the meaning of sovereignty: politics governs technique, society and culture always trump technology. Ends condition means, and technology is just a fancy word for means. The new telecommunications are less likely to alter and improve than to reflect and augment our current socioeconomic institutions and political attitudes. A commercial culture will entail a commercialized technology.[7] A society dominated by the ideology of privatization will engender a privatized internet.

Wishful thinkers at outfits like the Electronic Frontier Foundation fantasize an internet as free and democratic and horizontally organized as their own ingenuity and imagination. For internet technology *is* point to point and certainly can be said to have a democratic potential. But it will take political will to allow such tendencies to emerge and modify traditional attitudes and institutions, which in the meantime are likely to be determinative.

The internal combustion engine and electricity did not absolutely mandate a privatized, highway-strip, suburbanized, overmalled America. Those late-nineteenth-century technologies suited mass transportation systems (railways and buses, for example) equally well and thus could have also helped anchor an urban and town culture (as they did after World War II in Europe). It was not automotive determinism but specific political decisions taken in the first half of the twentieth century that translated the technologies of internal combustion and electric motors into a suburban society—perhaps most significantly, a critical decision by the U.S. Congress after World War II. Under pressure from the postwar steel, rubber, cement, and automobile industries, and possessed of a spirit of individualism that predated the new technologies, the Congress voted to fund an immense interstate highway system that privileged the automobile and the social environment it mandated.

Who knows how different America might look today had that same Congress opted for an equally extensive interstate rail system? During the cold war, Deputy Secretary of State George Ball once justified investment in the Soviet Union's automobile industry by proclaiming, "The automobile is an ideology on four wheels." But it was not the automobile that created the ideology but the ideology that created the automobile. A car is radical individualism writ large, the internal combustion engine turned to the purposes of private liberty rather than (to name some alternative ideologies) to such public ends as environmental protection, or the preservation of cities, or social cooperation, or war.

Is there then really any reason to think that a society dominated by profit mongering and private interests will exempt the new telecommunications technologies from the pursuit of profit or constitute them in a more public-spirited manner than will the society at large? Bill Gates's vision in *The Road Ahead* omits any reference to the civic good, prophesying instead a "shopper's heaven," in which "all the goods in the world will be available for you to examine, compare, and, often customize" and where "your wallet PC will link into a store's computer to transfer digital money."[8] And even where it can be shown that the technology inherently holds out the promise of civic and democratic potential, is it not likely to reflect the thin, representative, alienating version of democracy that currently dominates political thinking?[9] For without a will toward a more participatory and robust civic system, why should technologically enhanced politics not produce the same incivility and cynicism that characterize politics on the older technologies, radio and television, for example? (Recall that radio too once promised a more egalitarian and democratic form of communication, written into the Federal Communications Act of 1934 as a commitment to broadcasting as a public utility.) The internet promised new forms of civic discourse, but political chat-room banter on the internet today is as polarized and rude as anything you can hear on talk radio.

It remains true that technology can assist political change and may sometimes even point in new political directions. Interactive computer-based television hookups "point" in a certain sense to the feasibility of direct democracy, but unless there is a political will directed at greater participation, the potential remains only that: a potential. Nor will interactive technology do anything, on its own, to cure the primary defect of unmediated participatory politics—the danger of undeliberative majority tyranny and thus a kind of plebiscitary dictatorship.

One-way information retrieval via the net may expand for some the orbit of available resources; the Library of Congress achieved an instant success by making millions of items including Matthew Brady's Civil War photographs, Gershwin's musical scores, San Francisco earthquake pictorials, and memorabilia from the Yiddish Theater available on its new net site (www.loc.gov). Yet retrieval is at best an improvement on access to information, not a move toward genuine interactive communication.[10] Indeed, while Umberto Eco uncritically assumes that new technologies will render obsolete many kinds of books,[11] publishers who were originally excited by the rush to digital publishing and CD-ROMs have recently pulled back from the brink, arguing that "the business has been a huge bust for book publishers."[12] If then technology is to make a political difference, it is the politics that will first have to be changed.

THE NEW MEDIA: DIVERSITY OR MONOPOLY?

Much has been made over the apparent diversification of media and the multiplication of communication spectrums that has accompanied the evolution of advanced telecommunication technologies. In place of three networks in America, or two or three state networks in many other countries, we now have cable- and satellite-based systems that can offer up to five hundred or more channels. Even the traditional broadcast media are soon to be subjected to a digitalization that will yield five or six channels for every one that currently exists on the broadcast spectrum—a change that led U.S. Senator Bob Dole, fearing the "giveaway of the century," to exempt the question of what is to be done with these new spectrums from the recently enacted 1996 Telecommunications Bill, leaving it for the new Congress to debate. Moreover, the multiplication of available channels of communication is clearly abetted by an internet that offers literally endless millions of interconnected sites that promote point-to-point communication of a kind that seems in turn to promise endless diversity.

In short, the technology is clearly capable of exerting a pluralizing influence on communications. Yet though the technology may be inherently disaggregating and devolutionary, ownership over the technology's hardware and software is aggregating and centralizing. As delivery systems diversify and multiply, program content becomes more homogeneous, and digitalization will not in itself change that. As the laterally organized net expands, commercial carpetbaggers move in, ready to turn its horizontal and interactive communications networks into an opportunity for vertical one-way "we-sell, you-buy" commercial control (sometimes called "push" rather than "pull" techniques). So that kids logging onto playroom sites owned by companies like Toys 'R' Us that are supposed to be educational and fun are in fact being used as unwitting subjects of cyber-tot market surveys they fill out as their password to play.

More conduits, more hardware, and more outlets do not mean more diversity. Imagine a one-hundred channel cable system in Nazi Germany. "Yes, we Nazis prize diversity!" a Goebbels would say. But turn on the system and you find Himmler on Channel 1 for talk show fans, Hitler Youth Programming on Channel 2 for the kids, the Oberkommando Wehrmacht on Channel 3 for military buffs, Leni Riefenstahl documentaries on Channel 4 for history fans, the Party Platform as Hypertext on Channel 5 for C-Span devotees, and an exhibition of *Entartente Kunst* (decadent art) on Channel 6, the arts channel. And so on. Some "diversity"!

Free-market advocates defend this commodification of cyber-space by insisting on what they call the "synergy" between markets and the new technologies that supposedly turns markets into engines of efficiency that advantage public interests by maximizing competition and choice. But late capitalism is neither entrepreneurial nor competitive. It flourishes by selling singular, mass-produced goods like athletic shoes, electronic hardware, and colas to everyone on the planet: the same movie, the same book, the same burger—and the same software platform, the same program—to as many billions of citizens as can be turned into consumers. And when it can no longer push goods, it starts manufacturing needs so that there is a demand for the endless goods it must bring to the market if it is to flourish. No wonder that, as governments bow out of the communications regulation business and new technologies globalize in a manner that makes them resistant to regulation, ownership patterns are growing more rather than less monopolistic.

Software understood as computer programs, information and data banks, films and videos, entertainment, music and images is at the heart of technological change in the postindustrial era. And in the sector that supplies the new technologies with this software, production is controlled by a handful of powerful corporations that, quite literally month by month, grow fewer in number and more encompassing in scope and ambition. The concept that drives the new media merger frenzy carries the fashionable name "synergy."

The idea is to gather together the production companies turning out product (programming content), the telephone and cable and satellite companies transmitting product, and the television sets and computers and multiplexes presenting product to the public all into the same hands.[13] Synergy, however, turns out to be a polite way of saying monopoly. And in the domain of information, monopoly is a polite word for uniformity, which is a polite word for virtual censorship—censorship not as a consequence of political choices but as a consequence of inelastic markets, imperfect competition, and economies of scale—the quest for a single product that can be owned by a single proprietor and sold to every living soul on the planet. (In the United States, the popular C-Span channel that allows Americans to watch Congress around the clock is being forced off many cable systems by the new Rupert Murdoch–owned Fox News Channel as well as by burgeoning home shopping channels); or the search for a "safe image" that avoids all controversy in the name of broad consumer acceptance.

The quest for image safety manifests an all too common corporate anxiety about controversy and a tendency to support the bland and the plastic over the disputatious and the risk-taking. Postmodern capitalism is preternaturally risk-averse, anything but entrepreneurial. This means that just as Hollywood makes sequels to successful megahits rather than experimenting with new "art" films, that publishers seek megabooks by celebrities rather than serious "middle list" nonfiction and new novels, and that television is hostile to anything that appears too far out: too politically radical or too reactionary, too religious or too insistently atheist, too eccentric and far out and thus too far from the mean, too (quite literally) unpopular.

The consolidation of ownership in the infotainment telesector, well documented by Ben Bagdikian and others for the period from 1945 through the 1980s, has actually accelerated as technologies have multiplied and the possibilities for transmitting information have diversified. Conglomeration had reduced the number of mainstage telecommunications players from forty-six in 1981 to twenty-three in 1991. And of these, a handful like Time-Warner/Turner, Disney/ABC, Bertelsmann and Murdoch's News Corporation dominate—genuinely intermedia corporations with a finger in every part of the business.[14] So that, for example, when Rupert Murdoch wanted to accommodate the Chinese on the way to persuading them to permit his Asian Television Network to broadcast, he was able to instruct the publisher HarperCollins (a News Corporation subsidiary) to withdraw its offer to Harry Wu—a dissident thorn in the side of the Chinese—for his political memoirs.[15]

The recent erosion of boundaries between telephone, cable, and broadcast transmission has accelerated the conglomeration process even more radically, and the orphans of Ma Bell, cut loose in 1984, are now energized by deregulation and are threatening to supplant their aging mama as they enter and compete in the long distance telephone field. In fact, the new telecommunications bill allows any company to compete in more or less any field of communications so that AT&T (Ma Bell) can pursue cable television or satellite, the local telephone companies can go after long distance or cellular, and anybody can buy pretty much anyone or anything as long as they can cut the deal and pay the freight. And in February of 1997, sixty-eight nations agreed through the World Trade Organization to remove barriers that prevented private companies from competing with state telecommunication monopolies—good news for consumers in the short run, but better news by far for the powerful, technologically advanced American telecommunications cartels poised to take over much of the world's long-distance business and further secure their hold on global communications.[16] The proposed merger of MCI and British Telephone is a test case, and if it is permitted to go through, the global cartelization of communications will be well underway.

In the name of free markets, private profit is once again being permitted to displace public utility (or is assumed to be synonymous with it). An eighteenth-century version of free-market ideology is thus used to legitimate anti-entrepreneurial monopoly practices of a twenty-first-century global capitalism that has lost its taste for real competition.

THE SOFT NEW TOTALITARIANISM OF CONSUMERISM

The new trend toward monopoly signals then not synergy but vulnerability to a kind of commercial totalitarianism—a single value (profit) and a single owner (the monopoly holder) submerging all distinctions, rendering all choice tenuous and all diversity sham. Carriers want to control and profit from what they carry; cultural creators want to control and profit from the entities (stations and networks) that carry what they create; software purveyors want to control and profit from the hardware on which their wares are purveyed. Everyone wants a piece of the creative core, where the "content" that drives everything else is manufactured. The result is more talk about variety—and far more uniformity in product and content. Why be a pipe for someone else's music when you can own composer and composition alike? There may be one hundred or even five hundred channels on the new cable systems, but if the content providers are gargantuan monopolies whose products bear a strong family resemblance, what difference does it make that the conduits are multiple? And so Bill Gates buys Washington pundit Michael Kinsley to put a magazine on his internet network (*Slate*) and then purchases the rights to the Barnes Collection, along the way taking an option on filmmakers by purchasing a significant minority share in Dreamworks, the new creative "content provider" established by director/producer Steven Spielberg, record titan David Geffen, and former Disney magnate Jerry Katzenberg.

The men who dominate this extraordinary new world of technologized culture are mostly American (though there are the Murdochs and Bertelsmanns and Burdas to be reckoned with as well). America may have been down in the eighties, but as power has softened and soft information and entertainment products have replaced durable industrial goods, it has become the world's postindustrial economic superpower. American media moguls like Michael Eisner, Ted Turner, Sumner Redstone, Barry Diller, Martin S. Davis, George Lucas, Michael Ovitz, Bill Gates, Jeffrey Katzenberg, H. Wayne Huizenga, John C. Malone, and Steven Spielberg are surely as powerful today as Vanderbilt, Carnegie, Rockefeller, and their Gilded Age cousins were in the late-nineteenth century,[17] except the new titans of telecommunication exercise monopoly control not just over material goods like oil, coal, steel, and the railroads but over the essential instruments of power in an information-based civilization: ideas, images, words, and pictures. Such monopolies not only destroy capitalist competition, they also corrupt the diversity and pluralism of information on which democracy depends.

Behind the beckoning diversity of their media empires lurks a new form of totalism all the more dangerous because it boasts of "choice" and is sold in the language of freedom. The claim is that in the marketplace, with government out of the way, we are all equals. I have a home page on the net just like Bill Gates and the Disney Corporation, market devotees remind me. But does anyone really believe that the common capacity to produce a home page is the same thing as the common power to affect the world? Is power a question of who is speaking or who is listening (and who can get whom to listen)? In a world of communications leviathans, democracy requires more than "one man, one home page"![18]

Yet why in times when monopoly passes as synergy should we expect technology to produce genuine diversity? Or universal access—without which, income and education disparities are likely to be reproduced by information and technology disparities, with cleavages between rich and poor being replicated as cleavages between the information rich and the information poor. Who represents the public good in a world of privatized information production? Is there a global equivalent of even so reluctant a defender of the public interest as the FCC? Which institutions can exert countervailing pressures on media monopolies in the name of quality or diversity or community? There appear to be no easy answers, even on the rare occasions where the questions get asked.

WHAT IS VIRTUAL COMMUNITY?

In the solipsistic virtual reality of cyber-space, commonality itself seems to be in jeopardy. Not only does commerce tend toward monopoly; it mandates privatization, and privatization is the death of democracy. For democracy is always about *public* willing and *public* goods and the *common*weal. Decentralization can enhance democracy; privatization only corrupts it. Little is no better than big when it is private and for profit rather than public (but local) and for the common good (not personal benefit). You can be eaten alive by piranha as well as by a great white shark: it just takes a little longer.

Here commerce is reinforced by certain technical features of telecommunications technology that it in turn reinforces. How can there be "common ground" when ground itself vanishes and women and men inhabit abstractions? There may be some new form of community developing among the myriad solitaries perched in front of their screens and connected only by their fingertips to the new web defined by the internet. But the politics of that "community" has yet to be invented, and it is hardly likely automatically to be democratic, certainly not as a result of market imperatives. It has yet to be shown that anonymous screen-to-screen interaction can do for us what face-to-face interaction has done. The out-of-body nature of virtual communication is both a virtue and a vice. It can marginalize bodies—as when college roommates sit side by side conversing via their screens, or when wired campuses watch social clubs and local recreational centers atrophy because students are glued to their computers. My own test for a virtual community is this: I will believe in the virtual community when someone shows me virtual community service.

Enthusiasts for internet chat rooms or cyber-tot playpens prattle on about "community," but can an anonymous exchange with strangers whose identity is a matter of invention and artifice replicate the kind of conversations that occur spontaneously among fellow PTA members about a school board election or even mimic a gossip session across a back fence? If good fences make good neighbors, virtual neighbors may turn out to make good fences against real neighbors. The *New York Times* recently reported that "E-Mail is becoming a conduit of prejudice on many campuses."[19] Is the social trust that is eroding in our social and political world likely to be rekindled on the net, where identities can be concealed and where "flaming" and other forms of incivility are regularly practiced? Civility means taking responsibility for one's views (their virtues and their vices): the net is far more anonymous than talk radio, and neither medium seems much interested in social responsibility.

My own painfully time-consuming and colossally unrewarding visits to the net in search of deliberative dialogue and meaningful political talk netted little that would support Lawrence K. Grossman's happy conclusion that "the transformation to participatory democracy has been helped by the remarkable increase in the speed of information, pushed along" most recently by "digital convergence."[20] Information seekers are mostly after porn and pulp while chatroom visitors, when not also pursuing sex, seem to be asleep. In a typical conversation:

> *On-Line Host.* You are in Town Square . . .
> *DeepPhaze.* Which guy wants to eat me out?
> *Jr. Twety.* What's everyone talking about?
> *Iceburn 911.* Me.
> *Lodino.* I don't no [*sic*].
> *DeepPhaze.* Fuck me.
> *DWHKY.* No problem.
> *Lodino.* OK.
> *Iceburn 911.* Deep is a gay.
> *Bjanyeats.* No way pal.
> *DWJLY.* I'm a girl.
> *Hulk Dog.* Hi.
> *JmwIck001.* I am a new AOL User from Long Island. Where are any of you from?
> *Bjanyeats.* Big fat hairy deal.
> *Lodino.* Bye.
> *Lene77.* Dork.
> *Iceburn 911.* Let's have cyber-sex.
> *Otterhawk.* Get a clue.
> *Bjanyeats.* What clue?

(This conversation is concluded by the posting of an ingenious digital image provided by "Kyoung Pro" of Hulk Dog apparently being fellated by his "little sister.")

Even on the handful of "serious" sites that can be found, what is available is mostly superficial information about political parties, platforms, and candidates of the kind you can get by mail, or polarized debates around the conventional talk radio extremes with little in the way of real facilitation, discussion, or persuasion.[21] There are, to be sure, a handful of sites that have tried to create new formats for interactive political education, including PROJECT VOTESMART and MINNESOTA E-DEMOCRACY. But even these sites seem better geared to serve citizens during elections, and often do little in the long periods between them. There is no better guide to the apparent futility of hopes for cyber-democracy and genuine political dialogue than John Seabrook's new account of his disillusionment with the medium he initially celebrated. In a memoir called *Deeper,* he confesses that his hopes for a "many-to-many" technology "uniquely capable of inspiring" new hope for human relations were dashed by the reality that the net offered people only new ways to "be just as cliquish and exclusionary as they ever were."[22]

Finally, the economic trends of our world tend toward radical commercialization of values and behavior in a fashion that compromises not only civic politics but family values, education, and spirituality. The technology is not per se commercial or commercializing, but *commercialized;* it becomes one more weapon in the arsenal of corporations for whom consumption is the only relevant human behavior. When *U.S. News and World Report* trumpeted on the cover of its special issue on the internet "Gold Rush in Cyberspace!" it mixed nineteenth-century frontier imagery with twenty-first-century cyber-jabber on the way to revealing that for the telecommunication corporations, the only significant question is how to make money off of the innovations that utopians and idealists believe will usher in a new world of democracy.[23]

The frontier has been a powerful image in American political iconography, and it is no surprise that radical individualists and decentralist democrats like to deploy it in thinking about the net—as in the Electronic Frontier Foundation. But in reality, the Wild West frontier was opening up after the Civil War at the very moment when the concentration and conglomeration of capital in oil, coal, steel, and railways that defined the Gilded Age were getting underway. And by the end of the nineteenth century, it was not the frontier but the cartel that defined America, and the products of the cartel—railroads, industry, urbanization—had been the very commodities that closed the frontier down.

There is little reason to think that, in the absence of political will, the metaphoric electronic frontier will fare any better in the face of monopoly capitalism than did the historic frontier. Are the new monopolists like Gates and Eisner and Malone any less ambitious or talented than Carnegie and Rockefeller? Is capitalism any less interested today in the kinds of control that breeds big profits than it was a hundred years ago? The electronic frontier is not a metaphor; it is a dream, a myth, and a deeply misleading one at that: a perfect smoke screen for those busy closing it down.

The young history of music video offers a particularly instructive lesson for those who believe the net is likely to remain free from commercialization because it is a new, creative medium developed and used in its early incarnation by electronic frontiersmen and cyber-pioneers. In the 1970s, music videos were the playground of artists and countercultural dissidents — a medium for new wave creative explorers working at experimental studios like the Kitchen in lower Manhattan. Like moving pictures, which in their own time were celebrated as a democratization of aristocratic theater, music video was to be a peculiarly "democratic" medium. Its early experimental users insisted that, unlike film, it was inexpensive, flexible, erasable, and reusable, and, hence, accessible to everyone.

Yet within ten years, the television, cable, and music industries had moved in and expropriated the "experimental" medium, and today MTV and its imitators are wholly owned subsidiaries as well as the selling arm of the global music industry: a twenty-four-hour-a-day advertisement for a globalizing and ever more homogeneous pop music, as well as for the soft- and hardware it takes to play that music. Why should it be any different with the internet? Just because today it is the playground of intrepid cyber-explorers, that will not insulate it tomorrow from corporate ambitions.

Computer shopping has already become the fastest growing part of the World Wide Web. Even the usually technologically upbeat Aspen Institute, in a report celebrating "The Future of Electronic Commerce," warns that while "the business rush to colonize the Internet will surely invigorate cyberspace and make it more accessible to mainstream Americans . . . it may also marginalize the vast 'third sector' of nonprofits, civic groups and public institutions who generally do not have the money and expertise to participate fully in the on-line culture."[24]

Does this portrait of global commerce and growing monopoly mean then that all technological innovation is inimical to democracy? Not necessarily. It means only that without directives aimed at taking advantages of its democratic potentials, the global socioeconomic forces that are today shaping the world will also shape technology's usages.

IS THIS PROGRESS?

Science has been linked to progressive liberalism and democracy at least since the Enlightenment, when pioneers standing on the threshold of modernity believed that through their new science they could command the world and liberate the human race from prejudice, ignorance, and injustice. At the beginning of the century now ending, Bertrand Russell thought he saw in scientific skepticism a source of democracy's epistemological humility, but even then he worried about technology's association with power and manipulation. Advocates of the consumer society might ponder his warning that having once "delivered man from bondage to nature," science was in danger of delivering him "from bondage to the slavish part of himself."[25]

Less cautious heirs to Russell have become Panglossian democracy futurologists, unknowingly mouthing Candide's ditty, "This is the best of all possible worlds." Taking their cue from the eighteenth-century Frenchman Condorcet (who died in a French revolutionary prison writing a book about the ten stages of inevitable human progress), enthusiasts like Walter Wriston, Alvin Toffler, John Naisbett, and Bill Gates have all composed odes to the emancipatory, democratic powers of the startling new technologies that drive McWorld and have transformed capitalism from a system that serves needs into a system that creates and manipulates them.[26]

Walter Wriston thinks that "the information age is rapidly giving the power to the people[,]" speeding us along on "our journey toward more human freedom,"[27] while Bill Gates is certain that "technology can humanize the educational. . . . The net effect [of the new technology] will be a wealthier world . . . [and] the gap between the have and have-not nations will diminish. . . . Somewhere ahead is the threshold dividing the PC era from the highway era. I want to be among the first to cross over."[28]

Technology's mandarins are correct in seeing improved information and communication as potentially useful in improving democracy. From the time of the Greeks, who believed Prometheus's theft of fire from the gods lit the way to human civilization, technical gadgets have been made to support democratization. In ancient Athens, small machines that randomized the selection of white and black balls were used for jury selection. During the Renaissance, movable type, gunpowder, and the compass helped society transform itself through forces that both equalized and mobilized the population. Democratic trends already underway were thereby reinforced.

Twentieth-century technologies have mimicked those of the fifteenth and sixteenth centuries, further democratizing transportation, communication, and war. Combat has become the democratic burden of civilians as well as soldiers, while the internal combustion engine has given Everyman a horse and buggy and the mobility that goes with it. Most significantly, radio and television and in time mass-produced computers have offered an ongoing technically enhanced democratization of words and pictures that spreads effective literacy and political knowledge even to those who cannot read, and thus strengthens the will to govern (if not necessarily the deliberative competence) of democratic electorates. Television, one might say, does not so much enhance literacy as render it irrelevant—bypassing the black and white of the word to bring a bright color world of pictures to Everyman, adding "imagineering" (as the Disney Company likes to put it) to word crafting as a defining element of human literacy.

The net still seems wedded to words. Scrolling text with how-long-do-we-have-to wait-to-get-them?-pictures are the net's medium, suggesting a technology that is little more than a souped-up telegraph. But of course that is only a technical glitch resting on the medium's immaturity. As its capacity to carry more information at greater speeds increases, it is likely to become motion-picture based—just like television and the movies! Pictures are clearly the favored form of information on what are after all *moving picture* screens, whether they are found in quad cinemas or aboard laptop computers. Clever kids already use their keyboards to design character-generated graphics, deploying what are supposed to be the building blocks of words (and thus thought) to compose pictures. So it seems fairly obvious that the technology is wasted if all it does is transmit text. Yet many of the new technology's virtues have been associated precisely with this text-based character, its most retrograde feature.

Live picture interactive hookups beat electronic bulletin boards for some purposes of democracy—although it clearly depends on what we mean by democracy and whether we are looking for affective interaction or rational deliberation. Video teleconference capabilities allow local town meetings to interact with similar meetings across a region, a nation, or the world, breaking down the parochialism of face-to-face interaction without entirely sacrificing its personalism. I recently hosted a four-site interactive discussion of immigration and American identity in Arizona, with groups participating from Tuba City, Flagstaff, Tempe, and Tuscon, where it again was demonstrated how interactive television can transform a passive medium aimed at complacent consumers of entertainment and advertising into an active theater of social discourse and political feedback. Members of the World Economic Forum (the convening of economic and political elites at Davos each winter) are being offered their own communications network called Welcom (World Electronic Community), which promises to inaugurate a "secure, private, high-level, reliable network of active face-to-face global video communications" that will connect members "with cabinet members, heads of international organizations and central banks, and the foremost experts and knowledge-producing centres across the globe."[29]

The new technology does then open up the possibilities of democracy. For example, home voting by interactive module can facilitate and personalize voting, if we are willing to pay the costs of privatization (too little public deliberation, views voted on before they are exposed to public scrutiny). Interactive technologies foster lateral as well as vertical communication. This means citizens can interact with one another and not simply listen passively to leaders and elites. Project Vote Smart, a national citizens clearinghouse for election information, recently moved from 800 and 900 number technology to a "Vote Smart Web" on which the politically curious can access a welter of vital political and electoral statistics, data, and candidate information.[30] There are also web sites for the White House, Congress, and the new international CIVITAS network of global nongovernmental organizations.[31]

Satellite dishes the size of a dinner plate put a global ear at the disposal of peoples imprisoned in the most despotic regimes, and have proved their worth in places like China and Iran, where despite an official government ban, they continue to multiply—and as they do, to spread unfettered images and words to information-starved consumers. To be sure, much of what is spread is consumer information and banal entertainment rather than political debate and news, but this is the fault of those who use it rather than of the technology itself.[32]

WHICH DEMOCRACY? PROGRESS FOR WHOM?

In combination then, the new technologies and the software they support can potentially enhance lateral communication among citizens, can open access to information by all, and can furnish citizens with communication links across distances that once precluded direct democracy. Yet there is a formidable obstacle in the way of implementation of these technologies: unless we are clear about what democracy means to us, and what kind of democracy we envision, technology is as likely to stunt as to enhance the civic polity. Is it representative democracy, plebiscitary democracy, or deliberative democracy for which we seek technological implementation? The differences between the three are not only theoretically crucial, but have radically different entailments with respect to technology.

Do we aspire to further the representative system, a democracy rooted in the election of accountable deputies who do all the real work of governing? Most advocates of this form of indirect democracy are properly suspicious of the new technologies and their penchant for immediacy, directness, lateral communication, and undeliberativeness. Or is it plebiscitary majoritarianism we seek, a democracy that embodies majority opinions assembled from the unconsidered prejudices of private persons voting private interests? New technology can be a dangerously facile instrument of such unchecked majoritarianism: the net affords politicians an instrument for perpetual polling that can aggravate the focus group mentality that many rue as Dick Morris's political legacy. Will any politicians ever again gather the courage to lead in the face of a technology that makes following so easy?

Yet if we are in search of what I have called "strong democracy," a democracy that reflects the careful and prudent judgment of citizens who participate in deliberative, self-governing communities, we will need to tease out of the technology other capabilities. If democracy is to be understood as deliberative and participatory activity on the part of responsible citizens, it will have to resist the innovative forms of demagoguery that accompany innovative technology and that are too often overlooked by enthusiasts, and listen carefully to those like Theodore Becker and James Fishkin, who have tried to incorporate deliberative constraints into their direct democratic uses of the technologies.[33] In other words, it turns out there is no simple or general answer to the question "Is the technology democratizing?" until we have made clear what sort of democracy we intend. Home voting via interactive television might further privatize politics and replace deliberative debate in public with the unconsidered instant expression of private prejudices, turning what ought to be public decisions into private consumerlike choices; but deliberative television polling of the kind envisioned by James Fishkin can offset such dangers, while the use of the internet for deliberation across communities can actually render decision making less parochial.[34] In politics, fast is often bad, slow sometimes good.

Strong democracy calls not only for votes but for good reasons; not only for an opinion but for a rational argument on its behalf. Those who once preferred open to secret ballots, who preferred open debate about well-grounded viewpoints to closed votes aggregating personal interests, will today prefer technologies that permit frank interactive debate with real identities revealed to technologies that allow game playing and privately registered, unsupported opinions.

Traditional proponents of Madisonian representative democracy are likely to find much of the new interactive technology intimidating, since it threatens to overwhelm what they regard as a pristine system assuring government by expert politicians with a free-for-all among "ignorant" masses who swamp the polity with their endless demands and overheated prejudices. Such critics already complain that traditional broadcast television is destructive of party identity and party discipline, and they will properly worry about technologies that further erode the boundaries between the governors and the governed. Plebiscitary democrats will be mindlessly enthralled by interactive instant polling and imagine a time when private consumers make precedent-shattering public choices with no more serious thought than they give to which button to hit when they are surfing a hundred-channel cable system. "Let's see," mutters the glib new net surfer, "do I want to play checkers or outlaw abortion? Do I prefer Sylvester Stallone to Bill Clinton? Shall we download the 'Playmate of the Month' or vote to expand NATO to the Russian border? Time for a mock battle with Darth Vader on my Star Wars simulation. . . . Or should I just declare war for real on Libya?" Deliberative democrats can only shudder at such prospects, insisting that they do more to destroy than to enhance democracy. Deliberation, on the other hand, does require intervention, education, facilitation, and mediation—all anathema to devotees of an anarchic and wholly user-controlled net whose whole point is to circumvent facilitation, editing, and other "top-down" forms of intervention.

Technology can then help democracy, but only if programmed to do so and only in terms of the paradigms and political theories that inform the program. Left to the market, it is likely only to reproduce the vices of politics as usual. How different is the anonymous flaming that typifies certain kinds of internet chatter from the anonymous vilification that characterizes talk radio and scream television? Will the newer technologies be any less likely to debase the political currency, any less likely to foster sound-bite decision making rather than sound political judgment?

By the same token, if those who deploy the technologies consciously seek a more participatory, deliberative form of strong democracy and a newly robust civil society, they can also find in telecommunications innovation an extraordinarily effective ally. The trouble with the zealots of technology as an instrument of democratic liberation is not that they misconceive technology but that they fail to understand democracy. They insist that market-generated technology can, all by itself and in the complete absence of common human willing and political cooperation, produce liberty, social responsibility, and citizenship. The viruses that eat up our computer programs, like sarin in the Tokyo subway, are but obvious symbols of technology's ever-present dark side, the monster who lurks in Dr. Frankenstein's miraculous creation.

With participatory interaction comes the peril of political and economic surveillance.[35] With interactive personal preference modules comes the risk of majoritarian tyranny. With digital reasoning comes the danger that adversarial modes of thought will inundate consensus and obliterate common ground. Computer literacy cannot finally exist independently of life-long educational literacy. The age of information can reinforce extant inequalities, we have noted, making the resource- and income-poor the information-poor as well.[36] The irony is that those who might most benefit from the net's democratic and informational potential are least likely either to have access to it, the tools to gain access, or the educational background to take advantage of the tools. Those with access, on the other hand, tend to be those already empowered in the system by education, income, and literacy.

And how easily liberating technologies become tools of repression. As consumers tell shopping networks what they want to buy and tell banks how to dispense their cash and tell pollsters what they think about abortion, those receiving the information gain access to an extensive computer bank of knowledge about the private habits, attitudes, and behaviors of consumers and citizens. This information may in turn be used to reshape those habits and attitudes in ways that favor producers and sellers working the marketplace or the political arena. Moreover, the current antiregulatory fever has assured that the new data banks being compiled from interaction and surveillance are subject neither to government scrutiny nor to limitation or control—a sunset provision, for example, that would periodically destroy all stored information.[37] The model of Channel One, an invidious classroom network founded by Chris Whittle's Whittle Communications (and now owned by the K-III Corporation), which extorts classroom advertising time from needy schools in return for desperately wanted hardware, suggests that the public is likely to be served by the new technologies only in as far as someone can make serious money off it.[38]

It may be a cause of satisfaction, as Walter Wriston insists, that nowadays it is the citizen who is watching Big Brother and not the other way around. But if Big Brother is no longer watching you, nor is he watching those who *are* watching you, and even adversaries of regulation may find reason to be disturbed by that omission. If the classical liberal question used to be Who will police the police? the pertinent liberal question in today's McWorld ought to be, Who will watch those who are watching the watchers? Who will prevent the media from controlling their clients and consumers? Who will act in lieu of a government that has demurred from representing the public's interests? These are issues for democracy deliberation and decision, not for technological resolution. For technology remains a tool allied to particular conceptions of democracy; if we know what kind of democracy we want, it can enhance civic communication and expand citizen literacy. Left to markets, (and that is where it is presently being left), it is likely to augment McWorld's least worthy imperatives, including surveillance over and manipulation of opinion, and the cultivation of artificial needs rooted in lifestyle "choices" unconnected to real economic, civic, or spiritual needs.

If democracy is to benefit from technology then, we must start not with technology but with politics. Having a voice, demanding a voice, in the making of science and technology policy is the first step citizens can take in assuring a democratic technology.[39] The new technology is still only an instrument of communication, and it cannot determine *what* we will say or to whom we will say it. There is a story about the wireless pioneer Marconi who, when told by his associates that his new wireless technology meant he could now "talk to Florida," asked, presciently, "And do we have anything to say to Florida?" Enthusiasts exalt over the fact that on the net we can talk to strangers throughout the world. But many of today's problems arise from the fact that we no longer know how to talk to our husbands and wives, our neighbors and fellow citizens, let alone strangers. Will our blockages and incivilities locally be overcome by the miracles of long-distance computer communication? Will virtual community heal the ruptures of real communities? Will we do on our keyboards what we have notably failed to do face to face?

If in the coming millennium—a millennium in which technology is likely to dominate our lives as never before—we want democracy to be served, then the bittersweet fruits of science will have to be subordinated to our democratic ends and made to serve as a facilitator rather than a corruptor of our precious democracy. And whether this happens will depend not on the quality and character of our technology but on the quality of our political institutions and the character of our citizens.

NOTES

1. See Anthony Corrado and Charles M. Firestone, eds., *Elections in Cyberspace: Toward a New Era in American Politics* (Aspen, Colo.: Aspen Institute, 1996).

2. More than a dozen years ago, I suggested that "electronic enhancement of communication offers possible solutions to the dilemmas of scale," and called for television town meetings, a "civic communications cooperative," and a "civic videotext service." *Strong Democracy* (Berkeley: University of California Press, 1984), chap. 10, pp. 273–280. Theodore L. Becker and his colleagues in the televoting project have developed effective pilots in which electronic voting is tempered by various deliberative strategies. See Becker's pioneering work on the Hawaiian and Californian televotes, in his "Televote: Interactive, Participatory Polling," in Theodore Becker and R. A. Couto, *Teaching Democracy by Being Democratic* (Westport, Conn.: Praeger Press, 1996).

3. Jean-Jacques Rousseau, *First Discourse, Social Contract and Discourses* (London: J. M. Dent and Sons, 1913), pt. 2, p. 140.

4. See for example Theodore Adorno and Max Horkheimer, *Dialectic of Enlightenment* (Amsterdam, 1947); and Herbert Marcuse, *One-Dimensional Man* (Boston: Beacon Books, 1964).

5. See the "Münchner Erklärung," Akademie zum Dritten Jahrtausend, Munich, February 1997.

6. President Clinton's intervention with corporate executives from the entertainment industry at his February and July 1996 meetings can be seen as politically successful since it not only elicited the promise of a self-generated rating system and a commitment to the V-Chip (allowing parents to identify and screen out material unsuitable for children), and got a weak agreement to secure three hours of "educational television for children" ("educational" to be defined by the broadcasters, however!), but acted as an implicit threat: if you don't do this voluntarily, Congress and the White House might do it for you. The same is true of his efforts to applaud and encourage private industry's voluntary efforts at funding the wiring of schools and libraries. However, government-encouraged market initiatives will always play a secondary role to the primary corporate ambition to augment earnings, and

this ambition will never be a sufficient source for securing public goods in the technological arena. In the case of hardwiring the nation's schools, for example, the industry has backed off from its early pledges, and the program appears today to be in jeopardy.

7. According to Gingrich in his ebullient 1984 book *Windows of Opportunity,* "breakthroughs in computers, biology, and space make possible new jobs, new opportunities, and new hope on a scale unimagined since Christopher Columbus discovered a new world. . . . hope for a continuing revolution in biology . . . hope for jobs, opportunities, and adventures in space." Newt Gingrich, with David Drake and Marianne Gingrich, *Window of Opportunity: A Blueprint for the Future* (New York: Jim Baen, 1984); cited in Thomas M. Disch, "Newt's Futurist Brain Trust," *Nation,* February 27, 1995. David Drake is a science fiction writer. His offhand suggestion that welfare might be licked by dropping portable computers into the laps of the poor is suggestive of futurological gusto and is fairly representative of the naïveté with which many novices view the new technologies.

8. Bill Gates, *The Road Ahead* (New York: Viking, Penguin, 1995), excerpted in *Newsweek,* November 27, 1995, pp. 59–65.

9. This is why the most important section of the Munich Declaration alluded to above is part 3, called "Citizen Politics," in which the Academy calls for citizen participation (Burger Engagement), not just on the net but in all our civil and political institutions.

10. See R. W. Apple, Jr., "Library of Congress Is an Internet Hit," *New York Times,* February 16, 1997.

11. Umberto Eco, "Gutenberg Galaxy Expands," *Nation,* January 6, 1997, p. 35.

12. Chris Garske, senior vice-president in charge of publishing at GT Interactive Corporation; Phyllis Furman, "Plugged In: Interactive Meltdown. Publishers Retreating from Digital Books," *Authors Guild Bulletin,* fall 1996, p. 39. The book turns out to be a remarkable little technology of its own, packing an extraordinary amount of easily accessed information into a portable format that goes anywhere and makes reading an aesthetic pleasure as well (something no one claims for the internet!).

13. For a full account of these tendencies, see my *Jihad versus McWorld,* (New York: Times Books, 1995), chap. 9.

14. Ben H. Bagdikian, *Media Monopoly,* 4th ed. (Boston: Beacon Press, 1993), p. 19.

15. The Disney Company seemed to exercise more autonomy when it resisted Chinese attempts to close down production of a Disney feature film on the Dalai Lama and repression in Tibet, but the company is extremely anxious to do business in China, which has expressed interest in a theme park, and this story is not over.

16. The agreement opens up the global telecommunications market, and permits outside companies to buy into (though not take over or buy out) national companies. In the name of free trade and open markets, nations are being asked to permit international cartels to move in and take over communications. The idea of a public utility is apparently dead. See "68 Nations Agree to Widen Market in Communications," *New York Times,* February 16, 1997, p. 1.

17. Although titles change quickly in this world, as of spring 1997 Ted Turner is chairman of Turner Broadcasting and TNT; Sumner Redstone is CEO of Viacom and was a feisty competitor for the Paramount takeover; Barry Diller is the QVC Network president; Martin S. Davis is president of Paramount; Michael Ovitz was chairman of the Creative Artists Agency and a key player in the M-G-M Credit Lyonnais deal and until his $90 million buy-out was Disney Corporation president; Bill Gates is the power behind Microsoft; and John C. Malone is president of Tele-Communication, part-time chair of Liberty Media, as well as a one-quarter owner of Turner Broadcasting, which makes him a major force beyond Barry Diller's QVC Network.

18. When cable was first introduced, many thought that if communities were given public access studios, they could compete with the networks and corporations who were cable's primary vendors. It did not happen that way.

19. *New York Times*, February 16, 1997, p. 40.

20. *The Electronic Republic: Reshaping Democracy in the Information Age* (New York: Viking, 1995), pp. 46–48. Digital convergence describes the easy interface between broadcast television, computers, and cable afforded by digitalization of signals.

21. You can visit webpages for White House or Congress or the British Labor Party or the Library of Congress and download information easily available through other sources.

22. John Seabrook, *Deeper: My Two-Year Odyssey in Cyberspace* (New York: Simon and Schuster, 1997). For the kind of cyber-enthusiasm Seabrook is puncturing, see the vituperative and polemical account of the net as a weapon of the young against the moralistic old by Jon Katz in his *Virtuous Reality: How America Surrendered Discussion of Moral Values to Opportunists, Nitwits, and Blockheads like William Bennett* (New York: Random House, 1997).

23. *U.S. News and World Report*, November 13, 1995.

24. David Bollier, "The Future of Electronic Commerce" (Washington, D.C.: Aspen Institute, 1996), p. 39. Companies like Pepsico, Nabisco, Toys 'R' Us, Nintendo, Time-Warner, and Disney have all developed web sites on the net aimed not only at selling their products but, in some cases, also designed to elicit market survey information from kids logging on. See Lawrie Mifflin, "Advertisers Chase a New Target: 'Cybertots,'" *New York Times*, Friday, March 29, 1996.

25. Bertrand Russell, *The Scientific Outlook* (London: Unwin, 1931), p. 279.

26. See Condorcet, *Sketch for the Historical Progress of the Human Mind,* (Paris, 1794); Alvin Toffler, *Future Shock* (1970), *The Third Wave* (1980), and *Power Shift* (1990); John Naisbett, *Megatrends* (1982) and *Global Paradox* (1994).

27. Walter B. Wriston, *The Twilight of Sovereignty* (New York: Scribner's, 1992), pp. 170, 176. Wriston also thinks "modern information technology is also driving nation states towards cooperation with each other so that the world's work can get done" (p. 174).

28. With him on his trek is of course Microsoft, a corporation the *New York Times* described in a Sunday magazine cover article title as "The Microsoft Monopoly"—with a subtitle asking "How Do You Restrain a 800-pound Gorilla?" Gates, *Road Ahead; Newsweek*, pp. 66–67. See James Gieick, "The Microsoft Monopoly," *New York Times Magazine*, November 5, 1995, sec. 6.

29. From the inaugural brochure printed by World Electronic Community, 70

Blanchard Road, Burlington, Massachusetts 01803; E-mail welcome@caavcinc.-com. Once again, corporate and elite uses of the net for commercial purposes are light years ahead of civic uses.

30. See Project Vote Smart, "1996 Election Year Guide to the Vote Smart Web," http://www.vote-smart.org.

31. The Aspen Institute boasts of a "new era in American Politics," but turns out to be concerned only with traditional elections. See Anthony Corrado and Charles M. Firestone, *Elections in Cyberspace: Toward a New Era of American Politics* (Aspen: Aspen Institute, 1996).

32. A Western diplomat in China says, "The Chinese Government has decided and I think logically that it really can't shut out satellite television entirely, whatever the threat. We're not talking about a few dissident here. Hundreds of thousands of Chinese have now invested their life savings in these dishes, and there would be a nasty public uproar if the Government really forced the dishes down." And in Iran, the *Teheran Times* concludes that "the cultural invasion will not be resolved by the physical removal of satellite dishes." Both quotes from Philip Shenon, "A Repressed World Says 'Beam Me Up,'" *New York Times,* Sunday, September 11, 1994. Note that the danger is not of political propaganda but of pop cultural contamination. Murdoch willingly took the BBC World Service off of his China service and in Iran the danger is not CNN, but *Dynasty,* which is the most popular program in Teheran today.

33. See Becker, cited above in note 2.

34. James Fishkin has devised a deliberative technique that brings citizens together for several days and permits them to interact with one another and with experts, so that their views are not merely registered but pondered and modified. In 1993, Channel Four in the United Kingdom broadcast an exemplary weekend of Fishkin's project; a similar broadcast is being planned on public television (if there is still public television) for the 1996 American presidential elections. For details, see Fishkin's *Democracy and Deliberation* (New Haven: Yale University Press, 1991).

35. Precisely because it is interactive, new telecommunications technology "learns" about its users as its users learn about it. A system that "knows" what you buy, how you pay for it, what your consumer and political preferences are, and even (in programs providing home security) when you leave and when you come home, and which then stores and disseminates such information in the absence of any regulatory safeguards, is hardly a system political skeptics should trust.

36. Robert Reich has drawn an American portrait in which privileged information/communication workers increasingly withdraw public support from the larger society as they move to insular suburbs, but private recreational, schooling, security, and sanitation services for their own walled communities, which the public at large can no longer afford. Their withdrawal (Reich labels it the politics of secession) leaves the poor poorer, the public sector broke, and society ever more riven by economic disparities that technology reinforces. Robert Reich, in "The New Community," in *The Work of Nations* (New York: Knopf, 1991), chap. 23.

37. An early and prophetic book about the problems of electronic surveillance is John Wicklein's *Electronic Nightmare: The Home Communications Set and Your Freedom* (Boston: Beacon Press, 1981).

38. Channel One currently is in about twelve thousand junior high and high

schools. It loans free televisions, VCRs, and a satellite dish to schools (usually needy ones) willing to dish up two minutes of soft news, three minutes of commercials, and nine minutes of infotainment to its students during regular school hours. Channel One sells spots for up to $195,000 for a thirty-second ad, and has attracted many of the corporations on McWorld's frontier, including Pepsi and Reebok. In 1994, Chris Whittle sold the network for nearly $240 million to K-III, an "educational" publisher.

39. This suggests that science and technology policy need themselves to be subjected to democratic scrutiny. Technology should not try to produce an appropriate democracy; democracy should try to produce an appropriate technology. Experts in technology are *not* experts in the appropriate public uses of technology. Richard Sclove's project on community science boards speaks to these issues: *Democracy and Technology* (Cambridge: MIT Press, 1995).